TRAILS AND TRAILBLAZERS:

Public Education and School Desegregation
in Lunenburg County, Virginia
1870-1970

Shirley Robertson Lee

DORRANCE
PUBLISHING CO
EST. 1920
PITTSBURGH, PENNSYLVANIA 15238

The contents of this work, including, but not limited to, the accuracy of events, people, and places depicted; opinions expressed; permission to use previously published materials included; and any advice given or actions advocated are solely the responsibility of the author, who assumes all liability for said work and indemnifies the publisher against any claims stemming from publication of the work.

Dorrance Publishing Co
585 Alpha Drive
Suite 103
Pittsburgh, PA 15238
Visit our website at *www.dorrancebookstore.com*

ISBN: 978-1-4809-1218-2
eISBN: 978-1-4809-1540-4

Heinemann, Ronald L., John G. Kolp, Anthony S. Parent Jr., and William G. Shade. *Old Dominion, New Commonwealth: A History of Virginia, 1607-2007*. Charlottesville and London: University of Virginia Press, 2007.

Wilkinson, J. Harvie III. *Harry Byrd and the Changing Face of Virginia Politics, 1945-1966*. Charlottesville and London: University of Virginia Press, 1968.

Dedicated in memory of:

Margaret Cushwa Cocks
(1911-2011)

Alfonza Webster Stokes
(1945-2011)

Hilda Bagley Hawkins
(1921-2012)

CONTENTS

ACKNOWLEDGMENTS

The author is the person whose name appears on a published work; however, the production of this book would not have been possible without the contribution of many others. To those persons not listed in the acknowledgments, but granted an interview or provided a photo, I fall short of expressing my total indebtedness.

Gratitude is expressed to Dr. Audrey Church, Associate Professor, Library Media; the Janet Greenwood Library staff; Dr. Larissa S. Fergeson, Professor of History and Moton Museum Historian; Dr. Theresa A. Clark, Associate Professor and Chair, Department of Social Work, Communication Sciences and Disorders; and Dr. Elizabeth "Lissa" A. Power-deFur, Associate Professor, Coordinator of the Communication Sciences and Disorders Graduate Program, and Director of the Longwood Speech, Hearing, and Learning Services—all of Longwood University in Farmville, Virginia.

Many, many thanks to Mrs. Dora G. Wynn, Superintendent of Lunenburg County Public Schools; Lunenburg County Board of Education personnel; Mrs. Roberta C. Rickers, former Branch Manager of the Ripberger Public Library, Kenbridge, Virginia who said, "Somebody ought to write about it [the school system]," and the library staff; Mr. Gordon F. Erby, Clerk, Lunenburg County Circuit Court and the office staff; Ms. Dorothy Tucker, Publisher, Kenbridge-Victoria Dispatch; and Mr. Lucious W. Edwards, Jr., University Archivist and Historian, Virginia State University in Petersburg, Virginia.

Special thanks are expressed to Mrs. Ruth W. Randolph, retired English teacher and middle school assistant principal; Mrs. Dorothy D. Hatchett, entrepreneur; Mrs. Lula W. Gaskin, retired School Librarian; and Mrs. Frances P. Wilson, Director of Student Services, Lunenburg County Public Schools.

I am grateful to Mrs. Bessie C. Hopkins, Mrs. Elloise M. Callahan, Mrs. Mildred H. Jenkins, Mrs. Cordelia W. Hopson, Ms. Rebecca L. Randolph, Miss Grace 'Chris' Wilkinson, and Mrs. Mary F. Watkins for their encouragement and "bedrock" support.

My appreciation is expressed to the late Mr. Oscar Wood, educator, for permission to glean from his insightful 1953 research—Development of Education For Negroes in Lunenburg County, Virginia 1870-1952; Ms. Agnes L. Whittle for her superb literary guidance, and Mrs. Cynthia W. Coleman for the videotaping of interview sessions.

Lastly, I offer the utmost respect and appreciation to my husband, Charles, who endured with patience every phase of this work—from conception to completion; and a big thank-you to our two adult children who supported me.

PREFACE

The time for the fortieth reunion of the Central High School Class of 1970 was approaching. A committee of volunteers met on Saturdays—over the course of several months—to coordinate the event and contact classmates for a fun-filled, enjoyable evening. The reunion was held at the Victoria Golf Club in Victoria, Virginia on August 7, 2010 commencing at 6:00. It was a warm, sunny Saturday with no forecast of rain or threatening weather. Classmates gathered at the club house mid-morning to rearrange the tables and chairs, and decorate the room. Areas were designated for registration, food and refreshments, a slide presentation, and entertainment. Small last-minute details were given attention. After hours of preparation—we were ready for the celebration!

As I entered the club house that evening, the room was filled with the sights and sounds of former school days. The *Sword and Shield*—class yearbook—along with other memorabilia, was placed on a table near the registration area. It seemed as if I had stepped back into a familiar time and place—a time of the song, "What the World Needs Now," and a place where public education was segregated, but now integrated. As I glanced around, I noticed that each table was arrayed with a rich purple-colored table cloth with a long gold decorative streamer and crystal candle vase in the center. Shinny gold confetti denoting the year 1970 had been placed carefully—in no particular order—near the flicking candle-lit centerpiece on each table. Glistening purple and gold streamers dangled from the ceiling—swaying back and forth—as if they were celebrating, too! On the wall, just behind the DJ's area, there were two four-foot plastic posters representative of the apparel and typical moves of the "Dance Fever" era of the 1970s.

A photo slide show of classmates and former school administrators, faculty, and staff members scrolled along on a big screen as classmates and their guests cheerfully greeted each other. There were smiles, hugs, brisk hand-shakes, and an occasional burst of laughter. I heard classmates engaging in conversations about their school days, family-life, and future plans. The table that drew the most attention was the one on which the photos of deceased classmates were placed. Seventeen of approximately 140 classmates were no longer with us.

The highlight of the evening was the two-minute share period for impromptu reminiscences. Some classmates were reserved, but others eagerly took the cordless microphone to share their thoughts with the group. I was in awe, and felt my heart skip a beat as I heard wonderful, stories and recollections about their personal and professional lives. When one of our white classmate talked about her positive experience of school desegregation—I wasn't sure if I had heard her correctly. Immediately, I thought of that different time and place. As she continued, however, there was a spirit of hope that grabbed my heart—a hope that people can change. I had a renewed faith that perhaps the old regime of hatred, bigotry and racism was meeting its long-awaited death—and I was that witness! Then it hit me! I started to ask myself: Who were the first African American students that enrolled in the county's white schools in 1965? What forces influenced public education in Lunenburg County, Virginia? Why had I not thought of these questions years before the reunion? Simply, I haven't a clue! However, over the years, I've come to realize how vital education is to the achievement of a better life and freedom in society—through the legacies of James Henry Callahan, my great-grandfather, and a West Hill School trustee in the early 1900s; Ellen Callahan Gee, his daughter, who received teacher training at the Thyne Institute in Chase City, Virginia and taught at West Hill; and Eleanor Callahan Williams, a granddaughter who was an educator in the Richmond City Schools in Richmond, Virginia.

As a life-long resident of Lunenburg County and a former student in segregated schools from first to the eleventh grade, and an integrated school during my senior year, it seemed logical to conduct research about public education. There has been no study conducted specifically on the subject except that of Oscar Wood's (1953) research— *Development of Education for Negroes in Lunenburg County, Virginia 1870-1952.*

Two events occurred approximately a week after the class reunion that led me to seek information about public education and school desegregation. First, I sought biographical and historical information about James William 'Willie' Edward Nash who was the first teacher at the West Hill School in the early 1900s. Second, this search steered me toward another trail—the unsung heroes who paved the way for public education in Lunenburg County.

The "historical narrative" approach to inquiry was used in this recounting because it is concerned with reconstructing the sequence of activities and events throughout the centennial period of the school system's history. The work aimed to convey a sense of another time and place while providing an understanding of why and how certain events occurred. The process has taken me on a journey of personal visits, phone calls, and hours of travel within Lunenburg County and the surrounding area. I have engaged in informative conversations with persons in the county; and received emails or letters from others residing in California, Georgia, Maryland, New York, New Hampshire, Pennsylvania, Washington, D.C., and other areas of Virginia. I have spoken with people in various settings— homes, churches, restaurants, rehabilitation and healthcare facilities, street corners, workplaces, and the post office—just to name a few. More than 150 face-to-face interviews were conducted. Informants included civic leaders; public workers; governmental officials; former and current school employees; parents; clergy; former students; and other members of the community. Audio and video-taping was conducted. The creation of an educational collection of school-related photos and other memorabilia is the second phase of the study.

The words naming the people of African descent will vary and may cause some readers to feel uncomfortable. African American is the term of choice where contemporary references are being made. Throughout this selection, however, the words "Negro," "black," and "colored" are also used. And yes, the word "nigger" will appear in the text based upon the recollections of some contributors. In general, the name used reflects the period being addressed.

This book provides an overview of public education in Lunenburg County, Virginia beginning in 1870 to school desegregation by 1970. It is unrealistic to assume a study of this nature is the "end all" and "complete accounting" of the school system's history. The development of public schooling in Virginia will be highlighted within its context as the story unfolds. The history of public education—from its rudimentary beginning to the provision of equal educational opportunity for *all* school-age children— is an integral part of the legacy of Lunenburg County. The telling of this story is both necessary and timely in the wake of such events as the first *Annual Report of the Superintendent of Public Instruction of the Commonwealth of Virginia*, 1871; Jim Crow laws, 1876;[i] *Plessy v. Ferguson*, 1896;[ii] *Brown v. Board of Education*, 1954, 1955;[iii] and *the Civil Rights Act of 1964*.[iv]

With this in mind, I firmly believe this book is of local, state, and national interest; and hopefully, will be the pride of Virginians and joy of Lunenburgers everywhere.

—Shirley Robertson Lee

CHAPTER 1
AWAKENING OF PUBLIC EDUCATION

"The public sentiment in the county is largely in favor of public free schools."[v]

-Robert Miles Williams

Lunenburg County, nicknamed Old Free State of Lunenburg, located in the Commonwealth of Virginia, is approximately 70 miles southwest of Richmond, the state capital.[vi]

The county is part of a vast region called "Southside Virginia" because of its location among other counties south of the James River, which lies in the plateau region between the Blue Ridge Mountains (west) and Fall Line (east) in the area called the "Piedmont," which is a French word meaning "foot of the mountains."[vii]

Lunenburg is bordered by the counties of Prince Edward (northwest), Nottoway (north), Brunswick (east), Mecklenburg (south), and Charlotte (west). The Nottoway River is located on the north, and the Meherrin River on the south.[viii]

Local Sentiment of Free Public Education

In 1870, after the Civil War, the General Assembly decreed that there would be a "uniform system of public free schools" in Virginia. Just the year before, the "Underwood Constitution" provided for a state superintendent of public instruction elected by the General Assembly, and a State Board of Education consisting of the governor, attorney general, and chief state school officer, who would have the authority to 1) appoint and remove county superintendents and district school trustees; 2) manage the school funds; and 3) regulate all matters involving the administration of the school system. The General Assembly also was authorized to adopt compulsory attendance laws and to levy taxes for the support of schools.[ix]

William Henry Ruffner was appointed the first state superintendent for public instruction. In Dr. Ruffner's first year (1870-1871), 130,000 students were taught in 2,900 schools, and within a five-year period enrollment had reached 185,000.[x]

Public schools were opened in all Virginia counties in November 1870. However, early efforts to operate a system of public education floundered on inadequate funding. Most rural schools were one-room with only one teacher.[xi]

The development of public schools in Lunenburg was widely supported by its citizens after the establishment of the statewide system in Virginia in 1870. In 1871, Robert Miles Williams, a resident of Victoria, Virginia, was appointed as Lunenburg's first school superintendent.[xii] A year later, in 1872, he gave his first report to the State Board of Education on the initiation of public education. Williams stated, "The public sentiment in the county is largely in favor of public free schools. The name of nearly every family in the county is on the school rolls. But there is shown some opposition to raising funds for their support."[xiii] No other information was available about Williams. Virginia's overall school-age population was growing. The establishment of schools for Negroes and whites increased everywhere in Lunenburg County, too. The need for education was viewed with great promise by Negroes, and whites found it to be a primary goal for their children. Neale (2005) wrote, "In 1870, there were only four schools on the list in a county promotion: Cedar Hill in Plantersville, Lochleven Seminary, Moss Hill in Roxton, and Miss Mattie C. Stokes' School at Whittle's Mill."[xiv]

Other Early Schools

Oscar Wood, educator, in 1953 documented, "There were ten schools established for Negroes in the county in 1871—six male and five female teachers. One of the earliest was Trinity School operated by Mary McFarland Jennings in a one-room log Episcopal Church. Her primary objective was to conduct teacher training. The first graduates were Carrie Jennings, Betty Brydie, George Crawley, Cordelia Smith, Rosa C. Marable, and McNoah B. Cralle in 1876. The church burned in 1880, and members of Trinity erected another small school on the same site. In 1915 this school was deeded to the School Board because the patrons could not support it."[xv]

The Lunenburg School, constructed in 1874, was another early school for white children. This simple place of learning—a one-room log cabin—was located on the land of John L. Yates. The teacher was Richard May, one of the county's gentlemen. May was a noted educator and later became a county superintendent for his district. It is not known how many years he taught, but teaching was his profession. Through a long and useful life, he held the office of superintendent until his death. From Yates, the school moved to the home owned by John R. Couch. The teacher was James Flippin. The school was later relocated to the courthouse and renamed New Court House School. It burned in 1910, but was rebuilt on a shoestring budget and lasted into the 1920s.[xvi]

In 1874, the Methodist Church School for Negroes was established in the town of Victoria, Virginia. Jacob Robinson, the pastor, made a house-to-house canvass to solicit contributions to construct the church. Since this was the only building in town suitable to hold school, members of the church permitted a school to be opened there to educate the youth of the community. The first teacher was Bettie Smith, who lived with different members of the church. In 1906, this school was abandoned after members of the church erected another school.[xvii]

In 1875, the Baptist Church School for Negroes in Victoria grew out of the First Baptist Church (white) in town. Through efforts of the pastor, Joseph Pulley, a school was opened in the Negro church. The first teacher was Mary McGee. The school remained in the church until an elementary department opened on the site of the Lunenburg Training School in early 1900s.[xviii]

In addition to segregated schools, Jim Crow laws were put into effect in 1876, which created separate eating and drinking places, separate railroad cars, and separate toilets—separate everything. After nearly eighty-eight years, these laws were abolished with federal legislation in 1964.[xix]

Other schools believed to have been established for white children in the late 1800s were Smith School, Robertson School, Ledbetter School, Reedy School, Bagley School, Hite School and a school at Walker Grange Hall in the Lochleven District. Many of these earlier schools closed or consolidated because of low enrollment.

By 1880, the number of schools for Negroes had doubled to twenty. Wood pointed out, "The multiplication of schools created a demand for good teachers beyond the supply. In order to obtain the required number of teachers the superintendent lowered the standards of qualification. Some of the teachers were so poorly prepared that the school system fell into disrepute and required several years to recover."[xx] In 1881, there were fifty teachers—thirteen white males; twenty-six white females; seven colored males; and four colored females. The average school term lasted about five months.[xxi]

A school for white children was constructed in Victoria, Virginia around 1895. It was a one-room frame building located just south of the former bridge over the railroad in the town. The teacher was the wife of James T. Waddill, Sr.; and there were about thirty-two children at the first school.[xxii] The earlier schools in the county were rudimentary and ill-equipped buildings and many of them were usually constructed of wood planks or logs chinked with mud or cement.[xxiii] Heat came from a wood or coal-burning stove. Most of the children walked to school, usually up to two or more miles.

In 1898, the Kenbridge Negro School League was organized to raise money to build a two-room school with the assistance of Berkley Turner and J. Harrison Bagley. The Kenbridge Graded School was constructed within town limits of Kenbridge, Virginia on two acres of land leased by William Franklin Kennedy, co-founder of the town. In 1900, the first teachers at Tinkling (renamed Kenbridge in 1908) were Bettie B. Allen and Ella Bagley—who taught grades one through seven. Other early teachers included Bettie Hicks, J. Harrison Bagley, McNoah B. Cralle, Anna Holcomb, Pearl M. Bagley, Elizabeth Cralle Turns, Geraldine Jones, Lucille Blackwell, Lucille Overby, Elizabeth J. Cradle, Leola Craighead, Lula Cralle, Myrtle C. Smith, and Adele B. Taylor. The principals were McNoah B. Cralle, Frank P. Lewis, and Margaret Lawing Collier, and Haywood R. Watkins Sr., was appointed the assistant principal under Collier's leadership.

In 1928, another frame building with a principal's office, library, clinic, and small eating area was erected on the site. The Kenbridge Training School (as it was also called), was constructed with contributions in the amount of—black $1,000; white $5,000; public $1,000 and Rosenwald $3,525. Funding was also received from the Kenbridge Negro School League to pay the teachers' salaries. In fall 1969, the name of the Kenbridge Graded School changed to Kenbridge Primary School as part of Lunenburg County's School Desegregation Plan.

Segregated Public Education

Dr. Ruffner was an advocate of public free school for both races. He designed a statewide system of racially segregated schools as mandated by the General Assembly.[xxiv] The idea of "separate but equal" was brought to the national stage in the 1896 case of *Plessy v. Ferguson*.[xxv] This case addressed the constitutional issue of states that allowed the practice of segregated public facilities on the basis of a person's ethnicity. This case put "teeth" into the upward mobility of African Americans in every aspect of life and laid the foundation for racial segregation well into the twentieth century. Heinemann (2007), wrote, "The racial makeup of the state also changed as new segregation laws encouraged the migration of black Virginians out of the state."[xxvi]

Dr. Richard R. Farr succeeded Dr. Ruffner as state superintendent (1882-1886). John L. Buchanan followed (1886-1890), and then John E. Massey (1890-1898). During these administrations, the number of pupils and teachers increased, and the patrons and citizens developed greater confidence in the educational system.

Joseph W. Southall was appointed state superintendent of public instruction in 1898. He aimed to improve and consolidate rural schools, increase state and local financial support for schools, provide higher salaries for teachers, and establish a State Board of Examiners to handle teacher certification.[xxvii]

A New Century Dawns

There was an awakening in public education as a new century dawned. The people of Virginia had a renewed and vested interest statewide.[xxviii] In Lunenburg County—farming, home life, and church attendance were major activities in the community. The economy had recovered from the exuberant cost of the Civil War to the extent that there was employment and profit for almost everyone who was willing to work.[xxix]

Heinemann (2007) pointed out "Farm problems paled alongside the trend toward urbanization in Virginia that would increase dramatically over the next two decades. The number of city folks rose from 18 to 30 percent of the population. Urban standards of living compared favorably to the poverty of rural areas with their poor roads and schools and absence of electricity. Problems generated by urbanization contributed to the progressive current sweeping the country in the early twentieth century. Progressivism was a broad-based movement directed at the industrial-urban revolution that had devastated the landscape, changed the nature of work and human relationships, and made the United States into a world power."[xxx] Life in Lunenburg remained the same as it had been the century before—an agrarian society.

In July 1901, Dr. Southall called a meeting of Virginia educators to make recommendations for constitutional provisions pertaining to the creation of a "uniform system of public education." The new State Constitution, (ratified in 1902), under Governor Andrew Jackson Montague, gave a mandate for public education by providing that "the General Assembly shall provide for a system of free public elementary and secondary schools for all children of school age throughout the Commonwealth." The Constitution authorized the board to divide the state into school divisions, each to contain not less than one county or city; the magisterial districts within the counties retained their separate school boards and segregated public education.[xxxi]

In Lunenburg, educational disparities for Negroes had been "the way things are" to those charged with the responsibility for the provision of education for all children. The lack of needed educational resources, inadequate facilities, and unreliable transportation helped to spawn racist ideologies by some that African American students were unintelligent, second-class citizens, who would make little or no positive contributions to society and global world. The school system mirrored society—*separate and unequal.*

In 1901, a one-room, frame building was constructed in the white populated Traffic community in the Rehoboth District. The citizens purchased one acre of land through the efforts of George Holloway and others at their own expense. Later, in 1910, white citizens constructed another school in the African American community. Both schools were identified as Traffic School. Today, the Negro school has been remodeled as a private residence. The one-room school for white children in the community closed in the 1930s, and the students were transported to other area schools. The land on which the school stood became the site of the Mount Olivet Church in Rehoboth, Virginia.

Joseph D. Eggleston, Jr. succeeded Dr. Southall in the early 1900s. Eggleston was the first elected superintendent of public instruction in Virginia. In March 1904, educational reformers in the state created the Co-operative Education Association of Virginia (CEAV) to publicize the need for nine-month terms, more high schools, improved teacher training, and agricultural and industrial training. The reformers also instituted teacher certification, school consolidation, and school privy requirements.[xxxii] There were increases in teachers' salaries, length of school terms, and per-pupil expenditures during Eggleston's administration. The state took control of the College of William and Mary and established three new normal or teacher education schools for women.[xxxiii]

The CEAV undertook a statewide campaign, the "May Campaign of 1905," with a series of conferences aimed at improving public education in the South. Reaching into ninety-four counties, Governor Montague and others delivered 300 addresses at one hundred meetings within thirty days for the support of public education.[xxxiv] Twenty later years, Lunenburg's school officials implemented school-based "May Day" celebrations in recognition of the early statewide efforts to support public education.[xxxv]

In 1905 there was not a graded school in the county—not one white male teacher.[xxxvi]

Other earlier schools for whites were Union Ridge, Wood Park, and Traffic. In the Pleasant Grove District several other schools existed. Many of these schools had the advantage of a superintendent and some financial backing from their district School Board. There was one teacher who taught several grades, usually from one to seven, at the elementary level. Many of these schools lasted only a few years and some teachers remained for only a brief period of time. There were few requirements to maintain school records; and some of the early records are sketchy and incomplete. School-related information is documented in the local newspaper—beginning in 1913—and archived at the Lunenburg County Court House. Also, some records—beginning in 1918—are archived at the Lunenburg County School Board Office.[xxxvii]

Isham T. Wilkinson

Plotting the Early Education Course

In 1906, Isham Trotter Wilkinson became Lunenburg's second superin-tendent of schools when he was twenty-one years of age. Wilkinson and his five siblings grew up on the family's farm in the Lochleven District south of Kenbridge, Virginia.[xxxviii]

Claude August Swanson was also elected governor of Virginia in the same year. Governor Swanson expanded Montague's reform efforts in ed-ucation by appropriating state funds to match local contributions that had a revolutionary effect—the passage of the *Mann High School Act in 1906*; and by 1909, the state had 345 high schools.[xxxix]

In the spring of 1908, Superintendent Wilkinson, on behalf of the School Board, published *Our School*. This was the first district-wide pam-phlet designed to provide information to the schools' patrons. The pub-lication contains a note from Superintendent Wilkinson to the teachers and students, thirty-eight letters from school children ages twelve through nineteen, a history of the rural schools, and a description of the conditions of school system.[xl] Wilkinson wrote, "Our school system is recognized as being far behind those of surrounding counties, but meritorious work that is now being done by our energetic trustees warrant a bright future in the educational work of the county."[xli] He noted the deep interest that many of the patrons were taking in the schools and suggested financial conditions will be greatly aided by the revenue from the Virginian Railway. The Virginia Railway system, when completed, was part of Lunenburg's landscape and provided needed revenue to the county."

There were only three frame buildings in the county. The others were log; and not a two-room school until 1908. By this time, Lunenburg had four graded schools; one high school; and five white male teachers. The enrollment of students was getting much larger. Plans were being drawn up to erect a high and grade school in the districts of Lochleven, Rehoboth and Pleasant Grove, and a joint school between the districts of Lewiston, Brown's Store and Columbian Grove. Arrangements were made to have music taught in several of the schools in 1909. Wilkinson continued, "Many other improvements were being made in various ways that would be of great help to the cause of education."

Wilkinson spoke of an experience he had as superintendent of schools during an interview with a *Richmond-Times Dispatch* staff writer in 1953. Wilkinson said, "I got $37.50 a month and drove two horses and a buggy. Of course, my father fed me and the horses, too!"[xlii]

The course of public education was being plotted by Superintendent Wilkinson when the towns of Kenbridge (1908) and Victoria (1909) were incorporated. *Our Town*, a 75-year history of life in Kenbridge and the area of Lunenburg County surrounding it, was printed by the Kenbridge Chamber of Commerce in 1983. This booklet describes the first public school in Kenbridge, Virginia, as a one-room, frame building with three grades and three teachers.[xliii]

Established in the spring of 1909, the one-room, West Hill School was constructed on one acre of land purchased for the sum of one hundred dollars. It is believed that the money was donated by James Henry Callahan. This schoolhouse operated as a place to educate the children of the community during weekdays, and served as a church for corporate worship on Sundays. There were many small community schoolhouses in the county that served as a place for education, weekly cooperate worship, and other community activities.

John "Shug" Willie Callahan, Sr., spoke about attending this school built by African American patrons with private funds. Callahan said, "My grandfather, James H. Callahan, was a West Hill School trustee. James William "Willie" Edward Nash was a family friend and the first teacher at West Hill." Nash was among the fortunate young people from Lunenburg to attend the Thyne Institute for his education and teacher training in the fall of 1905. With $11 tied up in a cloth rag, accompanied by his Uncle Douglas, he walked about 23 miles to Thyne from his home in Lunenburg County.[xliv] Thyne Institute was a four-year, liberal arts boarding school located in Chase City, Virginia that offered an outstanding education to blacks beginning in late 1800s until 1923. Courses offered at Thyne included physics, geometry, Latin, Greek, Roman history, moral philosophy, civil government, political economy, botany, psychology, mathematics, and literature, and the theory and practice of teaching.

In 1921, Nash left Lunenburg and relocated to Athens, Tennessee. He graduated from Knoxville College, Knoxville, Tennessee in 1914; and did post graduate work at Ohio State University and Tennessee State University. Nash received an Honorary Doctorate Degree from Tennessee Wesleyan College. Professor Nash died at 108 years of age in Tennessee on April 26, 1996.[xlv]

Other teachers at West Hill were Ellen Callahan (Gee), Ada Jenkins, and Mabel Reid Jennings. Jennings substituted for Jenkins from time to time, and taught at other small schools in the county. Mary Trotter Wood followed Jenkins, and Elizabeth Cain Jones was the last teacher at the school. The West Hill School closed in the spring of 1949, and students were transported to the Lunenburg Training School in Victoria, Virginia.[xlvi] David "June" Jones, Jr., reminisced about his school lunches when he attended West Hill. Jones said, "My mother would boil eggs for us to take to school for lunch. I'd put an egg in each pocket to keep my hands warm on those really cold days since we had to walk about three miles to school each day. Our teacher prepared something for us to eat at lunchtime—like hot soup. This was far better than a boiled egg or two!"[xlvii]

As public education evolved, record keeping became an important part of the system. One example of the earliest recordings of the students' school progress is that of Anna Thelma Harding at the Kenilworth School in November of 1910. Over time, these reporting forms became insufficient and antiquated as new courses and improved curriculum offerings were made available. Later, all schools were required to use a uniform system to document the students' attendance, academic, physical, and social performance.

Wilkinson experienced some difficult days as a school superintendent. Beginning 1916, *The Lunenburg Call*, local news weekly, printed several articles related to the newly formed Farmers' Educational and Cooperative Union of Lunenburg and its educational concerns. The union's education committee included D. M. Austin, W. P. Smith, C. A. Moore, and Dr. Edwin M. Mann. The operation of the schools under the leadership of Wilkinson had been questioned by the members and they wanted the matter investigated. Dr. Mann, as spokesman, attended the meetings of the State Board of Education in November and December of 1916, and in January and March of 1917. But he was not able to present the case until the March meeting. Mann—representing the farmer's union—presented the following charges and specifications. Mann said, "I charge that I. T. Wilkinson, superintendent of the public schools of Lunenburg County, for the past six years, has deliberately, willfully, and intentionally violated the state laws, the rules and regulations of the State Board of Education, and regulations of the State Board of Health." Mann contended that Wilkinson:

(1) Failed to see that health regulations were complied with in that privies of the schools had not been kept in sanitary condition. For example, from July 13, 1910 to July 13, 1912, only thirteen out of fifty-three schools in the county had a privy for the pupils. Some outbuildings had been constructed on hills close to springs that were used for supplying the school with drinking water.

(2) Engaged in occupations other than that of superintendent, i.e. member of the Kenbridge Town Council; Mayor of Kenbridge; co-owner, editor, and manager of the Free State News; and secretary and treasurer of the Kenbridge Spoke and Handle Factory.

(3) Wilkinson had not visited all county schools once a year and he had never made any report in writing to the superintendent of

public instruction including a responsible excuse for not doing so as required. Sixteen letters from public school teachers in the county were presented as evidence. Each teacher stated that her school was only visited once the past year, and many stated the Wilkinson only stayed about ten minutes.

(4) In a School Board tie vote to raise the superintendent's salary from $1,200 to $1,400, Wilkinson, as chairman, broke the tie when he voted in favor of a $1,200 salary and $200 allowance for traveling expenses, in addition to stamps and stationery.

On May 3, 1917, *The Lunenburg Call* reported that the State Board of Education informed Mann and others of their findings. The State Board of Education found that:

1) Wilkinson had performed his duty with a written notification (dated September 15, 1916) sent to School Trustees of Lunenburg County to call their attention to the requirement for sanitary outhouses at every school building;

2) Wilkinson would be required to devote himself exclusively to the discharge of duties in his office according to state regulations;

3) No claim was given by Wilkinson that any excuse was made in writing where he had failed to visit the schools as required; and

4) No violation with the vote by the school trustees in the raising of Wilkinson's salary in 1913.

Following the aftermath, Superintendent Wilkinson made a brief and pointed reply in the *Lunenburg Call*. He is quoted as saying, "I wish to say that I am heartily in favor of the election of all school superintendents by popular vote, and have on many occasions expressed my views. However, as long as I desire to fill the office under the present laws, I have to apply to the State Board of Education for the appointment. I shall heartily support a change of the law in order that all division superintendents of schools may be elected by popular vote in each county and city in Virginia."[xlviii]

Dr. Reamur C. Stearnes (1912 -1918) was succeeded by Dr. Harris H. Hart in 1918 as state superintendent of public instruction. During his first year in office, Dr. Hart, in addition to conducting a campaign to strengthen the public school system by eliminating the district school board system, was instrumental in enacting a statewide compulsory school attendance law and providing free textbooks. Although free textbooks were not approved, the General Assembly passed a new textbook law permitting local school boards to purchase textbooks directly from publishers at wholesale prices.[xlix]

In the spring of 1919, Isham T. Wilkinson ended his tenure in Lunenburg County. He continued working with his friend, Tom Ozlin, as co-owner and publisher of *The Free State News*, the county's weekly newspaper. Wilkinson became a member of the Virginia House of Delegates in 1934, remained for two terms until 1937, but refused a third term due to health reasons. Years later, Isham T. Wilkinson was identified as a "Weaver of Yarns" by Hamilton Crockford, *Richmond Times-Dispatch* staff writer, because Wilkinson had been a school chief, weekly publisher, mayor, and legislator, as well as handle manufacturer.[l]

Trend of Philanthropy

From 1870 to 1906, forty-two schools for Negroes had been established. Wood (1953) wrote, "In Lunenburg County, African American communities donated or purchased all of the land, contributed materials and equipment, completed construction work, and paid teachers' salaries from private funds. By the early 1900s, the number of female teachers had more than tripled. Increases were also noted in school term, enrollment, and average daily attendance, but monthly salaries for Negro teachers—male and female—had not significantly increased." The difference in pay for black and white teachers would remain discrepant for several more decades.[li]

In an attempt to level the playing field in public education for Negroes, a trend of philanthropy occurred in the rural South. It was through the efforts of benevolent societies that many blacks were given their first chance to prepare themselves for the new life that confronted them during Reconstruction.

The John L. Slater Fund, founded in 1882 by a Connecticut merchant, provided a million dollars to create the first philanthropy in the United States for Negro rural schools. Inspired by the success of George Peabody, Slater specified that his fund be used "for the uplifting of the lately emancipated population of the Southern States and their posterity by conferring on them the blessings of Christian education." Grants from the Slater Fund helped to develop black colleges and high schools, as well as institutions for teacher training and industrial education.[lii]

Jeanes Supervisors

The Anna Thomas Jeanes Foundation established in 1908, (later known as the Negro Rural School Fund), provided aid to the public schools of the South. This fund was used to help pay the salaries of Jeanes teachers or supervisors employed to improve instruction in shop work, homemaking, and other vocational skills.[liii] The Jeanes educational supervision was modeled on the work of Virginia Cabell Randolph, a Negro teacher in the Richmond area, who emphasized vocational education, visited her students in their homes, and helped to improve their health and sanitation. In 1908, Randolph became the first Jeanes Supervisor Industrial Teacher that provided the first formal in-service teacher training for rural black teachers anywhere in Virginia. She also worked in North Carolina and Georgia.[liv]

In 1909, McNoah B. Cralle—affectionately called "Professor" Cralle—was the first educator employed as a Jeanes Supervisor in Lunenburg County.[lv] He found that it was necessary to form school clubs, build a good relationship between the home and school, and raise money for building schools. Cralle faced many obstacles such as inadequate transportation, poor school conditions, and insufficient funds.[lvi]

Cralle created interest in building new schools by meeting with people in civic and social organizations, churches, and Sunday schools to proclaim the importance of education. Under his supervision—and that of other Jeanes supervisors—significant developments for Negro teachers were realized such as the organization of the Lunenburg County Teachers' Association (1909), improvements in teacher training and certification, school consolidation, longer school terms, and the equalization of teachers' salaries.[lvii] The organization of the Negro teachers into a unified group became a reality under Professor Cralle's leadership. This group held monthly meetings for demonstrations in teaching, helped to sponsor the Negro Organization Society and Negro History Week, purchased professional books for in-service training, and sponsored parent-teacher banquets.[lviii]

By the fall of 1917, Cralle had ended his tenure as a Jeanes Supervisor, but continued as a teacher and principal at the Kenbridge Graded School until the mid-1940s. On October 6, 1944, W. D. Garland presented a paper to the School Board signed by twenty-four patrons expressing their regrets at the retirement of Professor McNoah B. Cralle.

Lucy H. Morrison

In the fall of 1918, Lucy Mae Hinton Morrison was appointed Supervisor of Colored Schools in Lunenburg County following Cralle's resignation as Jeanes Supervisor. Morrison was born in Lunenburg County on May 20, 1886. Her early education was in the public schools of Lunenburg County and Bluestone-Harmony School in Keysville, Virginia. Morrison continued her studies at Virginia State College in Petersburg, Virginia, and Columbia University in New York. She began her teaching career in the small schools of Lunenburg County.

When Morrison became the supervisor in 1918, the teacher certificate system was reorganized, simplified, and strengthened by Dr. Hart's administration. There were twenty-eight types of certificates available.[lix]

Morrison was also called "superintendent" by many in the community because of her exclusive supervision of Negro schools in the county. She is credited with major improvements, such as her written contributions to the school-wide newsletters, improvements in teacher education and certification, and the successful consolidation of small schools. Her administrative title was changed by the School Board from Supervisor of Colored Schools to Elementary Supervisor in 1946.

Morrison was a highly respected member of the community and deeply committed to public education. In her honor, a sixteen-inch-by-twenty-inch canvas portrait in a golden leaf frame was placed on the wall above the water fountain in hallway of the Lunenburg Elementary School in the 1950s. It remained there until schools desegregated in 1969 and the portrait was removed—its whereabouts unknown. As the story goes, Morrison's portrait and the frame were spared from destruction by a school employee that picked it up from a trash pile. Fortunately, the school employee stored it at home for more than forty years until it was returned to Morrison's family in 2014. A reproduction of this portrait was donated to the Lunenburg County Historical Society for preservation. Morrison retired as an Elementary Supervisor in 1952 after thirty-four years of service in public education. She died in 1973.[lx]

By fall 1952, Clara A. Morse had been appointed elementary supervisor following Morrison's retirement. The focus of the elementary supervisor in Negro schools was more on academic instruction rather than vocational training, particularly at the secondary level. During her tenure, Morse supervised the assignment of new students, and conducted teachers' instructional workshops, and in-service training. In addition to her duties, she helped to coordinate the Goodwill school program at the Lunenburg Elementary and Kenbridge Graded Schools. Goodwill Industries—as in the past—is a *not-for-profit organization* that provides job training, employment-placement services, and other community-based programs for persons with a disability, lack education or job experience, or those who faced employment challenges. Goodwill is funded by a massive network of retail thrift stores which operate as nonprofits as well.

In the early 1950s, and for some years later, the School Board gave support to the "Goodwill Industries" school program. Approval was given by the Board for an annual weekly collection of new or slightly worn clothes and shoes donated by members of the community. Do you remember the "Good Willy" bags—as they were called? Barbara N. Shell experienced firsthand the opportunity to share "good will" with others in the community. Shell said, "I vividly recall the Goodwill bags during my elementary years at the Kenbridge Graded School. A large, duffle-shaped, brown paper bag with the Goodwill Industries logo in black ink printed on the front was distributed to all students at school. On Mondays, our teacher asked us to take the bags home and fill with usable clothes that we had outgrown. Bags were filled, returned to school during the week, and loaded onto the industries' truck on Fridays. The opportunity to help the needy was well-received by the parents."[lxi]

On February 18, 1960, Lewis Ovenshire, Executive Director of Goodwill, in a news article announced that Lunenburg County schools would again help the blind, crippled, and disabled workers at the Goodwill Industries. Pupils in the schools would take home paper "Good Will" bags on February 26. They were asked to fill the bags with all kinds of clothing and shoes, clean or dirty, and in any condition. The clothing collection for 1959 had provided work for forty blind, crippled, and disabled workers for a whole year. Ovenshire said, "Our work program has grown from forty workers a day to eighty workers a day since our School Collection started in 1952. The "Goodwill" program helped to provide vocational and rehabilitative training to disabled persons in the community."[lxii]

Morse was the last supervisor for which the School Board received monies through the Negro Rural School Funds (Anna T. Jeanes Foundation) to support Negro education and teacher training in the county. She returned to the classroom at Lunenburg High School as an English and dramatics teacher in the fall of 1956. Morse co-advised the junior class, served as drama club sponsor, and co-authored the 1960 Historical Sketch of Lunenburg High School with Leila M. Williams.[lxiii] The Jeanes programs, which became Virginia tradition, ended statewide in the 1960s.[lxiv] For a period of forty-seven years (1909-1956), the work of the Jeanes Supervisors in Lunenburg County included emphasis on vocational training; teacher certification; academic instruction; better home and school cooperation; and improving the health and living conditions of the people.

A fund for rural Negro education was founded by Julius Rosenwald of Chicago in 1917. Rosenwald, president of Sears, Roebuck and Company, initiated a school-building program that was to have a dramatic impact on the face of the rural South, and in the education of African Americans. Through the Rosenwald Fund, more than 5,300 schools, shop buildings, and teachers' houses were built by and for African Americans across the South and Southwest. Rosenwald became interested in philanthropy that addressed fundamental issues of equality, access, and opportunity. He wished to promote self-reliance among African Americans by requiring them to add their own sacrificial contributions to his. With a munificent endowment of more than \$4.3 million to construct schools across the region, and the more than \$4.7 million raised by African Americans themselves, the Rosenwald School Program has been called the "most influential philanthropic force that came in the aid of Negroes at that time."

West End School (1935)

Rosenwald Schools were built in many Virginia counties. Of 4,977 Rosenwald Schools built in the South, 367 were in Virginia. In Lunenburg County, Rosenwald Funds were used to support the construction of two schools—West End (1921); Kenbridge Graded (1928); and two frame structures—four-room building with auditorium (1924) and vocational shop (1927) at the Lunenburg Training School. The teachers at the West End School (photo above) included Estella Reavis, Gertrude B. Carrington, Catheryn Tisdale, B. L. Turner, Irene B. Ashburne, A. A. Kent, Jeanette Whitehead and Betty Bryant. West End closed in the early 1950s. The Rosenwald building program was discontinued in 1932.

Other prominent philanthropic gifts providing educational opportunities for many blacks were provided by the Presbyterian Church, American Baptist Home Missionary Society, and Stokes-Phelps Foundation. The Freedman's Bureau also gave money and moral support for Negro education beyond high school. They were aided in their efforts by almost 60,000 free Virginia Negroes—many of them literate and property owners.[lxv]

CHAPTER 2
BUILDING A PUBLIC SCHOOL SYSTEM

"Nine-months term for every boy and girl, whether in town or country. If we care to give all children their due we, too, must give them all nine-months term, and thus standardize our work."[lxvi]

-A. B. Wilson

Visionary and Catalyst for Change

In the fall of 1919, A. B. "Ben" Wilson became the third school superintendent in Lunenburg County. His family purchased a home in Victoria, Virginia. There is little information about Wilson's family and his educational background. Superintendent Wilson may be called a 'visionary' and 'catalyst for change' because he demonstrated noteworthy efforts to change the public education landscape for children although the practice of segregated schools existed. New initiatives in public education would take place such as state funding for school transportation; "five-point" child health program; increased school terms; and the Rosenwald funding of rural schools and buildings.

At the state level, the General Assembly passed what is known as the *County Unit Act of 1922*. Prior to this time, Virginia had operated school boards on a district basis. This act made the county the unit of administration rather than each district operating independently. School buildings in districts became the property of the county under one authority; and the School Board would be comprised of a representative from each magisterial district.

Dr. Hart also encouraged school consolidation, but left the debts acquired for construction of these buildings to be paid from the district levies. A tax levy was paid by the citizens of the county to support public education.[lxvii]

In 1922 and 1923, Superintendent Wilson and high school principals—George L. Walker, Kenbridge High; J. M. Tignor, Victoria High; and J.F. Kennedy, Lochleven High—were co-editors of the Lunenburg School Life newsletters. The newsletter cost was twenty cents per subscription. The newsletter was useful in keeping parents, school personnel, and members of the community informed of the various school activities, changes in the curriculum, and other important school-related information.

Wilson was concerned that eight months of school was not enough time for a proper education. In the *Lunenburg School Life* newsletter (October-November, 1922), he wrote, "We must admit, however, that Nottoway, our neighbor, is getting ahead of us in raising standards of schools, and in longer terms. The slogan is 'nine-months term for every boy and girl, whether in town or country.' If we care to give all children their due we, too, must give them all nine-months term, and thus standardize our work."[lxviii]

Superintendent Wilson urged the school supervisors and teachers to submit school-related articles to be printed in the *Lunenburg School Life* newsletter. There was a section provided for information about the education of black children under this heading:

THIS SPACE RESERVED FOR COLORED SCHOOLS OF LUNENBURG COUNTY

In the 1923 edition, Morrison provided a written report of the status of Negro schools. There was over-crowding in the twenty-seven existing schools. She wrote, "We have 1725 scholars, averaging about 51 to a room, this means an overcrowded condition. Fifty-one scholars are too many for one teacher to master successfully!" Morrison stressed poor school attendance as a key factor in the lack of student progress and achievement.

Morrison continued, "Our league work has been splendid this year, the patrons have rallied right along especially in the Kenbridge, where they have raised $45 each month for the teachers' salaries, and other leagues are doing similar work. The new West End School had been constructed in the Rehoboth District. This school was recognized as a Rosenwald School because of the generous monies donated to assist with its construction.[lxix]

This is a splendid building! I wish every person in the county could see it. The School Board contributed a desk and heater." The cost of the school building follows:

For land	50.00
For lumber and labor	1,050.00
For contractor	1,200.00
From Rosenwald Fund	500.00
Total	2,800.00

Included in the newsletter was a notice of an activity scheduled at the Lunenburg Training School on March 6, 1923. Superintendent Wilson, W. D. Gresham, and white friends from Kenbridge and Victoria were invited to attend the school program and see the students' display of work. The soloist to perform was Hermine Royall.[lxx]

A third newsletter was printed in February of 1924 with A. B. Wilson as editor; and the three high school principals—George L. Walker, Kenbridge; Hal J. Meredith, Victoria; and C. L. Parker, a representative from Lochleven—co-editors. In the section reserved for the colored schools of Lunenburg County—*A Bird's Eye View of the Victoria Colored School* was printed. It was written by Pearl M. Bagley and E. Pearl Evans, two teachers from the Lunenburg Training School. An excerpt follows: "During the last few years the children have been struggling through many disadvantages from the standpoint of school buildings. In the last one or two years, providence opened its arms of fortune unto us and enabled the people to erect a nice, two-room building near town. Fortune is smiling upon us and is now at the verge of giving to us and the future generation, the advantages of having a County Training School—something for which the entire county of Lunenburg has been suffering." Lucille C. Overby, principal, Kenbridge Graded School, also submitted "Early American Orators"—an article that appeared in this section.

These newsletters were the second major school publications available county-wide. A copy of each is archived at the Ripberger Public Library in Kenbridge, Virginia.[lxxi]

In 1924, the one-room schoolhouse for white children in the Traffic community was in operation. The teacher was Sarah Virginia Love.[lxxii] Other teachers included Lucille Bowman, Garland Spencer, Nellie Bigger, Elva Thompson, Gladys Ward, and Marion Love.[lxxiii]

When did May Day start and why was it celebrated?

The earliest recognition of the May Day celebration was printed in the local newspaper on April 23, 1925. Superintendent Wilson appointed a committee in the May Campaign for Lunenburg County to recognize and celebrate the *May Campaign of 1905*. The committee members were A. B. Wilson, chairman; George L. Walker, J. M. Tignor, Noah H. Moody, Fannie Phelps, L. A. Hardy, and J. T. Waddill, Jr. Wilson said, "The May Campaign was inspired by recalling the splendid results of 1905 when people of Virginia woke up to a new and intense interest in education." The progress of education in Virginia dates from the *May Campaign of 1905*. The school system adopted a resolution and encouraged school-based programs to commemorate this event. The actions of Superintendent Wilson ushered in the annual school-based May Day celebrations in Lunenburg County.[lxxiv] Traditionally, in the month of May during the first week, a wooden pole or young tree would be cut down and secured in the ground on the school yard. Students would be selected to dance to songs like the "Tennessee Waltz" as they wrapped the pole with long ribbons of red, blue, yellow, green, white and other bright colors.

On May 14, 1925, a public notice by J. M. Tignor, principal of the Victoria High School, was submitted to the local newspaper. Under the heading, *MAY DAY SCHOOL PROGRAM ON THE PUBLIC SQUARE FRIDAY* was printed, "A program put on by several hundred pupils and music by the Victoria Band. All free." Following the program there would be an educational meeting with the Honorable P. H. Drewery, Congressman for the District, as guest speaker. The article continued, "You cannot afford to miss this meeting if you are interested in the welfare of your children."[lxxv]

May Day was celebrated annually in some form at nearly all the schools. It did not matter whether the school was in town or located in the countryside. The principal and teachers worked diligently to support May Day activities. There were group presentations; field activities and athletic competitions—potato sack race, tug-of-war, softball; and the crowning of a queen—king and queen at some schools—was the highlight of the day.

Many of the schools held their school annual 'five point' health program on May Day when certificates were presented to children that had demonstrated improvement in their health. Most activities took place during the school day, but there were some celebrations held after school in the evening.[lxxvi]

In 1940, Richard L. Kirby posed for a photo in his tuxedo and top hat with Alease Passmore dressed in a formal gown during May Day activities at Victoria High. They were described as "Breath of the South" in *The Victorian*, the Victoria High School newsletter.[lxxvii]

Michael A. Tisdale said, "There was a big celebration at Victoria High School on May Day. Many students—especially the girls, 'dressed up' for the occasion. I remember riding the bus to school on this special day—the 'hoop' or 'bell' skirt the girls wore seemed to take up the whole seat. Some of the children got to wrap the maypole as they danced to music."[lxxviii]

Margaret C. Cocks, former English teacher at the Kenbridge High School, shared memories of how they celebrated May Day in the 1940s and 1950s. Cocks commented, "Field day—as it was also called—was a big celebration, too! The students at the Kenbridge High School participated in different kinds of physical activities and games, and the program ended with the wrapping of the wooden pole as symphonic music played. We always selected a king and queen for that day."[lxxix]

Two former students of the Kenbridge Graded School spoke about their experience during May Day activities held in the 1960s. They were Alvester L. Edmonds and Barbara N. Shell. Edmonds had a smile on his face when he said, "I still have fond memories of those special days when we traveled to play a softball game at our rival school—Lunenburg Elementary. We would always win, of course."[lxxx] Shell described her experiences as a "good time." "I vividly recall the time when our teacher constructed skirts for the girls using crepe paper in an assortment of five colors, but they wore their own blouse." Shell chuckled as she continued, "The girls wore the paper skirts—not the guys! Each class presented a dance or routine during the program. This was a time of fellowship when parents could come to support the school and see the activities. There were lots of treats available for the students to eat. The May Day activities included the selection of a "queen" for the day. The student selected was among several contestants, and the one who presented the largest donation was crowned "queen." All donations collected were used to purchase needed instructional materials and supplies for the school.[lxxxi]

May Day activities were still taking place at some schools as late as 1941—sixteen years after the first recorded celebration in 1925.[lxxxii] The black schools continued May Day celebrations into the 1960s. No information was found as to when these school-based celebrations ended. May Day celebrations still continue, but not as a school-related activity. May Day is sponsored annually by the Rosary Chapter #177 Order of the Eastern Star (OES) of Virginia, Prince Hall Affiliate in Kenbridge, Virginia. Barbara T. Reese, OES member, spoke of the organization's sponsorship. Reese explained, "Today, our May Day is a fundraiser activity that provides scholarship funds for deserving county high school seniors."[lxxxiii]

A. B. "Ben" Wilson remained as school superintendent for approximately six years and ended his tenure in the spring of 1925.

Lunenburg Native Appointed School Leader

James Thomas Waddill, Jr., was appointed the fourth school superintendent by the fall of 1925. Waddill was a Lunenburg County native, and grew up in Victoria, Virginia. He began his education where his mother was the teacher of the first school in the town.

James T. Waddill, Jr.

Waddill and his brother, J. Wade Waddill, were the only members of first graduating class at Victoria High School in 1913. J.T. Waddill would be confronted with a number of issues during his eleven years at the helm of the school system.[lxxxiv]

In September 1925, *The Victoria Dispatch* listed the schools and teachers of Lunenburg County under the heading: *School Teachers in Lunenburg County: A Complete Review of the White and Colored Teachers for the 1925-1926 Session.* The article stated, "The teaching force was the same as previous year, at least in number, although there were some changes for individual schools. Some are still running as one-room schools, where last year they had two teachers, and vice-versa. The personnel considerably changed; fully one-third of the teachers would be new to the county or new to the school to which they were assigned."

W. D. Dickinson, State Supervisor of Textbooks and School Libraries, was invited as the guest speaker at Victoria High School. During the teachers' initial annual meeting on September 25, Dickinson urged them to be especially careful with their diet and method of living so that they might always be in the best health and thereby be at the height of their efficiency in the classroom. He also warned the teachers against automobile riding at night and numerous engagements which took their attention away from their school duties thereby necessitating a low grade of instruction and poor discipline in their schools.[lxxxv]

In June 1926, the School Board met in the superintendent's office to complete routine work, select teachers for the ensuing year, and plan for the summer school session.[lxxxvi] In September—and earlier years—the pre-opening school meetings for white teachers were held at the Victoria High School and, on occasion, at Kenbridge High School; while colored teachers met at the Lunenburg Training School. Plausible reasons for the selection of these schools were segregation of facilities; space availability; and two of them were closer to the superintendent's office in Victoria, Virginia.[lxxxvii] On June 4, an announcement was printed in the local newspaper about summer school information for high school pupils. Superintendent Waddill wrote, "The pupil must be examined on the work done under a tutor or by the principal of the school or some person designated by him, or by the superintendent." The announcement was to benefit those students who expected to make up academic deficiencies through tutorial summer work.

The Meherrin School opened by the fall of 1926. It was a four-room school with an auditorium, housing students in grades one through four.

Teachers were required to maintain the cleanliness of the building and grounds and to make fires in the stoves to heat the rooms. In later years, the school had a custodian who made the fires and cleaned the building.[lxxxviii]

In 1926, there were twenty-four schools, including Meherrin, for whites in operation—Kenbridge High, Woodrow, Dundas Graded, Oral Oaks, Wattsboro, Nonintervention, Salem, Snead, Lochleven, Mizpah, Lunenburg, Reedy, Ragsdale, Victoria High, Marshalltown, Union Central, Nutbush, Ledbetter, Fort Mitchell, Williams, Kenilworth, Lee's Mill, and Traffic.[lxxxix] The thirty-one Negro schools were Kenbridge Graded, Varick, Asbury, Cherry Hill, Camp, Central, Cool Spring, Davis, Gill Hill, Pleasant Oak, Nutbush, Macedonia, Plantersville, Mount Bethel, Oak Grove, Trinity, New Grove, Gary, Wattsboro, Friendship, Rosebud, Mount Olive, Bethany, West End, Midway, West Hill, Reedy, Traffic, Unity, Lone Oak, and the Lunenburg Training School (sometimes referred to as the Colored Industrial School).[xc]

A week before schools opened, Superintendent Waddill requested principals to urge their teachers to visit every patron during the first two weeks of school and to do everything possible to interest them in school and school work. He said, "An attempt will be made to enroll every child of school age during the first week. A home visit prior to the first day of school meant that school officials were eagerly expecting students to attend school on a regular basis. This would strengthen the relationship between home and school, and garner the parents' support throughout the educational process."[xci]

Report of School Progress

School Superintendent J. T. Waddill, Jr. addressed the Victoria Kiwanis Club in Victoria on the status of the school system in the evening of September 3, 1926. He provided a detailed description of the progress made by the county. He noted that Lunenburg County had made noted growth in its public education during the years from 1900 to 1914. The amount spent for education had increased to $9,162.50, and the county was paying $7,409.24 in salaries because of new hires. The length of the school year had increased eight months. During the 1914-1915 year, $42,718.25 was spent for public schools. Teachers' salaries claimed around $22,387.40, while about $20,330.85 went to capitalization, maintenance, and operation.

Analysis of age and grade distribution of the pupils in the county during the 1914 school year revealed that 1,480 were over-age or "retarded" pupils. They were on average of two years behind the grade in which their chronological age would normally place them. One hundred and twenty-seven were accelerated or ahead of the grade in which they would naturally be placed, and 732 were in the grade corresponding to their chronological age. This large percent of over-age or retarded pupils was due to the four following factors: (1) irregular attendance; (2) poor home environment; (3) poor instruction; and (4) mental deficiencies. The first of these factors was the largest contributor to non-promotion or retardation, and the other three were named in order of their importance. The greatest number of cases of retardation occurred in rural districts that had one- and two-room schools with a seven-month term.

Significant growth on the part of the schools of Lunenburg manifested between the years of 1915 and 1926. There were sixty high school graduates, most of whom were expecting to go to college. Waddill continued, "But, there were still many sections of the county whose sole educational facilities consisted of a one-room school, operated seven months in the year by an untrained, inexperienced teacher. In these communities the children have only half a chance to secure an education, and in most instances, they drop out of school at an early age.

Throughout the State and Union, the sons and daughters of Lunenburg are scattered. Their hearts turn to fond recollection to the home of their childhood. Many of them left the county in order that their children might be educated. Many more will do so if better educational opportunities are not provided. Why should we not make all our schools—primary, grammar and secondary—so efficient, so permeated with that culture that has made our State famous, that not only will its citizens refuse to leave Lunenburg, but that people will be attracted from adjoining counties and states in order that their children may secure training in all that upholds the noble traditions of the past and make for the highest ideals of the future?"[xcii]

In 1928 the State Board of Education used five academic and five financial factors as a basis for determining the ranking and efficiency of the county school systems with the state. When schools in Lunenburg County were compared among one hundred (100) counties of the state, its ranking was 52nd in average annual teacher salary; 46th in adequacy in local support; 50th in to cost per room; 45th in per capita cost of instruction; 64th in capita cost on enrollment; 57th in per cent attendance of population; 39th in per cent of teacher holding above First Grade Certificates; 77th in length of term; 36th in percent of high school pupils on enrollment; and 37th in adequacy of educational facilities.

An analysis of the ranking of the school system shed light on its educational needs in the 1920s. Although Lunenburg ranked in the fifty-second place in average annual salaries of teachers, it must be remembered that this ranking takes into consideration the salaries of both colored and white teachers. One must be mindful that average annual salary paid to Negro teachers during the session 1926-27 was $248.43; it can be readily understood that the average annual salary paid to white teachers is higher than that paid in fifty percent of the counties.

In the total per capita cost of instruction on enrollment, Lunenburg ranked forty-fifth while in total per capita cost on enrollment it occupied sixty-fourth. It may be inferred that Lunenburg did not spend as much as other counties on the maintenance of buildings, and for fuel, lights, transportation, etc.

In the percent of attendance on population, Lunenburg ranked rather low, fifty-seventh place. The census showed a school population of 4,766, while the school enrollment for the school term of 1925-26 was 3,699, with an actual daily attendance of 2,056. Many of the children of the county who should have been in school were not enrolled, while many enrolled only attended school a few days out of the year, thus causing a waste of salaries paid to teachers. A great economic waste to the county and state was created when children were forced to repeat their grades, thus causing children to eventually drop out of school without securing an elementary education.

Lunenburg ranked in the thirty-ninth place in percent of teachers holding above a First Grade Certificate. If Negro teachers were not taken into consideration when making this ranking, Lunenburg would have ranked much higher. This ranking showed that teachers in Lunenburg were much better qualified than the average teacher of the state.

In length of school term, the county ranked lower than under any other heading, due largely to the Negro schools of the county, which had only a five-month term.

In percent of high school pupils on total enrollment, Lunenburg ranked rather high, in thirty-seventh place. This shows that even though enrollment and attendance were poor, when compared to other counties of the state, Lunenburg held a large percent of the pupils through the elementary school, instilling in them a desire for additional education after the completion of seventh grade. In adequacy of educational facilities, Lunenburg ranked thirty-seventh and was given a score of 77.83 percent.

As shown in the various rankings, it is fair to say that even though Lunenburg County ranked above a majority of the counties of the state, one must be mindful that Lunenburg was compared with counties of a state that ranked rather low when compared to other educational systems of the United States.[xciii]

New Challenges and Opportunities

The school year of 1927-28 was uneventful as the School Board made plans for the ensuing school session. The year of 1928-1929 brought new challenges and opportunities for Superintendent Waddill. An important change was made in the school system with the appointment of a school division leader. In June of 1928, an amendment to the Constitution by the General Assembly provided that the school superintendent is appointed by the local school board.

In an article printed in *The Victoria Dispatch*, April 1928, Governor Harry F. Byrd, Sr. wrote, "Important changes are made in the school system. It is provided by amendment that school superintendents shall be appointed by the local school boards instead of by the State Board of Education, and confirmed by the Senate, as required by the existing Constitution. This gives greater control of their local affairs."[xciv] The School Board, in accordance to the law passed in June of 1928, made its first appointment of a county superintendent of education. J. T. Waddill, Jr., was unanimously elected on February 5, 1929, beginning July 1 for a term of four years.

On February 5, 1929, another matter of general interest came up at the School Board meeting. It was the Board's adherence to a resolution passed in 1927 that married women could not teach in the county.[xcv] Many of young women would devote their lives to the education field and remain unmarried, but others teachers married and resigned from public education to take care of their family or pursued a different vocation.

In April 1929, Superintendent Waddill provided an explanation to the School Board of the school rating results complied by the State Board of Education the previous year. Waddill concluded his report with the statement: "These factors do not show conclusively the weaknesses or strong point of the Lunenburg County Public Schools, but a close study of the figures will reveal to the discerning mind some of its most outstanding needs."[xcvi]

Education and the Church

In Lunenburg County, the next public buildings to be erected, in addition to the water power grist and mills, were invariably the churches. Pulley wrote, "In many instances the miller and the preacher were one and the same person."[xcvii] The most oppressive limit on slave education was a reaction to Nat Turner's Revolt in Southampton County, Virginia, during the summer of 1831.[xcviii] The uprising generated fears of slave insurrections and the spread of abolitionist materials and ideology led to radical restrictions on gatherings, travel, and—of course—literacy. Not only did owners fear the spread of specifically abolitionist materials, they did not want slaves to question their lot; thus, reading and reflection were to be prevented at any cost. This action was to discourage the propagation of education and literacy for slaves through Bible reading. African American preachers would often teach some of the slaves to read in secret, but there were very few opportunities for a concentrated period of instruction. The preachers, abolitionists, and other community leaders provided valuable political, cultural, and religious information through spirituals, stories, and other forms of oral literacy. Out of plantation prayer meetings and slave-quarter wakes came spirituals and other unique expressions of the African American personality.[xcix]

The rise of the black church was one of the most enduring and important phenomena during and after the Reconstruction. In 1865, after the Civil War, one of the first things Negroes did was to build an Episcopal church by the Trinity Community League. Many of these churches played an active role in the social life of the community. The church provided an effective organization for the citizens as a forum for expression on many issues, a plan for social living, and it offered relief and hope.[c] The church was the first social institution controlled entirely by the African Americans. The church served as an important training ground for leadership, in addition to the spiritual benefits it afforded.[ci] Subsequently, the church and public education intertwined as many churches provided a place of education, and vice-versa.

Wood wrote, "The development of education for African American students in Lunenburg County was characterized by generous contributions from sacrifices of organized philanthropy and the Negro Baptist churches. Even though these interested groups made vital contributions, educational opportunities and facilities for Negroes continued to lag behind those for the whites. From 1871 to 1906, six of the forty-two Negro schools were first taught in the churches, and ten of these schools were constructed on church property. The Irby House was a school constructed on church property during this period."[cii]

Traditionally, the local church serves as a "center" for social, political, economic, and educational change in the community, and as a safe haven for those seeking a better way of life for themselves and their families. The church is still viewed as a place of worship and center for community activities. In the historic and traditional sense, religious institutions have played a vital role as a spiritual, educational, and cultural force in shaping wholesome and socially accepted patterns of behavior. This being said, it is safe to assume that some church members have a vested interest in the viability and operation of the school system as they are public school employees and regularly participate in their church assemblies or other religious groups.

CHAPTER 3
SCHOOLS AND THE GREAT DEPRESSION

The Great Depression (1930-1939) would shake the Commonwealth like no other event in the twentieth century, other than World War II. The Great Depression brought the American economy to a standstill and produced untold misery for Virginians. Virginia did not escape these trouble times. Although the crisis was late arriving, its impact was strongly felt by early 1931. Governor John Garland Pollard announced a possible budget deficit due to the continued downturn. By 1933, the United States economy had hit rock bottom. It became a time for rigid economizing on Virginia's farms despite their self-sufficiency. Private relief agencies like the Family Service Society and the Salvation Army exhausted their resources, forcing greater reliance on public relief.

Unemployed whites took jobs normally reserved for blacks, and some organizations were calling on employers to fire blacks and hire whites. Scarce relief funds invariably were unfairly distributed, sometimes denied altogether. Continuing a trend begun in the twenties, black farm holdings declined. The only consolation in all this was that the decades old discrimination and poverty made greater deprivation somewhat easier to bear; in fact, many blacks experienced very little change, being "used to hard times anyway."[ciii]

Roosevelt Crowder recalled what life was like during the depression years. He said, "As a sharecropping family, I remember in 1936 when we worked with our father on a white farm. Most farmers did the best they could with what they had; it was so bad that they couldn't accomplish much. My schooling at Unity School was limited because I had to work on the farm most days of the week. My father would say, 'Well, son, no school today.' So, there was no school for me!" In 1945, the Crowder family was able to purchase their own land and relocate to the Victoria area.[civ]

In 1930s, many of the teachers in the county resided in a neighborhood boarding house. The boarding house was usually a private home in the community where a room or rooms were rented to teachers. Bernice Stokes Charlton spoke about her schooling and the neighborhood boarding house. Charlton said, "I attended the Cool Spring School in the Rehoboth area. It was a single-room; frame building with about thirty students in grades one through seven. My teacher was Maude E. Valentine and she lived in a community boarding house. With no available transportation, our teacher walked to and from school about three miles each way."[cv] The neighborhood boarding house was usually within walking distance from the school, and it served as a "home away from home" for many educators. Margaret C. Cocks spoke about her life as a young educator. She said, "In the 1930s teachers beginning their teaching career in Lunenburg County did not make very much money, therefore, many of them rented a room in a local boarding house. The boarding house where I lived was on Fifth Avenue in Kenbridge, Virginia and within walking distance from the school."[cvi]

Dr. Sidney B. Hall succeeded Dr. Hart as state superintendent of public instructions in 1931. His appointment coincided with the Great Depression, which had serious repercussions on public education. The state's overall financial position at the beginning of the Depression had been favorable since its predominantly agrarian economy was less affected than the economy of the more highly industrialized states. However, tax income from both state and local sources declined sharply.[cvii]

Early Funding Woes

In late 1931 and early 1932, concerned with the lack of adequate state support for school funding, Superintendent Waddill submitted a series of articles to the local newspaper. In the first article, he wrote, "During the period of great financial depression, a request of $2,000,000 must be backed by sound reasoning and an emergency situation. Such a situation faces the rural districts of Virginia at the present time. Unless additional State aid is given, the rural school program—already inadequate—must be curtailed."[cviii]

In the second article, Waddill stressed, "Support of the public schools is a State function, because it is to the advantage of the State to have a well-informed and intelligent citizenry. It is to the advantage of the cities to be surrounded by prosperous rural areas. It is only through education of the right kind that these things can be brought about. Statistics showed that the farmer, in proportion to his wealth, was bearing a much heavier load in direct taxation than the city dweller."[cix]

In January 1932, the School Board sent a letter to representatives of the legislature—Hunter H. Watson and W. E. Nelson—about the lack of state funding. A shortened school term of six months was in consideration due to the uncollected 1930 and 1931 school taxes. Lunenburg County had attempted to provide for an efficient system of public free schools by levying the maximum amount provided by act of the General Assembly for schools. Unless the taxes were secured from sources other than farms, Lunenburg would not be able to operate an efficient system of free schools. The letter went on to read, "Since the State of Virginia is able to spend as much as twenty million dollars on its highway system, it should not neglect the education of its children. We, the members of the Lunenburg County School Board, trust that as its representatives in the general assembly of Virginia, you will do everything within your power to secure a state appropriate for our county schools, in order that the children of this county may be able have school facilities enjoyed by the children in more prosperous sections of Virginia."[cx] Lunenburg County's early funding woes were certainly influenced by the advent of the Great Depression of the 1930s. However, the Depression years were not noted for major changes or innovations in Virginia's public education.[cxi]

In February 1932, one of the topics at the School Board meeting was the financial status of the school system. The Board was informed that the teachers and truck drivers of the county were willing to volunteer a ten per cent reduction of their salaries provided this would enable the schools to operate the maximum term of eight months. During the meeting, it was learned that $36,000 of the school taxes were delinquent, and in order to operate eight months, it would be necessary to collect $23,000 of this amount or incur an operation deficit equal to whatever part of this $23,000 remained uncollected on May 8, 1932. After much discussion and with an uncollected amount of school taxes of $36,000, the Board agreed to cut all employees ten percent. This decision on the part of the School Board gave the children enrolled in the schools of the county an opportunity to complete a full year's work and it helped to keep the high schools on the accredited list for another year.

In March, with funding still an issue, the Board carefully considered on a school-by-school basis the number of teachers needed based on enrollment. The decision was made to drop one teacher at three schools, thus reducing the number employed for the next term. By these means, with a slightly reduced salary scale, the Board was hoping to run the high schools—Kenbridge, Lochleven, and Victoria for nine months and all other schools eight months.[cxii] Teachers had been approved for the schools of Victoria High/Elementary, Kenbridge High/Elementary, Lochleven High/Elementary, Dundas, Meherrin, Pleasant Grove, Fort Mitchell, Nutbush, Williams, Kenilworth, Oral Oaks, Court House, William Bigger, Traffic, Nonintervention, Salem, Reedy, Rubermont, Russell, Ledbetter, and most of the small Negro schools.[cxiii]

Waddill's Leadership Continues

In spring 1933, Waddill was re-elected as the school superintendent. In March, the Williams School, a three-room structure, was entirely destroyed by fire. All of the textbooks owned by the children were destroyed, which was a direct loss to the people of the community. Temporary arrangements were made to complete the school year in a residence near the site of the school property. Waddill said, "A new building will be erected to commence the 1933-34 school term."

The schools would operate for a term of eight and one half months during the session. This was an increase of teaching days compared to the number when Waddill became superintendent.[cxiv]

In a statement to the School Board in 1933, Waddill said, "In addition to school consolidations, the system of transportation also accounts for the large increase in high school enrollment, which had almost doubled over the past nine years. The fact that children from practically every section of the county are now accessible to one of the four high schools is worthy of mention. There is nothing more important to the welfare of a community than its public schools. The best farming practice, efficient direction of labor, constructive leadership, the best home-life, good churches and Sunday schools, and efficient government are but a few of the important social qualities and institutions depending upon education."

Lunenburg County had begun to operate a system of tuition for non-resident school-age children. Children from the outside were charged the per capita cost of education, which was paid by the district in which these children resided.

The Depression took its toll on teachers as well. Many unemployed teachers were in need of relief. The Federal Emergency Relief Administration Act (FERA) was formed in May 1933 to alleviate unemployment. In 1935, FERA was replaced by the Works Progress Administration (WPA). Virginia effectively used federal funds from the Public Works Administration (PWA) and the WPA to provide needed school buildings.

Plans for the immediate employment of needy unemployed teachers in Virginia had been completed through the cooperation of the FERA, the State Emergency Relief Administration, and the State Department of Education. The Relief Program was handled by the regularly constituted school authorities and the local emergency authorities. All needy, unemployed teachers who wished to obtain teaching positions were directed to contact their local school superintendent. Dr. Hall had hoped that many unemployed teachers would obtain work relief.[cxv]

In the spring of 1936, J. T. Waddill, Jr. wrote another series of articles that were printed in the local newspaper. These articles compared the administration of Lunenburg County schools with that of adjoining counties the state in regard to enrollment and average attendance per teacher, term in days per teacher, average term in days, per capita cost of instruction, operation and maintenance, and the per capita distribution of state funds on the basis of school census. He concluded that Lunenburg County spent below the state average for the administration of schools, instruction, fixed charges and capital outlay, and operation of school plant; and that it spent more than the state average for transportation and debt service.

Waddill believed that the increase in enrollment and daily attendance; the amount of training beyond high school, high school attendance and graduation; increase in school term, value of school property increase; number of volumes in school libraries; and the decrease in school indebtedness—all indicated healthy trends in the public school system. He stressed, "It will be necessary to find more money with which to purchase adequate teaching materials and pay salaries which will attract the best types of young men and women, because it cannot be reasonably expected that these will continue to be attracted to the profession that pays a smaller annual stipend than does the State of Virginia to laborers on the highway system."[cxvi]

Waddill also pointed out, "The school buildings, grounds and equipment in Lunenburg are in better condition than ever before in the history of the county. However, there were many buildings, especially for the Negroes, that were totally inadequate—should be repaired and some replaced." He suggested the county adopt a building program which should seek to gradually remedy this situation on a pay-as-you-go basis.[cxvii] Progress in public education at the state level continued throughout the Depression years.[cxviii] On September 19, 1936 Waddill was appointed Clerk of the Circuit Court of Lunenburg County to fill the unexpired term of R. G. Dimmette. The School Board accepted Waddill's resignation. Under the law, the Board would elect the superintendent of schools from a list furnished by the State Board of Education.[cxix] James T. Waddill, Jr., had served as school superintendent for eleven years.

Adapted for School Leadership

Thomas Floyd "T.F." Crittenden was selected as the fifth superintendent of Lunenburg Schools in 1936, succeeding J. T. Waddill, Jr. Crittenden was born on March 30, 1908, in Crewe, Virginia. He was a graduate of Virginia Polytechnic Institute. After leaving college, Crittenden became principal of Ebony High School in Brunswick County before coming to Lunenburg as the principal of the Lochleven High School.[cxx]

Crittenden was appointed school superintendent by the School Board on October 2, 1936 to fill the unexpired term of Waddill, Jr. By March 1937, Crittenden was officially named the school system's leader for a four-year term ending in 1941. He was particularly "adapted for school leadership" and described as "an exceptionally fine student" by a Board member. Crittenden brought with him into the profession new methods and practices of teaching. Members of the Board felt that Crittenden was intellectually capable and he [Crittenden] would devote his best energies to the position of responsibility and trust. Crittenden was a school leader with experience as a high school administrator.[cxxi]

As the school system prepared to move into a new decade, Crittenden was faced with some of the previous school issues—pay disparity, school consolidation, transportation, school funding, supervision of Negro schools, and school attendance. There would be an opportunity to provide educational services to returning World War II veterans.

Lunenburg County had employed approximately sixty-five white teachers and forty-one colored teachers by the school term of 1937-1938.[cxxii]

In May 1938, a certificate of completion was awarded to students at the Lunenburg Training High School who had completed the elementary level course of study. The awarding of this certificate indicated that a student was ready to move on to the course of study at the secondary level.

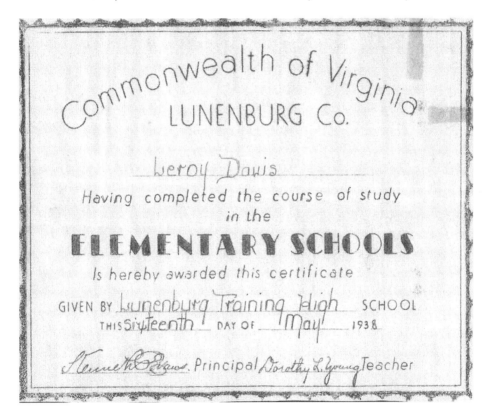

This 1938 Elementary Certificate was awarded to Leroy Davis for meeting the academic requirements for promotion to the secondary level at the Lunenburg Training High School.

In 1938-39, the Department of Education established a Division of Rehabilitation and Special and Adult Education which was to have far-reaching effects on the state's educational program. The division included a director and four supervisors of rehabilitation education, two supervisors of special education, and a supervisor of adult education.

In Lunenburg, teachers were appointed to fulfill positions for the school year. There were three high schools—Kenbridge, Lochleven, Victoria—and eleven elementary schools for whites; and for Negroes—Lunenburg Training High School and twenty-nine elementary schools. The small one-, two-, and three-room schools were often over-crowded with one or two teachers, and maybe a principal that provided the instruction. It was not unusual for the work of the principal to include both administrative and instructional duties. Eventually, this trend would change with the principal assigned to administrative duties only.

In January 1939, a group of Victoria High School students presented petitions requesting the School Board to permit the Agnes Winn Paschall to continue teaching the remainder of the school year. The Board received Paschall's resignation, and having passed a resolution at the beginning of the school year against the retention of women teachers after marriage, refused the request of the high school pupils. However, arrangements were made to have Paschall conduct examinations to students on that portion of the courses covered under her instruction.[cxxiii]

Dr. Hall, state superintendent of public instruction, was concerned to find that many children of school age were not enrolled in school and that the daily attendance in the state was only 83 per cent. He also recognized the need for an intensive program to improve instruction. Dr. Hall reorganized the Department of Education into six divisions—Research and Finance, Higher Education, Instruction, Vocational Education, School Buildings, and Libraries and Textbooks. The department was enlarged to include a total of twenty-eight staff members. The superintendent assigned the Division of Instruction the primary responsibility for initiating and developing a program to improve instruction.[cxxiv]

Dr. Hall stirred wide discussion throughout the Old Dominion when he advocated for a plan for a twelve-month school term. Hall believed a stagger system could be worked out under which children could attend school 189 days each year and ultimately might attend 200 days or more, using the property every month. Dr. Hall remarked: "As it is now, teachers work nine months a year and starve three months." Under his plan, teachers would be paid twelve months each year. Hall continued, "A twelve-month term is simply making the summer school an integral part of the school term." Dr. Hall called for better teacher pay, a study of the question of a later school entrance age or "money for nursery schools and kindergartens," the furnishing of free textbook and learning materials, and the expansion of adult and vocational education.[cxxv]

In other local matters, Superintendent Crittenden received a notice from the state that Lunenburg County would receive funds to be used for 1938-39 (instruction only) in the amount was $47,000, and of which $507.50 for Negro rural supervision. The rest of the cost of school operation was paid out by the county, including thirty percent of the instructional cost. Crittenden stated, "In making out the budget for the coming year, the Board was faced with the increase in requirements and demands, and that the levy for school purposes was already as high as the law allowed."

The Department of Education's expansion during the late 1930s and early 1940s reflected improvements in the economy. Curriculum revision at the state level was a major focus during the Depression years.[cxxvi]

Thomas F. Crittenden continued his employment as school superintendent into the World War II in spite of the depression years experienced by the district.

CHAPTER 4
SCHOOLS, WORLD WAR II AND POST-WAR DEVELOPMENTS

"Education is the most powerful weapon which you can use to change the world."

-Nelson Mandela

World War II, also called "The Second World War," was a global military conflict which began on September 1, 1939. Lunenburg County was impacted by the war on many fronts and played its part with the sacrifice of life and service of its native sons—men and women. The war-time efforts of all segments of the Lunenburg community—the Red Cross, County Department of Welfare, Victoria Fire Department, War Finance Committee, Virginia Railway Company, Lunenburg churches, and many citizens—are notable. The work of these agencies, religious organizations, and individuals was primarily with the needs of the civilians.

Schools in Wartime

Community organizations and various agencies were deeply committed to the war effort. The schools were often the object of support as men reported to their duty stations. For example, the Red Cross, in cooperation with other agencies in the county, helped to finance a program by which each underprivileged child of school age would be furnished one-half pint of milk a day and held a dental clinic for all school children.[cxxvii]

There were shortages everywhere. The schools experienced problems such as the lack of drivers—many of whom had gone to war. Some of the buses had to be driven by young men who were still attending school themselves.[cxxviii]

In 1934, Helen W. Buchanan graduated from Westhampton in Richmond, Virginia. Her first teaching job was in the Pittsylvania County Public Schools. She married O. M. Buchanan in 1937, and the young couple moved to Kenbridge, Virginia in 1939. Buchanan said, "I remember how difficult it was to get a teaching job in 1939. There was a policy that married women were not allowed to teach in the public schools. So, I started a child care preschool in the basement of my home—serving nineteen three-year-olds. Eventually the School Board changed this policy, and in 1957, I returned to the classroom as a seventh grade teacher at the Kenbridge High School." Buchanan began teaching fourth-grade students in 1963 and she semi-retired in the spring of 1977, but continued to teach part-time. Buchanan completely retired in 1979.[cxxix]

William W. Craighead, a faculty member at the Lunenburg Training School, wrote an article on the contributions of the Negroes during the war effort. An excerpt from his article states: "One of the first wartime measures inaugurated on the home front was the rationing of various essential items. Rationing systems were set up in various parts of the county, with the colored people setting up a board at the Lunenburg Training School under the direction of Kenneth P. Evans, Lucy M. Morrison, and local teaching staff throughout the county for the issuing of ration books and stamps for items such as gasoline, fuel, oil, sugar, meats and essential clothing obtained through rationing. It was through such rationing that a greater flow of essential goods reached the war front in unlimited quantities.

The effort of the colored people in aiding the war is best described under a group of headings as the colored citizens developed their efforts through a thorough organization of the county, of which practically all of our colored citizens so wholeheartedly contributed. Without such cooperation, the war effort among the citizens would have been a total failure. Much credit is due to the colored people of Lunenburg County for the success of the Rural War Food Production Training Program.

This program was set up within the county with the general idea of training citizens to further food production on their farms and also to preserve that food. The program was successful through the uniting efforts of the agricultural agencies of the county. Programs of this type helped relieve the larger centers of the State, which were engaged in all-out production for the armed forces. Much credit is due to the colored people of Lunenburg for the success of this program."[cxxx]

On October 16, 1940, the schools of Victoria High, Kenbridge High, Meherrin, Nonintervention, Kenilworth, Fort Mitchell, William Bigger, and Pleasant Grove were closed for the day because they were used as a place to register all young men between the ages of twenty-one and thirty-five, inclusive. The principals were urged to give all assistance possible in getting Registration facilities arranged in their schools as requested by the County Electoral Board. Crittenden said, "During these days of peril to our 'democratic way of living,' we as teachers wish to do everything within our power in cooperating with national and local authorities on our program of National Defense." Some of the teachers volunteered to assist with the Registration for National Defense."[cxxxi]

By January 13, 1941, a Defense Training Program was set up in the county by the United States Office of Education through the School Board. Classes were organized at Victoria in the Victoria Supply Company shop building; Kenbridge High School shop building; and at the Lunenburg Training School shop building fifteen hours per week for a period of approximately sixteen weeks.[cxxxii] Competent instructors conducted classes in woodwork and carpentry; metal work; care and repair to tractors, trucks, and automobiles; and electricity. Interested persons ages seventeen to twenty-five had to complete an application form posted in the local newspaper. Approximately $2,000 worth of power equipment had been purchased for these classes, and the shops were to be fully equipped.[cxxxiii] Fifty-two young men took advantage of the opportunity and enrolled in the Defense Training classes with P. B. Matthews as instructor at Kenbridge High School – fifteen pupils; N. Tanner, instructor at Victoria High School – eighteen pupils; and Archer Morrison, instructor at Lunenburg Training School – nineteen pupils.[cxxxiv]

In March 1942 the School Board also resolved that, due to the national emergency and the shortage of teachers, it was considered in the best interest of the school system that the existing rule against the employment of married women teachers be rescinded upon approval.[cxxxv] During the meeting, a citizen said, "It is an essential part of our war effort to keep our schools, churches, and libraries in a healthy and vigorous condition. As a matter of fact, it is largely for the privilege of having such things that this war is being fought. Using married teachers would free male teachers for service." As a result of this impassioned plea, the Board lifted the married teacher ban.[cxxxvi] The reversal of this rule directly impacted the number of married women who returned to the classroom. For other women, for the most part, the war meant learning to do new things such as working at a public job or running the farm for their husband.[cxxxvii]

By the fall, the teachers were one hundred percent in their pledges to have varying amounts deducted from their salary checks each month for the purchase of War Savings Bonds. During the year, more than $5,000 worth of War Bonds were purchased by the teachers of Lunenburg to support the war effort. Carl Hardy Jones remarked, "We cannot hope to win peace without sacrifice—give as never before!"[cxxxviii]

Thomas Floyd Crittenden resigned his position as the school superintendent in the spring of 1943, after serving for approximately six years. When Crittenden left Lunenburg, he became a captain in the army during World War II and was stationed overseas for two years. After the war, Crittenden was appointed executive officer for veterans training with the State Board of Education for about a year, and then he was employed with Selective Service. In 1952, Crittenden died at age forty-three as an Administration Officer for Virginia Selective Service in Richmond, Virginia.[cxxxix]

New School Chief

Macon F. Fears succeeded T. F. Crittenden as the acting superintendent on March 1, 1943. He began his new role as the sixth school leader at the height of World War II. Fears had been a teacher at the Fort Mitchell School, and principal of the Jefferson High School in Culpepper County. He also served as the principal of the Lochleven School to fill the vacancy of James "Jim" Hall Revere, who had been appointed principal of Kenbridge High School in July of 1940. Fears married a local school teacher and the couple resided in the Fort Mitchell area. The Lochleven High School secondary department closed after a couple of years because of low enrollment.

On December 3, 1943, the School Board at a regular meeting reappointed Elsie Judy as elementary supervisor. Elsie Judy, J. H. Revere, and H. L. Blanton were asked to present a plan at the meeting in January 1944—for improving the schools' offering for a post-war world.[cxl] No information is available with regard to the development of such a plan.

In spring 1944, school report cards were standardized, and reports indicated more than grade level completion. It included the scholastic

Macon F. Fears was the principal of Lochleven School from 1940–1943.

achievement, social attitudes and habits, health and home report of each pupil per marking period. Teachers received cards at the beginning of the school year, and they were required to complete a report for each child. The Board approved the purchase of 2,000 cumulative record cards to be used in the schools beginning the next school term.[cxli]

Florence L. Hayes Hatchett is a former student of the West Hill School. Hatchett said, "Our school had one teacher who taught several grades at one time. Each row of students represented a different grade, and we were allowed to help the students in the lower grades from time to time. Some of us would be placed in two grades if we didn't have enough students for a single grade. My teachers were Ada A. Jenkins, Elizabeth Trotter Wood, and Elizabeth Cain Jones. I think my teachers were excellent educators— they cared about the students."[cxlii] In 1944, 'A Report to Parents' from Acting Superintendent Fears was printed on the back of the report card and it was signed by the teacher, Elizabeth T. Wood.[cxliii]

The war had taken its toll on the local economy. In 1944, the Victoria High School cafeteria was aided by a committee of the Victoria School Parent-Teacher Association to secure and can all food possible for use in the cafeteria for the winter. Donations such as tomatoes were given by citizens.[cxliv] Negro educators had also set a $1,000 quota for the Virginia War Fund, with Lucy M. Morrison as chairman.[cxlv]

Road to Recovery

World War II was over in May of 1945. Some of the servicemen did not return home alive, but many did. Pulley (1949) noted, "The returned veteran, granted the numerous advantages which are his due, is rapidly changing the business, agricultural, and to some extent, the political and religious outlook of the county."[cxlvi] Some veterans took advantage of the opportunity through the *Servicemen's Readjustment Act of 1944* (G. I. Bill) to complete the high school requirements and continue their education. The school system offered education classes to veterans who had returned from the War.

Richard L. Kirby shared his experience of when the government offered this educational opportunity to veterans who had returned home from the war. Kirby said, "I taught World War II veterans who had returned to Lunenburg after the war. My classes were held in the evening for those who were being assisted by the G.I. Bill to complete their schooling." Kirby's eyes brightened as he continued. "I specifically remember my contract with the school system as an agriculture teacher in the shop at Victoria High School in 1940s. My job was to help returning veterans with developing needed work skills. I did not remain in education a very long time." Kirby became an insurance agent, selling a number of policies to many of the school teachers in Lunenburg County and surrounding areas.[cxlvii]

In 1945, school children took part in the war effort as well. They were expected to make a county-wide canvass during November, in which they would accept checks, cash (or pledges) with the applications, and arranged to deliver the bonds to the purchaser. "We are tremendously pleased that the school children of Lunenburg County will assist the Victory Loan. This service by the children means more to them than a patriotic assistance. The experiences in contacting the public and in selling Bonds will be an education in good citizenship," said A. B. Chandler, Victory Loan Chairman.[cxlviii]

World War II had revitalized the national and state economies and prepared the way for new opportunities.[cxlix] Lunenburg County was on the road to recovery. Although the county experienced economic growth and renewal following the war, many of the county's schools did not fare as well. Neale wrote, "After World War II, the schools were in disrepair and needed work done. The lack of manpower and the focus on war efforts had taken a toll."[cl]

Throughout the Commonwealth of Virginia, educational problems grew out of the war and post-war years. The shortage of qualified teachers that developed at the outbreak of World War II had become critical by the end of the war. The widely held belief that most of the absentees would return to teaching after the war proved to be a false hope, for the number returning was insignificant compared to the serious deficiency that existed. Inflation continued into the post-war period, and despite pay increases voted by the General Assembly, teacher salaries were not competitive with those in other states or with salaries in the private sector. Recruitment of new teachers became increasingly difficult as enrollment in teacher-training colleges declined. Following the war, the need for more teachers was accentuated by the increased birth rate during the "baby boom," the improved holding power of the schools, and the change to a twelve-grade system. Broader curriculum offerings and the need to adjust the heavy pupil loads that had been carried by teachers during the war aggravated the situation.[cli]

Despite impediments, some forward steps were taken during this period at the state level. The State Department of Education initiated visiting teacher and conservation education programs, increased emphasis on guidance, and started a statewide testing program.[clii] In the spring of 1945, the School Board authorized Fears to secure a visiting teacher for Lunenburg County, with the state paying two-thirds of the salary. On June 1, 1945, the School Board employed Virginia Price as the visiting teacher. Price had been principal of the Meherrin School for four years, and would become the first visiting teacher for the county. She worked for twelve months with a monthly salary of $170 plus five cents per mile for travel.[cliii] Her duties included promoting regular attendance on the part of the pupils, working with the classroom teachers, and helping parents in cases where circumstances indicate the need.[cliv]

The Board also accepted a recommendation of Superintendent Fears that an eighth grade be made a part of the high school, thus creating a system of twelve years of education—seven in the elementary grades and five years at the secondary level. The eighth grade was an orientation period and a time to take care of weaknesses by giving diagnostic tests. It was believed children would benefit from instruction under several teachers instead of only one; thus, enabling individual students to concentrate on subjects they may have failed to make satisfactory progress in the preceding year.[clv]

In June 1945, a letter from R. F. Williams, State Supervisor of Elementary Education, was read to the School Board by Fears, stating that funds were available for employment of a Negro visiting teacher for the county with the state paying two-thirds of the salary. One visiting teacher had been already employed for the county, and since this was a new program, the School Board decided not to employ another visiting teacher. On May 6, 1949, the Board accepted the resignation of Virginia Price as visiting teacher effective June 30, 1949.

A number of years later, Anne Terrell would be appointed the visiting teacher following the resignation of Virginia Price. In a statement during a general meeting of Lunenburg County teachers held at the Victoria Elementary school on September 1, 1966, Terrell said, "Among several causes for poor attendance were the child's and the parent's attitude toward school; poverty or lack of funds for books, clothes, medical and dental bills; lack of credit at stores; babysitting for parents; social misfits and boredom. There is definitely a relationship between the child's achievement and attendance." Terrell asked teachers to help promote good attendance by visiting the home of the child who attends poorly; and also to help give the child a feeling of achievement in some area as an incentive to attend school.[clvi] Lunenburg County approved the staff for the 1945-46 school year. There were twenty-six schools for Negroes, and six schools for whites in operation.[clvii] The number of schools in operation and teachers approved did not change for the following school of 1946-47.[clviii]

In 1947, with carefree summer days a memory, pupils throughout the county trudged back to school on September 6 to face now nine months of study. Schools for Negroes included the Lunenburg Training School, Kenbridge Graded School, and eighteen other small schools (grades one through seven). There were two high schools—Kenbridge and Victoria (combination elementary level) and four elementary schools—Lochleven, Meherrin, Fort Mitchell, and Kenilworth for whites.[clix] The Negro schools—Mount Olive, Bethany, Macedonia, Cool Spring, and Gill Hill—closed in the spring of 1948.[clx]

The state entered the World War II and the postwar periods with a tremendous backlog of school building needs. War priorities allocated manpower and materials to the defense program and forced a suspension of new school construction "for the duration." Postwar efforts to meet the critical shortage of buildings encountered serious difficulties. Residential, commercial, and industrial construction needs had been deferred during the war, resulting in postwar competition for labor and inaccurate cost estimates added to the difficulties. All of this occurred at a time when additional classrooms were needed to accommodate the rapidly increasing enrollments during the early 1950s. Shortly after his election in 1950, Governor John S. Battle carried out his campaign promise by recommending that seven million dollars in state aid be given to localities for school construction. The General Assembly approved his proposal.

Three state superintendents served during the war and postwar years. They were Dr. Dabney S. Lancaster (1941-1946), Dr. G. Tyler Miller (1946-1949), and Dr. Dowell J. Howard (1949-1957).[clxi]

Superintendent Fears ended the school year on an optimistic note with the prospect of new school construction, and the modernization of some existing buildings.

CHAPTER 5
SCHOOL TRANSPORTATION

"Fix in your heart the deep conviction that the welfare of this community depends upon a constantly rising level of participation by its citizens in public education."[clxii]

— Macon F. Fears

School transportation has been a major part of free public education since the "horse and buggy" days or when the first paneled truck was used to transport children to and from school. One major hurdle in equal accessibility to public education was inadequate school transportation. In the earlier years, many children walked to and from school for several miles because there was no school bus provided.

The best information about the earliest school transportation is that of Accomack County, on the Eastern Shore. It was probably the first to begin with the use of covered wagons in 1902. Three years later, the same kind of transportation—in horse drawn wagons—was begun in Highland and Norfolk Counties. Highland County was the first of the school divisions in the mountainous areas to begin transporting students. Twelve other school divisions, all in the eastern part of the state, including Highland and Norfolk Counties, had begun transporting pupils by 1920.[clxiii]

James Saunders spoke about the conversion of his Ford panel truck into a vehicle for transporting children to school in Lunenburg County. The truck was equipped with three wooden benches on the back—one in the center and two on each side—all parallel to the length of the truck. Saunders thought he was among the first school bus drivers in the county.[clxiv]

It is believed that the first Lunenburg County School Garage was a frame building constructed in the early 1920s near the Lunenburg County Bank (now Benchmark Community Bank Administrative Offices) in Kenbridge, Virginia. Four school buses were added to the school's fleet because of an increase in the enrollment of children in the county schools.[clxv]

The second building—constructed in the 1930s—was a cinderblock structure located on Oral Oaks Road (#635) a few hundred yards from Highway 40 (K-V Road). It was a service station with an office area, automotive supplies, three cargo bays, gas and air pumps—a place for the repair and maintenance of the buses and other school-related vehicles.

This former Lunenburg County School Garage was constructed in the 1930s, and remained in operation during the school desegregation era. In later years, it was abandoned and demolished in September of 2013.

The *County Unit Act of 1922* also appeared to give impetus to the provision of transportation. By 1930, more than half the counties in the state—fifty-seven in number—were providing transportation by some means. The consolidation of schools was greatly accelerated, and the improvement of roads also contributed to the rapid growth.

Minutes of the State Board of Education (September 1926) contain a statement of policy that the transportation of pupils was left to the judgment and discretion of local school boards. These minutes also contain some requirements for the school bus drivers, which seem to be the first time that such requirements were established. The only requirement that transportation is provided has been contained in the *Compulsory Attendance Law*, which exempted children from attending school unless transportation was provided for those living beyond certain distances.[clxvi]

In July 1927, a special meeting was held in the Superintendent Waddill's office for the purpose of providing school transportation. The School Board accepted bids on three bus routes—Pleasant Grove and two in the Fort Mitchell area. The bids went to B. L. Winn, W. A. Edwards, and R. F. Colbert.[clxvii]

Hilda Bagley Hawkins and her family lived near a dirt road west of the town of Kenbridge, Virginia. School bus transportation was limited when she began elementary school. Hawkins reminisced about having to walk about two miles to and from school with her four brothers each day. She said, "I started first grade at the Kenbridge Graded School in the fall of 1928. Schools were segregated and so were buses. There was a bus, but only for white children. Back then, we walked the dirt road that got very muddy when it rained. There were times that the white bus passed us, and we got mud thrown all over us. We would often hitch-hike a ride with Elizabeth Cralle Turns, a teacher at Kenbridge. She drove a Model-T Ford, and she'd often stop to offer us a ride to school. The five of us would climb in the rumble seat. I felt very proud to ride in the teacher's car. I remained at Kenbridge from the first through seventh grade, and in 1935, I was promoted to the high school level. By then, there was an old "raggedy" bus that stopped at the intersection of our road (now Hickory Road) and Highway 40 (Main Street) to take us to Lunenburg Training School in Victoria, Virginia."[clxviii]

In the 1930s, the legislature appropriated monies from the State Equalization Fund to aid localities with transportation, among other costs of education.[clxix]

Two Dollar Fare

In early 1932, Negro patrons organized county-wide leagues to provide transportation for their children because there was no public transportation available. It was decided funds would be raised to purchase a school bus. Four of the seven districts participated, and the patrons agreed to pay a transportation fee of two dollars per month for each child that rode the bus.[clxx]

A two-dollar receipt was written for the parents of Norma Elloise Marable (Callahan) and signed by Lelia M. Williams. Williams was an elementary teacher at the Lunenburg Training High School and treasurer of the Parent-Teacher Association as shown:[clxxi]

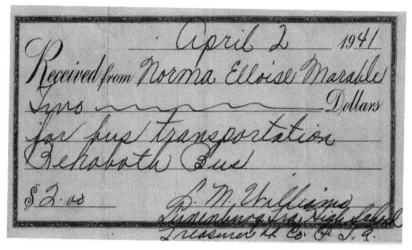

Many African American parents in Lunenburg County had to pay two dollars for their children to ride the school bus.

The patrons in the rural areas realized the importance of bus transportation since there was only one high school for Negro children in the county. It was not feasible for the children to attend the secondary school or either of the two elementary schools in the towns because of the distance. Negro supervisors worked with the county leagues to help obtain adequate school transportation.

In August 1932, Roger Gee, a patron of Russell School, requested the Board to furnish transportation for all children of the neighborhood. The Board agreed to allow transportation at the rate of two dollars per month for every child that attended school not less than fifteen days per month. The Board also agreed to allow C. E. Hardy an additional amount of eight dollars per month for this purpose. A committee of L. A. Hardy, J. T. Waddill, Jr., and H. S. Powers was appointed by the Board to make arrangements for a bus route for the school year. F. F. Redmond was given the sum of fifteen dollars a month to transport the high school children of the Ledbetter neighborhood to the Victoria High School. Lucy Hazelwood also requested that the Hardy truck be sent to her home in order that her children might attend school in Victoria. The Board agreed to renew W. H. Flowers' contract to operate a bus to Meherrin and set his compensation at fifty dollars a month.[clxxii]

The issue of public transportation for Negro children would again be brought to the School Board's attention in late summer of 1939. Shaffer Peter "S.P." Jones and a committee of school patrons appeared before the Board to ask for consideration of public transportation for Negro children. Jones was a local businessman, and leading citizen in the Kenbridge area. After consideration, the Board decided to allow each colored bus—of which there was a limited number—fifty dollars per month, provided the bus route was approved by the school superintendent.[clxxiii]

Initially, the School Board did not provide any buses in response to a petition from some of the Negro patrons.[clxxiv] Wood stressed, "Secondary-school enrollment for Negro students had increased from 92 in 1920 to 236 by late 1940. There were only four buses available to transport these students."[clxxv]

Russell L. Callahan described his school days before the availability of school transportation as "hard" because he had to walk a long distance to and from school. The school system operated a bus near his home, but he was not allowed to ride because he was a black student. School transportation was segregated; and few buses were provided for blacks at the time; therefore, Callahan went to the nearest schools of Gary and New Grove for his elementary education. He attended the Lunenburg Training School after his seventh-grade year. Callahan said, "In most cases buses, school furniture, and textbooks were passed down from the white schools—as I was told. Eventually, a bus was provided by the school system—two buses in the same area—one for blacks and the other for whites."[clxxvi]

Again, in April of 1940, a delegation of colored men appeared before the Board representing the school bus leagues with "S. P." Jones as their spokesman. They requested the School Board to take over the operation of buses beginning in fall of 1940. The matter was tabled. A patron of the West End School also appeared before the Board to request transportation allowance for his children. The Board informed the patron that it was the parents' obligation to see that their children got to school. Due to there not being enough children in the vicinity to maintain a school, the request was not granted.[clxxvii]

In January of 1941, the Lunenburg County Public Schools' transportation department experienced a serious bus accident. A school bus transporting students from of the Lunenburg Training School sideswiped the trees in the yard of a Victoria resident completely demolishing the right side of the bus. The accident resulted in serious injury to two students—one a broken leg and another with a broken arm. The driver received head and scalp lacerations, and five other students had minor injuries.[clxxviii]

Women were employed as bus drivers for the first time by August of 1941.[clxxix] The School Board also decided to employ a maintenance man to keep school buildings and buses in repair.[clxxx] W. Harry Cruise was hired as foreman at the Lunenburg County School Bus Garage. Cruise organized the bus shop under the supervision of Superintendent Crittenden. He remained in this position for twenty-one years, retiring in 1961.[clxxxi]

In September 1941, the school board expected a savings of $2,000 in bus operation for gas and oil. The plan called for five dispensing stations located at the schools—Victoria, Kenbridge, Lochleven, Meherrin, and Lunenburg Training. The pumping was done by the National Youth Administration (NYA) worker at each school, in the presence of the principal.[clxxxii]

By March of 1942, Lunenburg County received $5,672 in state aid toward the cost of transportation of public school pupils. School transportation costs had risen steadily in the rural sections of the state, and this assistance was the result of a generally felt need. The School Board had supported this legislation by a resolution sent to its representative in both the House and the Senate.[clxxxiii] The state expenditure had increased to $2,095, 240.72. The year 1942 marks the first state appropriation directly for transportation.[clxxxiv]

The School Board at its May meeting in 1942 voted to eliminate the two-dollar transportation fee for Negro students as of September 1.[clxxxv] A couple of years earlier, the Board paid all outstanding debt from the Negro bus leagues and decided to run the buses. But they continued to support Superintendent Crittenden's plan of charging two dollars per month per student for all high school children transported.[clxxxvi] The community leagues, Negro supervisors, and school patrons—working together—led to the elimination of the transportation fee and availability of more buses to transport students.

In August of 1942, Lunenburg County school buses were used to transport county (Kenbridge, Victoria) girls—who were "highly chaperoned"— to the United Services Organization (USO) dances set up on weekends at Camp Pickett (now Fort Pickett in Blackstone, Virginia). The School Board was reimbursed by the Blackstone Defense Committee for the cost. However, transporting county girls to the USO dances was discontinued by October.[clxxxvii]

In November of the same year, two representatives from the Victoria Baptist Church appeared before the School Board to see if the Board could help in any way toward continuing the use of a bus to transport some of the rural people to Sunday school and church in Victoria. The School Board voted to cooperate in doing whatever possible to transport people in Victoria and Kenbridge to Sunday school, but in January 1943 the matter was tabled. Although this practice was supported by the Board, it was short-lived.[clxxxviii]

In September 1943, Lunenburg schools posted its bus schedule in the local newspaper. There were approximately twenty-four buses—eighteen for whites and six for Negroes in operation for the 1943-44 school term.[clxxxix] The pay for all Negro bus drivers would be twenty dollars per month based upon the School Board approval of a recommendation from Superintendent Crittenden.

In other matters, the children at Pleasant Grove were transported to the school in Victoria after a fire had destroyed their school before the end of the school term. They were assigned to classes held in the auditorium. However, arrangements were made whereby the children would be transferred to classrooms with their two teachers from Pleasant Grove School. Elizabeth Hart would continue to teach first through third grades, and Iva Perkins instructed students in the fourth through seventh grades just as it had been at Pleasant Grove.[cxc]

A group of petitioners from the P. M. Snead's bus route requested that the School Board do whatever possible to have the bus on this route run in a more efficient manner. The superintendent explained that the securing of bus drivers and replacement of bus parts had caused the irregularity of transporting the children.

The transportation of Negro students was still a problem—not enough buses! With only six buses operating and a need to transport at least four hundred and fifty students—more buses were needed. The buses were overcrowded. There were long routes; and double runs that caused students to arrive to school late and at erratic times.[cxci] The drivers were Harlis Gee,

Sr., Sam Fierce, Horace Bagley, Joseph E. Taylor, Sr., E. T. Spencer, and W. C. Thompson.[cxcii]

In February 1943, the school board requested the State Department of Education to make a survey of the school bus transportation system in Lunenburg within sixty days to show if consolidation of any routes was economically feasible. The Board authorized the division superintendent to use his best judgment in shortening bus routes and cutting out stops wherever possible, according to the requirement of the Office of Defense Transportation.[cxciii] A resolution was also passed by the School Board prohibiting high school boys from driving school buses except in cases of an emergency. Adult contracted drivers were responsible to drive and to notify the principal or superintendent whenever a student was used to drive in an emergency.[cxciv]

On June 7, 1943, Joseph E. Taylor, Sr., from Meherrin, Virginia, would be the first African American employed by the School Board to assist at the bus garage with overhauling school buses. Taylor worked as a bus mechanic and driver. He retired after more than forty years on the job.[cxcv]

Issues surrounding the transportation of black students continued. Some children were still being transported by community volunteers to the Lunenburg Training School because of inadequate bus service in their area. Verna Hurt Spencer commented, "In fall 1944, my brother, James Hurt drove our father's B-Model Ford pick-up truck to take children back and forth from the Lone Oak School to the school at Lunenburg when they didn't have a bus to transport them. There was no top on the back of the truck, so they put a wagon cover on it to protect students during bad weather."[cxcvi] Tom Hardy, a Negro school patron from the Lewiston District, also appeared before the School Board to request transportation for his five or six children to attend the school at Lunenburg in Victoria. Apparently, there was no response from the Board.[cxcvii]

Wood's research on the transportation of Negro children documents that for the school year of 1951-52, ten buses were operated and the drivers averaged 54.7 miles per bus daily. There were nearly one thousand elementary and high school students that needed transportation. The average number of pupils per bus was eighty-five.[cxcviii]

The safe transportation of children to and from school was of utmost importance to school officials, drivers, and parents. There were three important facts that faced the transportation department: (1) safety of pupils;

(2) efficiency of transportation; and (3) economy of operation. In keeping with the conservation progress of the Office of Defense Transportation, mileage traveled by school buses was reduced as much as possible, consistent with efficiency and safety. The Board made every effort possible to prevent unnecessary mileage by the bus in order to eliminate needless travel. To make this possible, some drivers had to park their bus on the school grounds during the day. There was no justification in having the School Board furnish transportation for the bus drivers going to their other work after having delivered the pupils to the schools.[cxcix]

E. Mason Reese, life-long resident of the county, shared his experience as a bus driver for the school system. Reese said, "I remember when the first school bus shop was located in a frame building next to the Lunenburg County Bank in Kenbridge, Virginia. I started driving bus #7 in 1956, and by then the county school bus garage had moved to cinderblock building located on road #635 (now Oral Oaks Road). My pay was $50 per month with no benefits, and seven years later, a pay of $90 was reduced to a monthly pay of $80. Due to the pay reduction, I drove the school bus for the last time in 1962. Alfred C. Stokes and other students often worked as a substitute driver and attended school during the day." During WWII many of the bus drivers had gone to war and some buses were driven by young men who were students themselves.[cc]

A Dream Comes True

"Riding a big, yellow bus to school was a 'dream come true' for me. Traveling across the old, squeaky, wooden bridge over the Norfolk-Southern Railway on Road #635 seemed terrifying. The thought of the numerous stops to refuel, times waiting after school for a substitute bus [because of mechanical problems], or riding on a second load because of over-crowdedness lingers still. Yes, my dream came true in September 1957 with my first ride on bus #10 with John 'Booster' Mills as the driver."

— Shirley Robertson Lee

Lunenburg operated fifteen buses from various locations within the county for students in the fall of 1966.[cci] The sixteen black students that enrolled at the white schools in Kenbridge and Victoria in 1965 had the option to ride the bus or to be transported privately. The next school year, there would be approximately 110 of these students enrolled in the newly consolidated Central High School in Victoria, Virginia. There were reports of segregated seating on some buses. The Virginia Students' Civil Rights Committee (VSCRC) newsletter reported: "In 1967, black children who attended the previously all-white schools were forced to accept segregated seating on the buses. After a direct confrontation with Superintendent Fears, Nathaniel L. Hawthorne, Sr., president of the Lunenburg County Branch NAACP, was able to stop this practice."[ccii]

In 1968, research was conducted regarding transportation. Superintendent Thweatt reported to the School Board that there were six students and eleven women drivers. The rest were men. The monthly pay was $70 for the students; and ranged from $115 to $120 for adult drivers.[cciii]

In 1969, an article appeared on the front page of *The Kenbridge-Victoria Dispatch* with regard to the new bus routes and pupil transportation. Edward Grey Thompson was approved by the School Board to take care of bus routes and to recommend the employment of bus drivers, etc.[cciv] The buses had been entirely rerouted for each school and vicinity. R. A. 'Buster' Bynum, State Department of Education, assisted the county with a map showing all bus routes and the school attendance areas (see Appendix G – School Attendance Areas Lunenburg County, Virginia, 1969-1970).

The drivers were—West End Rural Area—Asa Holloway, Mabel Price, Morris Beck, John B. Forloines and Juanita Stokes; Victoria Elementary Rural Areas—William Marable, Lewis Hurt, Frances Williams, Polly Dowdy, George Armstrong, Samuel Stokes, Martha Gaulding, J. E. Harshman, Joe Smithson, John Mills, Thomas Hoover, Alice Yeatts, James Gee, W. McCoy Ghee, and William Hardy; Kenbridge Elementary Rural Areas—Arvin Bell, Violet Walker Johnson, Frank Spencer, Clarence Bowen, William Hines, Nancy Estes, Daniel Booker, Fleta Smith, Ellington Churchill, Edward Gray Thompson, Geneva Covington, Pattie Bridgeforth, Gertrude Gordon, Katherine Morgan, Barney Quinn, Thomas Brydie, C. W. Elliott, and Gussie Abernathy. Some substitutes or student drivers were not listed by name in the news article.

All regular bus drivers were responsible adults; some of them would be driving for the first time, and others had been serving in that capacity for a number of years. Students who walked to the neighborhood school, but needed transportation to another school were picked up and transported to their respective school. Others did not use public school transportation.

Some of the high school students drove to school or they were transported privately.[ccv]

Thompson reported to the School Board that he had thirteen women and twenty-five men to operate buses for the school year. He stated, "Each bus driver was responsible for getting his or her substitute and the substitute would have to be approved the same as the regular driver."[ccvi]

Now, public school transportation was desegregated as well!

CHAPTER 6
EDUCATIONAL DISPARITIES
AND OTHER ISSUES

*"Public education is the means by which our society guarantees
all of our children that they shall have the opportunity to learn,
to grow and develop."*[ccvii]

—Dr. Neil V. Sullivan

There were noted educational differences from the onset of building a public school system at the turn of the twentieth century. These inequalities were evident in funding, facilities, school terms, educational resources, teachers' pay, training, and certification.

School Funding

Disparity was noted in cost of instruction for some of the schools. This discrepancy was not only in segregated schools, but among white schools as well. In 1926, Superintendent Waddill called the School Board's attention to the wide discrepancies in the instructional costs of schools in the county. The per capita cost in the elementary grades of the nine-month schools ranged from $26.50 at the school in Victoria to $58.37 at the Nonintervention School; and in the seven-month schools it varied from $24.50 in Traffic School to $61.25 in the Marshalltown School. The per capita cost of instruction in the high schools varied from $48.96 at Victoria to $64.96 at Lochleven School.

Virginia provided thirty dollars per pupil for instruction, operations and maintenance at the time. Public school funds had been supplemented by local donations in order to extend the school term or by tuition charges in the high school grades. A news article reported, "These methods of financing schools have to be reported in some instances, but they do not constitute in any respect a satisfactory method of financing an institution as important as the public school system, nor can a good school system be operated upon the chance of raising enough to take care of the necessary expenditures."

In 1938, a report to the School Board from the governor's committee on the schools in Lunenburg County revealed some striking figures on the comparative cost of instruction in three different high schools. It appeared that Lunenburg County was spending a considerable amount of money unnecessarily. The conclusion of the committee and its recommendations were based on the fact that the school population of the county was decreasing, and that any program for the future must take this into account. The 1936-37 annual cost of instruction per pupil in Victoria High was $33.55; in Kenbridge High $63.16; and Lochleven High $47.58 (though Lochleven provided fewer advantages than the other two schools). Taking into account the number of pupils in the Kenbridge High School (111), and in Lochleven (82), the report stressed that fact that it is not economically sound to attempt to maintain a high school with an enrollment of less than 250 pupils. Providing a central high school meant a saving of $4,437.17 per year to the taxpayers of the county.[ccviii]

Here a Little . . . There a Little

For African Americans pupils, funding differences when compared to white children were even more obvious. The difference in cost of instruction depended willingness of citizens in each district to pay school levies in a timely manner, state appropriations, and the School Board's funding decisions. Educational facilities and resources were usually inferior, with little or no support from the district school board. School patrons and members of the community made contributions to the education of their children out of necessity because neither the state nor the county would support the school. The School Board promised to make significant contributions, but for one reason or another, including insufficient funds, they often did not.[ccix]

Denied public support, African Americans were often forced to raise their own funds to build schools. Public education was made available because of the patrons that often donated or purchased all of the land, contributed the materials, equipment, and construction work, and paid teachers' salaries. Many of these schools were named in honor of the person who donated the land, for example, Denkins Town, Morton, Henry May, Irby House, etc. The condition of the schools was determined by the amount of money available for the schools, and the contributions from private funds were usually collected through community leagues. In the early 1900s, the urgent demands on the capacity of the system to educate an ever-growing population increased faster than the educational funds to support the schools. At the state level, more attention would be given to address public education. In the late 1920s, Dr. Michael Vincent O'Shea, professor at the University of Wisconsin, conducted an exhaustive study on public education in Virginia with the cooperation of the Virginia Education Commission.[ccx] O'Shea's study would lead the state superintendent to take a hard look at the educational status among blacks and whites. Dr. Hall placed Negro education under the leadership of a director of instruction when he reorganized the Department of Education in the 1930s.[ccxi]

In 1944, the Virginia Education Commission, headed by George H. Denny, appointed a committee to study Negro Education in the Virginia. The committee found that, because of poor facilities among both whites and Negroes, the system was inadequate. The Commission concluded that "[t]he complications of present day culture demand that those who live in it must keep abreast of it, not only that they survive individually, but that they may not retard the advancement of the group through their inability to cooperate." The report stated further that "[e]conomic progress without education is inconceivable. The present condition and relative national position of Virginia's educational system is a matter of knowledge and deep concern. Negro education obviously lies at the lowest level of the whole system."[ccxii]

Education facilities were needed as well as local and out-of-state funding to provide adequate schoolhouses and resources for Negro children, as suggested in Denny's report. Wood revealed, "The educational opportunities and facilities for Negroes lagged behind that of whites even though interested groups, such as organized philanthropy and the Negro Baptist churches, made vital contributions.[ccxiii]

School Terms

In 1871, the school term only lasted about five months.[ccxiv] By 1900, the term had increased to six months—operating the months of October through March; however, the five-month term continued in some schools.[ccxv]

On March 1, 1927, the School Board decided to reduce the all colored schools to the same length term as that of 1926-27—five months; and to cut the white two-room, nine-months schools of Woodrow and Nonintervention back one month—giving them an eight-month term. The decision was based on the deficit in the salary fund in relation to length of the school term.[ccxvi] The school term was staggered. The schools of Victoria, Kenbridge, Woodrow, Nonintervention, Lochleven, Mizpah, Lunenburg Court House, Marshalltown, Union Central, Ledbetter, and Fort Mitchell opened September 12; The Meherrin School on September 13; and Dundas School commenced September 26. The other schools of the county began the school year on October 10. County schools still operated the staggered terms of nine, eight, and seven months for the term of 1928-29.[ccxvii]

By fall 1930, the high schools of Kenbridge, Victoria, and Lochleven operated for a term of nine months, and all other schools operated a term of eight months. The seven-month school term was eliminated.[ccxviii] In February 1931, the School Board decided to end the school year for all Negro schools by April 1 and all white schools on May 8. *The Victoria Dispatch* reported, "The School Board deemed it advisable to make such cuts in the school term because the county treasurer had estimated that not more than eighty percent of the 1930 school levies would be collected." Taxes were levied in each magisterial district to provide needed revenue to support schools. The amount was listed on the back of the county's tax payment form. The lack of adequate revenues had a direct impact on the school term.[ccxix]

A definite assurance had been received from the State Board of Education that the rating of the high schools would not be jeopardized, provided all schools are continued for eight months. This ruling made it possible for every high school pupil to received full credit for the work passed during the eight-month session of 1930-31. In order that the fundamental subject matter may be completed within the eight-month session, it became necessary to devote more time to actual classroom work. The high schools of Kenbridge, Victoria, and Lochleven agreed to lengthen the school day by one hour and fifteen minutes. The minimum requirement would be met; credit would be given for all high school work; and about $10,000 saved to the county. Many boys and girls were given an extra month at home during the summer. The earlier school-term closing created a disparity in the amount of time African American pupils received instruction for the school year.[ccxx] There were twenty schools for whites in operation during the 1931-32 school term—three high schools and seventeen elementary grade schools; and the Lunenburg Training School, Kenbridge Graded School, and at least twenty-five other elementary grade, schools for colored children.[ccxxi]

The School Board was informed that the teachers and truck drivers volunteered a ten percent reduction in their salaries beginning January 1, 1932 provided this would enable the schools to operate the minimum of eight months. The Board agreed to operate the school until May 8, 1932. This decision on the part of the School Board gave the children enrolled an opportunity to complete a year's work and helped keep the high schools on the accreditation list for another year.

One of the most outstanding gains in the education of Negroes was realized during the 1938-1939 school term through the operation of schools for nine months in ninety-eight Virginia counties. A few schools closed because of failure to make the legal average attendance. In Lunenburg, the average attendance was equal to that of the previous eight months. In some schools the average exceeded the previous months. The evidence showed that Negro children will, if given the opportunity, attend school regularly for a full nine months.

Eventually, the staggered school terms were no longer a barrier to equal educational opportunities. On September 6, 1939 all schools—white and colored—of Lunenburg County opened and closed on the same day.[ccxxii]

Teacher Salaries

Schooling in the early years was a family matter for the most part. Few of the young in the county went to any formal school, although some were taught reading, writing and arithmetic in their home. Many of the young men were taught about agriculture, a craft or trade, and often surveying by their fathers. More affluent families would join together and hire a tutor to instruct their children. Tuition fees, agreed on by the teacher and parents, financed the schools. In some cases, however, schools were organized and begun by teachers, many of whom were parsons attempting to supplement their income. By the late 1800s, the Board of Education for the Commonwealth of Virginia was formed and some funds were made available for teachers' salaries and school buildings.

Teachers' salaries or pay based on gender was already noticeably different. In 1871, monthly salary for colored teachers was twenty-nine dollars and eighty-seven cents (male teachers) and twenty-seven dollars and fifty cents (female teachers).[ccxxiii] In 1906, salaries ranged from twenty to thirty dollars per month for colored teachers; and for other teachers it averaged thirty dollars a month. During the 1910-1911 school term—teachers holding a first grade or high school certificate—the annual salary ranged from $840 to $2,745 for white teachers; and $125 to $160 for colored teachers in various districts.[ccxxiv] For the most part, a teachers' salary was based on the funding from patrons, with higher salaries paid to white teachers— male or female. The lowest monthly salary was paid to colored female teachers. In the districts of Brown's Store; Columbian Grove; Lochleven; Lewiston; Pleasant Grove; and Rehoboth, the total annual average salaries ranged from $410 for colored teachers to $9,320 for white teachers—male and female.[ccxxv] In 1922, the average salary for colored teachers ranged from thirty-five to forty-five dollars a month.[ccxxvi]

By 1929, no fixed or equalized pay for county teachers had been adopted by the School Board although salaries were approved. A teacher's salary was often determined in accordance with professional preparation, success in school, and the size of the teaching job. Their livelihood in terms of salary depended upon the individual community or school system's willingness to pay. The issue of the equalization of teachers' salaries was not different from the status quo—separate and unequal.[ccxxvii]

In spring 1940, Superintendent Crittenden gave a report on the sum of $4,850.00 appropriated for an increase in teacher's salaries for the school term of 1940-41. In December, a group of concerned citizens from the Colored Civic League appeared before the School Board to express concerns about the difference in teachers' pay. Negro teachers through their lawyer, C. W. Hill, requested the School Board to equalize the salaries of teachers within the period of two years—fifty per cent of the difference beginning

September 1941. As a result of the teacher's request, increases in teachers' salaries were given for the next two years.[ccxxviii] Negro teachers were paid a monthly salary of $108 beginning in the 1940s, with an increase to $225 by the 1952. Supposedly, beginning with the school term of 1943-44, teachers' salaries would be equalized, but this was not the case.[ccxxix] The annual salary paid to principals was discrepant, too. In 1942, the annual salaries paid on a twelve-month basis to white principals at the high schools—Kenbridge, Victoria, Lochleven—ranged from $1,920 to $2,400; and the Negro principal at the Lunenburg Training School received $1,250.[ccxxx]

There were forty white and thirty-six Negro teachers employed at the time. All teachers making an annual salary of $1,500 or less would receive a $10 monthly raise; and all making over $1500, a raise of $5 per month with School Board approval.[ccxxxi] The following teachers' salary scale was approved by the Board for the 1944–1945 school term.

White: Local Permit and Elementary Certificate: $122.50
       Normal Professional Certificate: 127.50
       Collegiate Professional Certificate: 142.50

Negro: Local Permit and Elementary Certificate: $100.00
       Normal Professional Certificate: 105.00
       Collegiate Professional Certificate: 112.50

Since there was a balance to have been spent for instruction, the School Board approved a bonus for all teachers except the agriculture teachers who received a $100 bonus from state funds. Those teachers who had taught less than a year would receive a bonus based on the number of months they had taught.[ccxxxii]

Salary increases still did not equalize pay across the board. For example: The substitute's salary printed in the special covenant section of a teacher's contract in 1945 reveals that whites received five dollars per day for the first ten days while the Negro substitute's pay was four dollars for the same amount of days.[ccxxxiii]

The School Board approved annual salaries for the two white high school—Kenbridge, Victoria—principals for the session 1945-46. The difference of $300 was paid to the Victoria High School principal because of a larger enrollment and greater responsibilities at his school. Also, there was a glaring discrepancy in the annual salary of $1,000 more being paid to the white elementary supervisor as compared to her African American counterpart. The annual salaries for teachers—white and Negro—remained discrepant with white teachers receiving $125 to $147.50; and Negro teachers paid $105 to $125 for the same certification.[ccxxxiv]

On June 1, 1945 the School Board recognized the teacher certificate of Local Permit & Elementary Certificate; Normal Professional; and Collegiate Professional. However, white teachers received more pay than Negro teachers although they had the same certification. For example, the monthly pay for white teachers holding the Collegiate Professional certification was $152.00; and Negro teachers received $132.00 although the Board of Supervisors had appropriated an additional $5,700 for teachers' salaries.[ccxxxv]

The School Board approved 9.5 months for the 1947–1948 school term. Negro teachers continued to lag behind their colleagues in earned annual income. The salary scale ranged from $1400 to $1600 for white teachers, and $1250 to $1550 for Negroes. The Board approved a change in the high school principals' annual salaries with the state paying one-sixth, however, a significant difference remained:[ccxxxvi]

On recommendation from the superintendent, the Board appointed the high school principals, supervisors, and visiting teacher. Their approved salaries for the same school term of 1947–'48 were:

Victoria High School Principal	$3600
Kenbridge High School Principal	3300
Lunenburg Training School Principal	2500
Supervisor (white)	3000 plus $180 for travel
Supervisor (Negro)	2100 plus $120 for travel
Visiting Teacher	2500 plus $400 for travel

Considerable progress was made towards equalizing the salaries of white and Negro teachers statewide. The salary scales for elementary and high school teachers equalized in nearly all school divisions in the state, but not in Lunenburg County.[ccxxxvii]

On April 1, 1948, the School Board officially equalized all teachers' salaries! An annual salary scale was set up by the superintendent for teachers—white and colored—ranging from $1540 to $1770. In May, the scale was revised for the year 1948-49 with a ten-dollar reduction for each certification grade. The next year, in 1949, the School Board adopted the teachers' salary scale based on years of experience and certification. A salary increase of $300 was approved for high school principals.

In 1951, the teachers' annual top salary had increased from $1770 to $2200; and the pay ranged from $1800 to $2400 for a four-year college degree in 1952.[ccxxxviii]

Teacher Training and Certification

In 1881, there were four grades of certificates. The professional certificates were issued first for two years, and could be renewed for a period not exceeding five years. They were designed to represent scholarly excellence and professional skills tested by experience in the classroom. Other grades were issued each for one year only. Moral character as well as scholarship was taken into account. Wood pointed out, "Most of Lunenburg's first teachers were those who had completed public school in the county. In 1885, there was only one Negro teacher in the county who had received training beyond that offered in the public schools of the county."[ccxxxix]

At the turn of the century, the State Board of Education designed a uniform examination for teachers' certification. The examination was different for colored teachers in terms of the questions presented (see sample examination questions Appendix A - Table 1: Uniform Examination For Teachers' Certificates, 1900).

By 1918, there were twenty-eight types of certificates available for teachers. In spring 1923, a school-wide notice for the renewal of elementary teaching certification was printed in the *Lunenburg School Life* newsletter. One may assume that all county teachers participated in renewal of the elementary teaching certification when it was offered at Victoria High School. Realistically, this may not have been the case for colored teachers since public education was segregated.[ccxl]

On November 8, 1929, a report by the State Supervisor of Teacher-Training suggested improvements in the training of Virginia teachers, as witnessed by the increase of the number of certificates issued during the school year ending June 30. The State Board of Education had adopted one year of college normal school training as the minimum requirement for teachers in Virginia. The Farmville State Teachers College (now Longwood University) headed the list of state institutions during 1928-29, with

2,296 of the teachers trained and employed; Radford State Teachers College (now Radford University), which trained 2,202, was second; and Harrisonburg State Teachers College (now James Madison University), where 1,900 were trained, was third.[ccxli]

In 1868, the Hampton Normal and Agricultural Institute (now Hampton University) was established by the American Missionary Association of New York, which had conducted schools for Negroes on the Hampton River since 1861. Hampton had been founded as a teacher-training school by the American Missionary Association guided by Samuel Chapman Armstrong. At Hampton, eighty-four percent of its first twenty classes became teachers. Other Negro colleges that trained teachers—Virginia Normal and Collegiate Institute (now Virginia State University) founded in 1882, in Petersburg, Virginia, was supported by state funds; Virginia Union University (1899), in Richmond; Virginia Theological Seminary (1823) and College (1888), whose alumni serve many of the churches in the Commonwealth; and in 1888, James S. Russell, an Episcopal minister, established the Saint Paul's Normal and Industrial School (St. Paul's College) in Lawrenceville, Virginia. This was a coeducational college and teacher-training institution, but is no longer in operation.[ccxlii]

The Presbyterian Church controlled the Ingleside-Memorial Institute (1877) at Burkeville, Virginia, which gave an accredited high school course and two years of college work. The Roman Catholic Church maintained the Saint Emma Industrial Institute for Negroes (1895) at Rock Castle on the James River; and Thyne Institute (1876), which had its birth at Chase City, in Mecklenburg County, Virginia, was a teacher-training and boarding institution.[ccxliii]

Virginia's predominately white colleges and universities did not admit African American students until the 1960s. There were few, if any, white students enrolled in a historically black college or university (HBCU) until years later. Over the years, many of Lunenburg's educators have received training from one of these institutions of higher learning.

In the late 1920s, Virginia had a significant increase in the number of trained teachers. Dr. Thomas D. Eason, Secretary of the State Board of Education, made a statement about teacher training. Dr. Eason said, "There are a number of professionally trained teachers employed in the Virginia Public Schools during the school term of 1928-29. While there was marked improvement in the preparation of teachers employed in both the counties and cities of the state, the teachers in the cities, as would be expected because of larger financial support, were better trained than the teachers in the counties. With respect to the source of supply of teachers, it is interesting to note that Virginia relied chiefly on her own institutions for the training of teachers. For example, sixty-seven percent of the teachers employed during the 1928-29 session were trained in state institutions. However, the private and out-of-state colleges provided a considerable number. Twenty-three percent of teachers were trained in Virginia's private institution; nine percent in out-of-state institutions; and one percent without any college or normal school training."[ccxliv]

In 1931, during Dr. Hart's administration, the teacher certification system was reorganized, simplified, and strengthened. The twenty-eight types of certificates available in 1918 were reduced to three—collegiate professional, collegiate, and normal professional. Teacher certification standards were raised from a level where applicants who had completed only the eighth grade could be certificated to teach by passing an examination, to one where no applicant who had completed less than two years of college could be certified. This was the beginning of Virginia's modern period of teacher certification, and the system developed at that time has required few changes to the present. In 1934-35, the requirements for division superintendents were raised to include the master's degree, training in administration and finance, and a minimum experience of three years as supervisor or principal.[ccxlv]

On April 2, 1948 four certification grades—Elementary and Local Permit, Normal Professional, Collegiate, Collegiate Professional—approved at the state level were recognized by the School Board. The teacher certification grades of Local Permit, Emergency License, Normal Professional; Collegiate and Collegiate Professional; and Master's Degree were acceptable in 1951; and in 1952, the Normal Professional and Collegiate Professional certification was recognized.[ccxlvi]

In the mid-1960s, Dr. Woodrow W. Wilkerson had succeeded Dr. Davis Y. Paschall as state superintendent of public instruction. In an effort to improve the quality of education in Virginia, Dr. Wilkerson recommended upgrading the minimum qualification requirements for teachers as part of his nine-point plan. This plan called for: (1) upgrading the minimum qualification requirements for teachers; (2) upgrading the salary schedule; (3) providing more teacher scholarships (recruitment program); (4) expanding the in-service training program; (5) improving library services and materials; (6) expanding special education; (7) establishing a uniform reimbursement rate for all state-aid positions; (8) encouraging extended use of educational television; and (9) providing more time for teachers to devote to planning instructional activities. In 1966 the General Assembly made record appropriations for public education, approving those proposals of the State Board of Education that required additional funds.[ccxlvii]

By fall 1969, there were 146 teachers in Lunenburg County—3 with Special License, 16 with Master's Degrees, 15 with a Normal Professional, Elementary or Vocational Industrial Education Certificate, and 112 with Collegiate Professional Certificates.[ccxlviii]

School Attendance

Regular school attendance was one of the most important factors in developing an educated, productive populace. The school attendance issue was brought to the School Board's attention in February 1927. Members of the School Board had an earnest discussion about the extremely poor attendance of school children throughout the county and the steps needed to be taken to remedy the situation.

Superintendent Waddill reported that there were at least five schools not making the attendance average of twenty pupils for a one-room school, which in most cases was not due to the lack of children in the neighborhood. During one school visit by Superintendent Waddill, there were only three scholars present. "Schools there, teachers there, throughout the county, but where are the children?" he asked.[ccxlix] On September 29, 1927, an annual report of the Superintendent of Public Instruction indicated that a marked variation in public school attendance was noted among the counties in Virginia. For example, the average daily attendance, with regularity of eighty-eight percent of all children between the age of seven and nineteen, was noted in one Virginia County, while the lowest average was 38.8 percent in one of the smaller counties. This wide variation among the counties in the regularity with which the children attended school gave concrete evidence of the need for school officials, teachers, and parents in seeing that every child of school age attended school regularly.[ccl]

School officials, in their analysis of the education system, found that the attendance situation in Lunenburg County showed a large waste of funds from the non-attendance of school-age children. The school term of 1926-27 school term was 151 days. With 3,699 pupils enrolled, the average attendance was 2,656. Since the per capita cost of instruction based on enrollment was $20.41, the county paid out $21,287.63 in tuition for the 1,043 students who were regularly absent from school.

Schools throughout the Commonwealth began the 1927-28 school term with an increase in enrollment. *The Victoria Dispatch* reported, "555,000 children of school age were expected to be enrolled in Virginia's public schools." The compulsory age for school attendance was eight to fourteen, and too many children dropped out of school upon reaching the fourteenth year. In many cases, physical facilities were not sufficient in the schools to encourage larger enrollments because of poor financial support.[ccli] As a result of Virginia's survey of public education in the 1920s, recommendations were made with regard to the compulsory-attendance laws such as the change for school age attendance from age eight through fourteen to seven through fifteen; minimum school year of 160 days; compulsory attendance through the school term; abolition of exemption on the basis of ability to read and write; and a provision that exemption for physical and mental disability be granted by the county or city board.[cclii]

By the spring of 1930, the number of students attending Woodrow School had dropped to less than thirty.[ccliii] The school closed, and the students were transported other area schools in the county.

Some schools experienced high attendance rates of ninety percent or better during the school year in 1938-39. The Williams School led the county's white schools in average attendance records for the month of December 1938 with an average attendance of 94.17 percent; Lochleven – 93.76; Victoria and Dundas – 93.13; Meherrin – 93; Pleasant Grove – 91.97; and Kenilworth with 90.87 percent. Several Negro schools reporting high attendance were West Hill, with the highest attendance of 98.78; Gary School – 98.22; Lone Oak – 97.57; New Grove 96.88; Varick - 95.40; Nutbush – 94.85; and the Lunenburg Training School, with an average attendance of 93.24 percent. No reason was available as to the cause for the elevated attendance rates in these specific schools during this term. Crittenden was concerned about student absenteeism in some of the other schools. He said, "I wish to urge the parents of the school children of Lunenburg County to cooperate with the county school authorities in securing regular attendance to the schools of the county. I would like to express my appreciation to the parents for the improvement made in attendance in 1938-39 when compared to the 1937-38 term. Although the previous year showed a considerable decrease in enrollment, the attendance was so much improved over the preceding year that the state made an increase of $1,000 in their appropriations for the schools of Lunenburg County."[ccliv]

In 1940, *The Victoria Dispatch* reported, "Absentees costly to the school system and $10,000 was lost during the previous (1938-39) school session. Attendance figures released from the office of the superintendent, in connection with the recent school census, revealed that there were 6,119 white and colored children of school age in the county. Of this number, 2,062 are white and 2,122 Negro. The number of white children who attended some state-supported institution was 1,689 and thirteen attended private school, while 360 attended no school. Of the Negro children, 1,568 attended public school, forty-two attended private school, and 512 attended no school. Besides the children who were too young to attend school or who had graduated from high school and were attending no other school, there were a number of children classed as handicapped and could not attend school.

The following figures include all children from birth to the age of twenty. Under the heading of 'handicapped children' were the impaired hearing—ten white and seven Negro; impaired vision (uncorrected)—forty white and ten Negro; crippled—thirteen white and eight Negro; mentally defective—seven white and five Negro. One of the outstanding facts of the school census was the finding of the children between the ages of seven and twenty—two whites and twenty-nine blacks were unable to read."[cclv]

The Victoria School reported a large enrollment. In spite of the fact Victoria school had the smallest number enrolled in the first grade than at any time over the past twelve years between 1927 and 1939. The total enrollment was 351 in high school and 411 in the other grade building. The enrollment as reported by Davis Y. Paschall, principal, in September 1940 showed a decrease from the previous school session. Enrollment was approximately thirty pupils less during the opening days of school. The peak of school enrollment was 767 in 1939, and 730 were reported for the year 1940-41. Paschall said, "The children are well-adjusted, with the exception of the commercial department, which is suffering an overflow of students. This situation necessitated the teaching of one class after school."[cclvi]

The "baby boom" after World War II in 1945 led to even higher enroll-ments in the schools county-wide.[cclvii] *The Victoria Dispatch* reported, "The county schools opened their 1949-50 session with 3400 pupils enrolled with an increase of nearly 200 over the last year.[cclviii] The county school showed an increase of eighty-four pupils." The number of African American pupils enrolled had increased from 1492 in 1940 to 1607 by 1950.[cclix]

On September 23, 1969 the enrollment figures were presented to School Board by John H. Wells, Director of Instruction (see Appendix E – Table 5: Lunenburg County Public Schools Enrollment, Fall 1969). These figures show the enrollment of Negro students at 56.3 percent; and white students at 43.7 percent of the total school population of 2,750. There were 137 teachers, with 77 white (56%) and 60 Negro (44%) employed at this time.[cclx]

CHAPTER 7
NEW SCHOOL PROGRAMS

Summer School Program

It is believed that the first tutorial summer program in the school system was offered in June of 1926 at Victoria High School to secondary and elementary students who wanted to make up academic deficiencies (not more than two). No high school graduation credit was given for new work done privately under a coach or tutor.[cclxi]

In June 1943, the School Board approved the operation of a summer program at the schools of Victoria and Kenbridge with two teachers assigned to each school. The program lasted a six-week period for the benefit of pre-school children and children up to ten years of age. The summer program was approved to operate in the same schools in 1944.[cclxii] The Board did not indicate whether this program was available to all children in the county. However, the program was suspended the next summer because children in the rural areas of the county could not take advantage of it.[cclxiii]

In 1950, students had to register before attending the summer session offered at Victoria High School. The session allowed pupil who had failed to make up a limited amount of work; and permitted pupils of average or above average ability to enrich their high school experience by completing more than the minimum requirements for graduation. The session was conducted for eight weeks—forty school days—and pupils had to complete eighty hours of classroom work for one unit in a repeated subject. There was a tuition charge.

In June 1962, *The Kenbridge-Victoria Dispatch* announced, "Summer School At Victoria High School." A summer session was made available for white high school students in Lunenburg County from June 18 – August 10, 1962. The pupils had to register at the school for make-up work in the subject of General

Math, Algebra I, and English 9, 10, 11 and 12. No pupil was permitted to carry more than two (2) repeat subjects of one unit each. The tuition charge for each pupil registered was thirty dollars per subject.

The U.S. Department of Education enacted Title I (Public Law 89-10) under the Elementary and Secondary Education Act (E.S.E.A.) in 1965. The purpose of the law was to ensure that all children have a fair, equal, and significant opportunity to obtain a high-quality education and reach, at a minimum, proficiency on challenging state academic achievement standards and assessments. In May 1966, Lunenburg County received a grant amount of $183,000 under the Title I provision. A portion of the funds in the amount of $41,040 was used during the summer to offer courses at Lunenburg High School; and operate summer programs at the Lunenburg Elementary and Kenbridge Graded Schools in remedial reading, remedial mathematics, music appreciation, and library services.

The qualification of schools for the use of these funds was based primarily upon the concentration of children from families with incomes less than two thousand dollars a year. Title I was designed as a supporting factor in the anti-poverty program, but was left entirely in the hands of local officials for administration. *The Kenbridge-Victoria Dispatch* reported, "While the direct benefit from such a program may seem limited, the indirect and not-so-easily seen benefits are county-wide. A prime example of this is that every dollar spent for capital outlay under this special program can free a local tax dollar for improvement of the overall school program."

In 1966, the General Assembly appropriated money for the first time to help localities conduct summer school programs. This aid made it possible for more students to take courses they could not schedule during the regular school terms; and enabled more students to move toward graduation on an accelerated basis.

Superintendent Thweatt gave a report to the School Board about the 1969 Summer Program at Central High School. The total enrollment was 182—1 Campbell County; 1 Dinwiddie County; 28 Blackstone High School; 43 Crewe High School; 16 Kenston Forest (private school); 51 Central High School; 28 Lunenburg High School; and 14 Luther H. Foster High School. Haywood R. Watkins, Sr., E.S.E.A. Coordinator, reported on the summer program at the Lunenburg Elementary School, which was a six-weeks program that began June 26. Watkins said, "Eighty-four children had attended in grades five through seven. It includes reading, mathematics, physical education, band instruction, and health services. There are four buses for transporting children to Lunenburg Elementary School."[cclxiv] There was no report that other county schools were operating a summer program.

School–Based Health Services

The health and well-being of children has been a concern of school officials. In fact, as early as 1907, McNoah B. Cralle discovered that his work depended upon doing much more than teaching and supervising instructional work. In addition to his other responsibilities as a Jeanes supervisor, Cralle found it was necessary to visit homes and encourage better health and living conditions within the Negro communities.[cclxv]

In the early 1920s, the first organized school-based health program was initiated by George Luther Walker, principal at the Kenbridge High School. Walker created the "five-point" health program for school-age children to target five areas—teeth, weight, vision, hearing, and throat. This program was proven to be one of the best means of preventing and correcting the bodily defects.

The program was later adopted by the State Board of Health and featured in every county within the Old Dominion, and in many adjoining states. A nurse from the state spent approximately a week in the county to check all "five-point" children at various schools; and on "health day," during the May Day activities each child was recognized with the awarding of a certificate for meeting the standards.

A number of schools had bought into the health program with strong community support from businesses, organizations, and interested citizens offered additional prizes to the contest winners.[cclxvi]

On May 6, 1927, Kenbridge High School was awarded the silver cup for what was believed to be the highest percentage of children in the state to meet the health standards, and the Snead School won a banner for the elementary school with highest percentage of "five-point" children. Six hundred certificates were awarded county-wide. About twenty-five percent of the children of Lunenburg County had met the standards. In addition, about one-third of the children had teeth with no unfilled cavities; good eyes; ears; throats; and up to the standard in weight. Several other schools reported more than seven hundred corrections of physical defects of school children were made during the school term.[cclxvii]

The next year, on May 4, 1928, Victoria High School observed the "health day" with a parade through the town of Victoria with a program and activities that followed. A contest for the best program in the schools ended with Salem School being the white school with the most "five-point" children, winning $25, and $5 going to the Lunenburg Court House School for the highest amount of black "five-point" children.[cclxviii]

Efforts were made to arrange for dental clinics for the school children at the beginning of each school year. Neale (2005) wrote, "A strong health program cut down incidences of disease and contagion in the schools. Schoolyards were kept clean, because of the dangers of hookworm "in the fall and spring when the children are barefooted."[cclxix] The teachers were urged to make daily inspections of school children so that those in the early stages of infection might be isolated; and efforts are made to provide hot school lunches that included well-balanced diets.[cclxx]

The standards were still being kept in 1939; however, some principals reported an appallingly low percentage of "five-point" children due chiefly to the lack of dental care. In the previous year there were only five "five-point" children in a school population of sixty. In a school of twenty children or less, there were no children who achieved the required rating. But all was not lost. The Parent-Teachers Association arranged to raise a minimum contribution of $300 to support dental examinations for school children. Sixteen years following the first implementation of the local plan, the State Department of Health had begun to sponsor county dental clinics, making accessible to rural school children dental care at a nominal cost. The expense of such a clinic was one-third paid by the parent, one-third by the county, and one-third by the state.[cclxxi]

The only first aid and health service provided in many of the small county schools was performed by the principal or teacher. Bessie Chatmon Hopkins reminisced about her days as a teacher at the Trinity School. Hopkins said, "There was no school nurse, sick room, or health services available in the one-room schools when I began teaching in the 1940s. I took the responsibility to care for sick children and the ones who got a scrape or two. I did what I thought was best at the time."[cclxxii]

In 1941, the Lunenburg Chapter of the National Red Cross felt a particular need for first aid to be taught in the county. With the cooperation of the school superintendent and the School Board, first aid was taught at Kenbridge and Victoria High Schools. A total of 278 certificates were issued in the county in first aid, with sixteen persons qualified to teach the subject. Two classes in Accident Prevention were taught—one to adults and one to juniors at Kenbridge High School. Fifty persons in these two classes received Red Cross certificates. The shortage of doctors and trained nurses during the years of 1943 to 1945 was acute in the county. The realization of the need for training in home nursing resulted in seven classes being taught. Two of these classes were taught to juniors and seniors at Kenbridge High School and Victoria High School.

During World War II, members of the Home Demonstration Club were also interested in the betterment of conditions of rural people and worked faithfully to improve the standards of nutrition in the county. They worked to establish lunchrooms in rural schools with the result that all schools in the county—with one exception—would have a hot lunch served each day.[cclxxiii]

Title I provided funds for health and psychological services at the Kenbridge Graded and Lunenburg Elementary Schools during the summer of 1966.[cclxxiv] These funds were also used by the state for strengthening the Department of Education.[cclxxv]

Ann W. Jackson

The School Board would employ its first full-time school nurse through Title I funds. Ann W. Jackson was that person. She was assigned to provide school-based health services in specific schools and conduct home visits. Jackson was quite aware of the Board's policy on school desegregation.

85

She described her assignment in Lunenburg schools. Jackson said, "During my tenure as a school nurse from 1966 to 1998, there has never been a time I did not feel welcome or comfortable visiting a home in the county. Even today, former students and their parents continue to address me as 'Nurse Weaver.' I will always remember my first day at the Lunenburg Elementary School where Ruby M. Ragsdale, first grade teacher, had placed a vase of flowers on my desk to welcome me. I've always thought of Sherman Vaughan as a wonderful school leader and caring person."[cclxxvi]

African American students now had access to some health services at school. Jackson was assigned to visit all county schools beginning in the fall of 1969. Later, additional school nurses would be employed to provide daily health services at each school.

Title I funds were also used to employ assistants in the schools. They were Brenda W. Ragsdale, secretary; Zenobia S. Bias, librarian; and Gloria J. Allen, Bessie R. Callahan, Mary R. Jackson, Janie L. Jennings, Ruth W. Jones, Bertha E. Seay, Mary F. Watkins, and Katherine Wynn were assigned to help in the classroom.[cclxxvii]

Vocational and Agriculture Programs

In the early 1900s, vocational education began to take root in rural communities. I. T. Wilkinson faced new, innovative school initiatives during his final two years as superintendent.

The *Smith-Hughes Act of 1917* established by United States Department of Education provided federal funds to support the teaching of agriculture in schools. The purpose of this Act was to train people "who have entered upon or who are preparing to enter upon the work of the farm." States had to establish a Vocational Board of Education to receive federal funding and segregate programs from traditional schools. This Act also led to the start of organizations such as the Vocational Industrial Club of America, Future Business Leaders of America, and Future Farmers of America. Vocational education became a major area of federal aid to schools. Funds were used to establish vocational rehabilitation in 1918; support vocational education in 1944; and provide educational assistance for veterans with the *Servicemen's Readjustment Act of 1944*.[cclxxviii]

It is believed that the Lunenburg Training School was the first to implement a vocational-agricultural program in the early 1920s. Stephanie

Deutsch wrote, "Booker T. Washington felt, that more than anything, black people needed to be able to support themselves. The book learning, they had been denied in slavery and that so many of them craved had to go hand and hand with occupations that would bring them to income that would allow them to build their own homes, raise families, and gain the respect of their neighbors. Trades—carpentry, laundry, cooking, sewing, farming—were to become as much a part of the Tuskegee education as English and math."[cclxxix]

Lucy M. Morrison thought the education program at Lunenburg Training School should be modeled after the school in Tuskegee. In the *Lunenburg School Life* newsletter (1923), Morrison wrote, "We need all the help we can get from our friends, white as well as colored; and we want to put this movement over and if possible make this a Booker T. Washington School." A plausible reason for Morrison's desire to transform the training school into a Booker T. Washington School was the view that both book learning and vocational training was necessary for the survival of Negroes and their ticket out of poverty.[cclxxx]

In 1927, a vocational education shop was constructed at the training school site for the cost of $1,400 with public and private monies. The sources of funding included contributions from Negro Community League ($600), Public Funds ($400), and Rosenwald Fund ($400).[cclxxxi]

Kenneth Portly Evans in his first year as principal, and school league raised money to build a science laboratory, agriculture shop, and six-room home economics cottage in the early 1930s. Two of the cottage rooms were converted into living space for Evans and his wife. The construction was done by the patrons and agriculture students under the direction of Grant Burk, agriculture instructor. These buildings were erected and equipped by the citizens, with a contribution of three hundred dollars from the county toward the home economics cottage. In the mid-1930s, Richard Pegram was employed as the agriculture teacher following Burk.[cclxxxii]

Franklin D. Roosevelt was elected the thirty-second President of the United States during the Great Depression in the 1930s. In his first "hundred days," he proposed the "New Deal" programs, and in 1933, Congress enacted this sweeping program to bring recovery to business and agriculture.[cclxxxiii] The Civil Works Administration (CWA), under President Roosevelt's new program, provided much valuable work on many of the school buildings in the county, and put them into first-class condition in 1933.

The CWA expended $12,987 for labor and $5,301.37 in materials. But there were no monies appropriated for building construction at the Lunenburg Training School through the CWA funds.[cclxxxiv]

In the spring of 1935, the School Board authorized the extension of fourteen school days to complete a standard nine-month term providing a federal appropriation was made for this purpose. Superintendent Waddill had received an assurance from the state that grant monies would be wired to Lunenburg County as soon as it was authorized.[cclxxxv] The Board also agreed to have the Marshalltown School moved during the summer months to Victoria, Virginia on Eighth Street—one-half block from the Victoria High School. The school was converted into a combination home economics cottage and agricultural shop building. The labor for moving the building was supplied by Federal Emergency Relief Administration (FERA), and the cost of the new materials would be paid out of the funds supplied by this agency and the State Agricultural and Home Economics Departments.[cclxxxvi] Federal funding was made available to localities; and vocational-agricultural education and home economics programs were in full operation at the schools of Kenbridge High, Victoria High, and Lunenburg Training School. L. E. Kent was employed as the agriculture teacher at the Victoria High School.[cclxxxvii] Later, U. K. Franken replaced Kent as vocational-agriculture instructor.[cclxxxviii]

In August of 1939, before the school session began, Davis Y. Paschall, principal of the Victoria school, announced a plan of establishing a Vocational Guidance and Placement Bureau in connection with the regular school work. Paschall explained, "It was not just 'another idea or project' to spend government money. The program would receive no financial assistance from any such agency. Likewise, the administrators expected no financial return for service rendered. It is, and should be, looked upon as a logical outgrowth of what school work should accomplish. It is an effort to keep 'square pegs out of round holes,' or, in other words, assist youth in finding something worthwhile to do at a time and period of life when so many are floundering around."[cclxxxix]

In fall 1939, classes were offered to the community for adults. Crittenden said, "A program of adult education was mapped out. It would be sponsored by the State Board of Education at no cost to the county." The classes were held at night and the instructors were chosen from the teaching staff at the schools. Classes were taught in typing, shorthand, business English and arithmetic, landscape, vegetable and flower gardening, English grammar, reading, arithmetic, English literature, and classes in other subjects to meet the demand.[ccxc]

Fourteen had enrolled in the adult commercial class, and ten in the English and arithmetic class, while the in landscaping and civics classes no one had enrolled. The school system also offered industrial arts classes for young men between the ages of eighteen and twenty-five. This was made possible through the School Board and the National Youth Administration (NYA). The agricultural teacher—L. E. Kent, with an assistant—conducted the classes in the shop building at Victoria High School. Appropriations were made by the NYA for the power equipment and tools for the shop. Twenty young men enrolled in the classes.[ccxci] The availability of services provided through the new program was thought to be beneficial and the school needed to take advantage of the opportunity.

Helen Ferguson Snead remembered the vocational offering at the Pleasant Grove School where her aunt was the principal. Snead said, "My aunt, Iva Perkins, was an outstanding educator. She started a successful program of vocational education at Pleasant Grove in 1942. The vocational program lasted throughout the school year. My aunt thought that the children 'learned by doing.' The work the children did included making towels, curtains, pillows for chairs, and so forth. Once a week was 'wash and ironing' day, and the children learned to cook and serve properly. The vocational program at the school was indicative of my aunt's concern for the children and her dedication to education."[ccxcii]

There were buildings for vocational-agriculture and home economics classes at Kenbridge High School. L. T. Shelton was a vocational-agriculture teacher at the Kenbridge High School in the mid-1930s; and in September of 1943, Mary Owen Cobb was employed to instruct the home economics courses.[ccxciii]

By 1944, Moses T. Poles was employed as the agriculture teacher at the Lunenburg Training School. Poles served as the Vocational Agriculture Agent Instructor for the Rural War Food Production Training Program. He not only furthered the production of food, but repaired or constructed classroom furniture at the school site. He is credited with the training of 246 volunteers on 2,738 pieces of farm machinery as part of the war effort.[ccxciv]

In the summer of 1948, classes were offered at the home economics cottage at Victoria High School to anyone who was interested in learning to sew. A class was organized for adults, and high school age groups—whether or not enrolled in home economics during the regular school session.[ccxcv]

In fall 1949, James W. Thweatt joined the Victoria High School staff as the vocational-agriculture teacher. He had three assistants—Andrew J. Eubanks, Richard L. Kirby, and Herbert W. Daniel. Mildred Ann Ritchie was employed as the home economics teacher.[ccxcvi]

Mary Owen Cobb was re-employed to teach home economics at Kenbridge High School. Rae Chick followed May Owen Cobb as home economics teacher at Kenbridge High in 1945, and later, another teacher replaced Chick. In the early 1950s—James C. Potts and G. Shirley Potts were employed as vocational-agriculture instructors, and Carl E. Vaughan as an assistant. Alma O. Gee was appointed the home economics teacher.[ccxcvii] Other teachers would be employed as the home economics teacher including Lois Marshall in the late 1950s.[ccxcviii]

In 1952, a new and improved vocational-agricultural program began at Lunenburg High School (formally Lunenburg Training School) with two new teachers—Galvin Lewis Jenkins and Rhoecus Leburn "R.L." Cousins. Jenkins served as head of the agricultural department with Leroy Davis and William A. Dillard as assistants and classroom teachers.[ccxcix]

N. Harvey Jeter joined the Victoria High School staff as a vocational agricultural assistant in the early 1950s. Jeter said, "My teaching career stated in Lunenburg County when I was employed to work in the agricultural and industrial shop at the Victoria High School in 1952. I replaced a teacher who had left teaching for health reasons. I am a World War II veteran, and in June 1948, prior to my teaching assignment, I had instructed war veterans who had returned home and needed vocational training. I also assisted Ralph Underwood with some school maintenance and repair jobs that were needed at some of the one-room frame schools. When the Unity School closed in the early 1960s, Underwood and I had to shut down the school." Jeter stated that he once repaired and replaced some of the missing wooden letters in the name Kenbridge High School posted on the front of the building.[ccc]

In January of 1955, a fifteen-week class in rural electrification for Lunenburg's young farmers was offered at Lunenburg High School once a week for two hours. The electrical workshop was sponsored and supervised by Galvin Lewis Jenkins, vocational-agriculture teacher. Vocational instruction was offered in the groups of twenty young farmers on electrical stud panels used to complete wiring exercises.[ccci]

The decade beginning in 1957 was a period of growth for vocational and technical education programs for high school students and adults, reflecting Virginia's rapid industrial development. After an extensive review of Virginia's vocational needs, a legislative commission headed by Delegate C. French Slaughter, Jr. of Culpeper, made broad recommendations for improving vocational and technical education in the public schools and at the post-high school level. This resulted in giving special attention to experimental programs for youth with special needs, upgrading technical institutes and area vocational technical schools, vocational guidance institutes, vocational training centers for high school youth and adults, and establishing a program of technical education to be administered by a new Board of Technical Education.

In 1963, Virginia inaugurated the Manpower Training Program and established an additional service in the Department's Division of Vocational Education to coordinate and plan construction of local vocational centers. New vocational centers have been constructed in rural and urban areas to provide facilities for educating high school youth and adults in business and office occupations, distributive occupations, and wage-earning occupations in home economics. The *Vocational Educational Act of 1963* provided approximately six million dollars annually for the construction of area vocational schools; purchase of equipment for high school and adult programs; for programs for persons with special needs; and for ancillary services such as teacher training, development of instructional materials, innovative programs, and research.[cccii]

By 1965 all high schools—Kenbridge, Lunenburg, and Victoria—offered courses in vocational and agriculture education, building trades, and home economics. However, after the consolidation of the Kenbridge High and Victoria High in fall of 1966, two secondary schools remained—Central and Lunenburg. Both schools offered vocational and agriculture education training, but not mechanical drawing and drafting. One former student from Lunenburg High School spoke of the time when some of Lunenburg's students were transported by bus each day to take advantage of the mechanical drawing and drafting courses at Central High School.

Distributive Education

As part of the State's vocational education initiatives in early 1960s, the Distributive Education (DE) Program was added to the course offerings at Central High School in the fall of 1966. This program was designed for students who were preparing for or engaged in distributing goods and services to the public, including all retail, wholesale, and service occupations. It centered on preparatory instruction for high school students desiring to explore distribution as a career, and seeking a broader knowledge of the principles of free enterprise for continuing education related to distribution.

The Distributive Education Cooperative Plan for high school students in their junior and senior years offered the opportunity to attend classes in the school for half of each school day. During the half day, each student would take two subjects required for graduation, and the DE course, in which the student received classroom instruction for performing a beginning job in distribution. In addition to the classroom instruction, students received fifteen to twenty-five hours per week of instruction and experience in a job in a local distributive business. DE offered vocational training and instruction in the Adult Training Program on preparation, employee, supervision, and management. This program was designed to improve the proficiency of personnel in retail, wholesale, and service businesses. Additional courses were offered in Personnel Management, Sales Promotion, How to Supervise an Employee, Salesmanship, Display, and Human Relations.

In August of 1966, Benjamin Lee Watson III was employed as the Distributive Education Coordinator for Lunenburg County Public Schools. Watson is credited with the implementation of the DE program and oversight of the Distributive Education Club of America (DECA).[ccciii]

Violet Johnson (Harris) spoke of her experience as a student in the Distributive Education Program at Central High School. She was a senior preparing to graduate in the spring of 1967. Harris said, "I enrolled in a new program called Distributive Education in the fall of 1966. I attended English and government classes in the morning, and worked at my assigned job site the rest of the day. I also became a member of the Distributive Education Club of America."[ccciv]

CHAPTER 8
CURRICULUM AND INSTRUCTION

In the late 1800s, recommendations were made by State Superintendent John E. Massey (1890-1898) for the preparation of courses of study in Virginia's schools. Wood documented, "The majority of the schools were small, and the principal or teacher gave all the instruction." The first course of study for elementary schools was published in 1907, and a revised edition was issued in 1909. Further efforts to strengthen the secondary program in 1917 included an approved program of studies.

In 1931, at the beginning of his administration, Dr. Sidney Hall recognized the need for an intensive program to improve instruction, chiefly through curriculum revision. Therefore, he organized the Department of Education into six divisions including a Division of Instruction to unify secondary education, elementary education, Negro education, and health and physical education. The superintendent assigned to this division was primarily responsible for initiating and developing a program to improve instruction. Within two years more than 10,000 of the state's 17,000 teachers had participated in curriculum planning workshops and seminar groups, for which state and local supervisors served as advisors and discussion leaders.[cccv]

Development of High Schools

In Virginia, before the educational awakening of in the early 1900s, opportunities for an education beyond the elementary level were severely limited. Students went from grade one to grade seven. Some elected to go on to high school, but that was not a strict requirement. It was under Massey's leadership that the high school level was implemented. Although the number of high schools in 1900 is not known, Massey reported sixty in 1897, which probably included limited high school programs offered in elementary or grade schools. Only 10,210 white students and 1,031 Negro students—representing four percent of whites and seven-tenths of one percent of Negroes enrolled in public schools—were studying at "the higher branches."[cccvi]

A 1903 act establishing the minimum requirements for high school teachers was the first step in developing standards for high school accreditation. The *May Campaign of 1905* resulted in far-reaching legislation during the administration of Joseph D. Eggleston, Jr. with the passage of the *Mann High School Act of 1906*. The legislature authorized funds to match local contributions for high school programs, where localities furnished adequate buildings and teachers' salaries. By 1909, the state had 345 high schools.

High school courses of study were published in 1906 and 1910. The latter publication listed minimum requirements in subjects and units of three grades of high school: first, second, third. Requirements for first-grade high school included twelve required units: English, four units; mathematics, three units; history, three units; and science, two units. Five elective units were to be selected from the following subjects: Latin, German, French, Spanish, history, physical geography, agriculture, manual arts, botany and zoology, physics, chemistry, and mathematics. The development of these early courses of study indicated a trend toward state-level leadership and guidance in improving classroom instruction. An example of these is listed on the 1910 Monthly Report for the Kenilworth School. At that time, the unit of study included the courses of reading, spelling, arithmetic, geography, penmanship, grammar, history, physiology, and composition. Other courses—not graded—included physical geography, orthography, algebra, philosophy, rhetoric, botany, civil government, and Latin.[cccvii]

A comprehensive program of high school accreditation began in 1912 when the Southern Association of Colleges and Secondary Schools established a Virginia Commission on Accredited Schools. Lunenburg County operated the accredited high schools of Kenbridge, Lochleven, and Victoria; and in the early 1930s the Lunenburg Training School received its accreditation.

In 1915, the Department of Public Instruction issued a new course of study for high schools, superseding the rudimentary first course published in 1910. It consisted mainly of college preparatory work, but included subjects in business, agriculture, and homemaking. The number of high schools increased rapidly, and by 1917 there were 522 high schools enrolling 27,107 students. Wood wrote, "No provision had been made in the county for the Negro boy or girl of exceptional mentality to further his education if he so desired. Due to the efforts of Mrs. Morrison and the school leagues in various communities, plans were laid for the initiation of secondary education in Lunenburg County. The high school offered two years on the secondary level during the session of 1918-1919." The Jeanes supervisors aided in making shopwork, homemaking, and other vocational skills part of the curriculum in the schools for Negro children beginning in the 1920s. By the early 1930s, the Lunenburg Training School offered vocational training and work leading to general college courses.[cccviii]

Quality Education

Two major developments had a profound impact although many factors affected public education. One grew out of the U. S. Supreme Court decision in *Brown v. Board of Education*, and the other out of the launching of Sputnik by the Russians in 1957.[cccix]

The 1958 General Assembly, reflecting the public concern generated by Sputnik, enacted legislation providing for a commission to evaluate the curriculum, teacher training and certification, "and related matters" for the public schools in Virginia. The Commission on Public Education, headed by State Senator William B. Sprong, Jr., endorsed the State Department of Education's efforts to strengthen teacher education and the high school curriculum. Its report also emphasized the need for improving the quality of teaching and strengthening programs in science, mathematics, foreign languages, and English, while at the same time recommending a balanced curriculum.

By the school term of 1959-1960 the instructional emphasis would be on American government and economics with the development of materials and guidelines for instruction in education. The State Board of Education wanted a unit developed on basic principles of the American form of government and economic way of life. An outline for the unit was prepared for incorporation in the senior high school course in Virginia and United States government. Another was requested by the Board to be prepared for use during school term of 1962-1963.

The School Board employed S. M. Haga as General Supervisor to provide guidance in the implementation of the new instructional materials from the state.

The guide entitled "Communism in Contrast with the Principles of American Freedom," was distributed and regional meetings were held throughout the state to discuss its use. A third publication, "An Instructional Guide for Virginia and United States Government," was issued in November of 1964 to give teachers suggestions for selecting, organizing, and presenting content to further the study of the American political and economic system and to contrast it with totalitarianism and communism.

Upon recommendation of the state superintendent and with the board's approval, the program was redefined and expanded to include a guide for the required course in Virginia and United States history, a guide for the elective course in civics in grades eight and nine, a guide to stress economic education at the elementary level, and revisions of teacher certification regulations to provide a stronger background in economic education.[cccx]

Dr. Woodrow W. Wilkerson succeeded Dr. Paschall as state superintendent of public instruction in the mid-1960s. Major steps were taken to improve the quality of education in Virginia. In 1966, the Board of Education supported state aid for kindergarten classes operated as part of the public school program; and the General Assembly approved the principle of state aid for the full-scale operation of kindergartens. The next year, the state Board of Education adopted the first regulations in the state's history governing the operation of public school kindergartens. These regulations established standards for the certification of kindergarten teachers, length of the school day, and size of classrooms. In January 1968, a curriculum guide for kindergarten education was approved by the Board.

Dr. Wilkerson, in January 1967, recommended that the state accreditation program be expanded to include elementary as well as high schools. An accreditation program for elementary schools was approved in 1969 and became effective in September 1970.

A statewide conference on education was called by Governor Mills E. Godwin, Jr. This historic meeting called for rapid improvements in education at all levels, and especially the elimination of disparities between public school programs in different sections of Virginia. In 1967, the state Board of Education authorized the superintendent of public instruction to appoint a committee to develop a plan to effect substantial improvements in public education, particularly those localities where the needs were greatest. The committee recommended visiting teams be assigned to evaluate programs for school divisions; and two studies—one of "ways and means" to effectively consolidate small school divisions and the other of the formula for distributing state aid to public schools.[cccxi]

System of Textbooks

There was no organized textbook system in the county prior to the 1900s. The teacher or hired tutor created his or her own instructional materials and educational tools for students. One of the earliest known textbooks in Lunenburg County was used by Annie Thelma Harding during her studies at the Kenilworth School in 1909. *Word Studies*, advanced edition, contains 127 pages with Section 1 – Syllabication; Section 2 – How to Become a Good Speller; Section 3 – Troublesome Words and Word Origins; and Section 4 – A Brief Dictionary. A statement on the back cover explained that the price of this book was fixed by contract with the state and any derivation there from should be reported to the State Superintendent of Public Instruction. The retail price was thirteen cents, with an exchange price of six cents.[cccxii]

Dr. Hart, in 1918, made three recommendations to the General Assembly. Two of his recommendations were adopted in 1922 when the General Assembly enacted the county unit law and a statewide compulsory attendance law. Although free textbooks were not approved, the General Assembly passed a new textbook law permitting local school boards to purchase directly from publishers at wholesale prices.[cccxiii]

In October 1925, W. D. Dickinson, State Supervisor of Textbooks and School Libraries, spoke at Victoria High School on the methods of distributing textbooks in the State of Virginia and the state's plan for the provision of libraries for public schools. The textbook system once controlled by the state agency was turned over to the local school board. In Lunenburg, school books were housed in the superintendent's office located on Main Street in Victoria, Virginia; B. L. Gee's Store in Kenbridge; and B. L. Winn's Store on the Victoria-Keysville Road (now Lunenburg County Road). Information as to prices, requirements, etc., could be obtained at the office from the clerk, Fannie Phelps. Parents were encouraged to buy the books ahead of the school opening week to avoid the rush.[cccxiv]

Willie Lucretia Maddux McAllister spoke of her school days at the Bethany School in the 1930s. McAllister said, "I vividly remember those days when we didn't have many textbooks to use. Mrs. Morison would visit our little schoolhouse and bring an armful of books and other learning materials. Back then, if we got any textbooks at all, they were usually 'hand-me-down' from white schools in the county. On many occasions we would use clear tape to try and repair as many of the torn pages as we could so we were able to read." Morrison visited the schools to monitor the academic instruction taking place in the classroom and delivered needed textbooks and other school supplies.[cccxv]

In August 1931, the School Board appointed teachers as they prepared for the new school term. To prevent any mistakes in purchasing textbooks as a result of changes made by the State Board of Education, a list was prepared showing the exact books required in each grade.[cccxvi]

Many of the white schools in Lunenburg opened with a new primer and first reader used in place of the *Everyday Classics Primer and First Reader*. New textbooks were available in arithmetic (grades three and five); language (grades three and six); and history for grade five; and readers in grades six and seven. At the Victoria High School, the *Dugger's Agriculture* textbook was dropped and no other textbook was adopted in its place. Textbooks were adopted for first year—mathematics, history, Latin and science; second year—Latin; and third and fourth year—history. Any patron wishing to purchase books before the opening day of school could secure a complete list for any of the grades by applying at Office of the Division Superintendent in Victoria, Virginia.[cccxvii]

In March of 1933, the Williams School, a three-room structure, situated near Ontario in the Rehoboth District, was burned by fire. It is believed that the blaze was of an incendiary origin. The contents, including textbooks owned by the children were destroyed. This was a direct loss to the people of the community. Temporary arrangements were made to complete the school year in a residence near the site of the school property; and plans were underway to erect a new building.[cccxviii]

In early 1939, C. W. Dickerson, Jr., State Director of Libraries and Textbooks, submitted a plan to the School Board by which Lunenburg County could have a book mobile furnished by WPA funds to work in connection with the public library. No decision was made by the School Board with regard to Dickerson's proposed textbook plan.[cccxix] Bernice Stokes Charlton spoke about her early education. She said, "I remember attending the Cool Spring School in the mid-1930s. There were about thirty students in our school from grades one through seven. My teacher lived with a neighborhood family and walked about three miles to school. We had a wood-burning stove that was used to keep us warm on those really cold days. Our special day was 'happy' Friday. That's when our teacher would cook a batch of homemade candy on the stove. Our teacher thought that reading was important so she started a book club although many of our books were 'second-hand' or 'hand-me-down.' One of the patrons constructed a small bookshelf for us to use in the classroom. We also had access to the county's Book Mobile that made stops at Kunath Store, in Rehoboth, just a mile or two from the school."[cccxx]

In December of 1939, Evelyn Nolley, a teacher at the Kenilworth School, submitted an article to the *Kenbridge-Victoria Dispatch* on the behalf of the students there. It stated, "We would like for everyone to know just how happy we were Tuesday morning when Mr. Lyons brought us our first unit of books purchased through the cooperation of the schools, the County School Board, and the State Board of Education. We feel that we have already—in one day—'gotten our money's worth.' We hope all the school children in Lunenburg County are going to have as much fun reading new books as we are having."[cccxxi]

On January 9, 1940, the county's elementary teachers held a meeting at the Kenbridge High School with Superintendent Crittenden and guest speaker, C. W. Dickerson, Jr., State Director of School Libraries and Textbooks. Dickerson said, "The tremendous growth of the school libraries and textbook program has largely been responsible for the increased success of the progressive education program throughout the state. No longer is it necessary for pupils to receive all of their instructions from one textbook. Instead, many different books are available, providing the material to carry on a much broader educational program.

With state aid, it was possible for schools to buy books at a cost of twenty cents for a one-dollar book—these books being purchased in sixty-dollar units. For each school to purchase its own units of books is a wasteful and an out-of-date practice. A plan used in a number of different counties and regions of the states in which there is one central collection that is circulated to each of the schools in the system, thus giving each school access to a much larger collection than would otherwise be available."

One hundred percent of the school boards that Dickerson visited had cooperated with him in the new textbook system; that is, the school library program that started a year earlier would work in cooperation with the Lunenburg Public Library. The payment of five dollars by each grade would be made, to be matched by the county and state funds for the purchase of books that would be the property of the county school board. These books would be circulated to all schools under the auspices of the county library.[cccxxii] No decision was made by the School Board to implement Dickerson's proposed textbook plan.

On August 2, 1940, the School Board approved the textbooks of *Modern School Arithmetic* in place of the *Problem and Practice Arithmetic* for use in the elementary grades; and for eighth grade—*Modern School Arithmetic III, Elementary English in Action III, Plain English Handbook, Eighth Grade Stanford Speller, United States At Work,* and *Our Environment—How We Adapt Ourselves To It.* School textbooks would continue to be available through a rental system and a list of text books would be published in the local newspaper.[cccxxiii]

At the state level, Wilbur C. Hall, Chairman of the Senate Finance Committee, had proposed a plan to provide free textbooks for every child in the Commonwealth of Virginia. He believed, however, that the time had arrived "when a provision for free textbooks in Virginia is absolutely necessary and essential." The bill failed passage because of insufficient funds for direct appropriations. In 1944—about a decade later—the School Board approved free textbooks for indigent children in the county whose parents could not afford the full cost of textbooks in September. The Board authorized Fears, with the assistance of H. S. Morgan, Superintendent of Public Welfare, to investigate and recommend children needing these free books.[cccxxiv]

In May 1945, the selection of textbooks was left to a committee consisting of the principals, supervisor and superintendent.[cccxxv] Fears also presented for consideration the plan of the School Board to furnish desk copies of textbooks for teachers in June of 1945. In addition to the adoption of textbooks, the school system would allow the patrons to purchase the Pilot Accident Insurance Premiums at cost per pupil for the school year.[cccxxvi] Textbook adoption and rental had become the norm.[cccxxvii]

In 1946, the General Assembly approved changes in the method of distributing school funds and free textbooks for elementary grades. An increase was made in the state's appropriation of $500,000 for free textbooks in the elementary grades with the counties matching one-third.[cccxxviii]

By the 1950s, students were requested to bring the fees on the first day of school or as soon as possible. A check was acceptable, written to the school. In addition, parents were allowed to bring any books they wished to sell with them. The book rent fee had more than tripled at each grade level, and the rates listed in the local newspaper did not include cost of consumable materials and art supplies in the elementary grades. The consumable materials included a supply of writing paper and an annual subscription to the *Weekly Reader* for $3.50. (see Appendix B – Table 2: Book Rental Fee and Consumable Materials Cost, 1957).[cccxxix]

The Board made plans to implement a new textbook rental process in the fall of 1958. All students had to report to their homeroom, where the book rent and consumable materials fee was collected instead of direct purchase from the School Board office. For the most part, the acquisition and distribution of textbooks and other instructional supplies for the Negro schools continued to be handled by individual school patrons. Sherman C. Vaughan was the assistant principal and teacher at the Lunenburg Elementary School. Vaughan said, "In late 1950s and early 1960s, textbooks were often purchased from the parent of a student in the next upper grade. New textbooks were often not purchased because some parents could not afford to buy them."[cccxxx]

By September 1966, the price for textbook rental at Victoria Elementary School was Grade 1 - $6.25; Grade 2 - $6.50; Grade 3 - $6.75; Grade 4 - $7.00; Grade 5 - $5.80; Grade 6 - $6.25; and Grade 7 - $8.70.[cccxxxi] No explanation was available for the lower cost in the fifth and sixth grades; however, a reasonable answer may rest with the requirement and cost of consumable materials at each grade level.

With continued concern about the education of African American students in the integrated schools, Nathaniel L. Hawthorne, Sr., President, Lunenburg County Branch of the NAACP, appeared before the Board in late summer of 1969 to request history books that were racially diverse be used in the classrooms. He said, "I would like to ask the Superintendent of Schools and members of the Board to consider trying to come up with a plan to use some of these books." The chairman of the board, J. W. Blackburn, replied, "We will give it consideration that some would be in the library and eventually can be worked out to have some in the schools."[cccxxxii]

The Lunenburg School Board continued to operate a rental system for all schools in 1969-70. The fee cost follows:

Book Rental Fee and Consumable Material Cost, 1969

First Grade	$2.54
Second Grade	$2.66
Third Grade	$6.21
Fourth, Fifth & Sixth Grades	$7.00
Grade Seven	$8.25
High School	$1.80 per subject

(These rates did not include the cost of workbooks, consumable materials, and dictionaries.)

Textbook adoption included new books for elementary (grades 1-7) in arithmetic, health and science; elementary dictionary; and high school (grades 8-12); physics; and a high school dictionary for the school session of 1969-70.

The Kenbridge-Victoria Dispatch reported, "Parents who wished to purchase books for their children could do so. The only stipulation is that a child must rent all or purchase all books. The rental system included all adopted basal textbooks. Workbooks and consumable supplies must be purchased as well. The rental rates could be obtained from the individual schools; and all textbooks were handled by each school."[cccxxxiii]

CHAPTER 9
TREND OF SCHOOL CONSOLIDATION

The consolidation of schools is not a new idea. This method has been used by school officials to ensure the most efficient use of available resources—materials, equipment, facilities, and personnel. Records show that school consolidation in the county began as early as 1908 during the leadership of Superintendent Wilkinson. In *Our School*, Wilkinson wrote, "I condemned one of those one-room buildings once. The examiner—from the state—and I went down there. People were walking around with pistols in their pockets. We had to be right careful about that. Had to tell 'em we weren't closing the school—just the building."[cccxxxiv]

When the Robertson School closed around 1915 or 1916, the students were transported to the Jonesboro School located on Jonesboro Road. The name of Jonesboro was changed to Woodrow in honor of President Woodrow Wilson.

In 1926, school consolidation continued to be a topic of discussion by Superintendent Waddill and district trustees—J. R. Featherstun, Lochleven; C. S. Barnes, Pleasant Grove; H. G. Fore, Rehoboth; and George Snead, Columbian Grove. Waddill stated, "The schools as operated under the present system are costing the county too much for the results obtained." Waddill's plan was to group all the children of the county into some eight to ten schools, instead of having them scattered in twenty-nine different schools. This would reduce the number of teachers about one-third, thereby saving the county $15,000 to $20,000 annually in salaries alone, and the grade of instruction would increase by one hundred percent.

In Waddill's opinion, "One-room school was as obsolete as the ox cart in the world of commerce and industry." The School Board made arrangements to transport the high school pupils of the Union Central School to Victoria so they could be given better educational advantages than they were receiving. This would be less cost to the county.[cccxxxv] The school term of 1927-28 was the last for the Snead School. Some children were transported to the school in Kenbridge and others enrolled at the Nonintervention School.[cccxxxvi] The Nonintervention School served students in grades one to eleven. The first school burned, and a new four-room school was built for grades one through nine. With a declining enrollment, even with the Snead School students, only two rooms were used. One of the remaining two rooms was used as an auditorium in warm weather, and the other for storage. The school closed in the spring of 1941 because of low enrollment and the students were transported to the school in Kenbridge.[cccxxxvii]

Beginning in 1931—at the state level—greater attention was being given to establishing schools of sufficient size to offer comprehensive educational programs at reasonable per capita cost. The Ledbetter school closed at the end of the 1931-'32 school year, and the teacher and pupils were transferred to Pleasant Grove School.[cccxxxviii]

In November of 1938, a committee appointed by the governor made a study and survey of the schools of Lunenburg County and made its report to the School Board. The recommendations follow:

The abolition of the Kenbridge and Lochleven High Schools, and the establishment of a single high school for the county to be located in Victoria; and the closing of several small, frame schools and the establishment of six consolidated, well-equipped elementary schools at various points in the county.

At the August 1939 Board meeting, it was decided to close the Lunenburg School near the courthouse. The teacher and pupils for this school were transferred to the school in Victoria.[cccxxxix]

In July 1941, the School Board announced the public auction school sale of Nonintervention, Russell, and Reedy because they were no longer being used. More high school consolidation occurred in 1942 when nine or ten seniors from Lochleven High School were transferred to Kenbridge High and graduated with the seniors there.[cccxl]

The successful consolidation of Negro schools was among the many accomplishments of Lucy M. Morrison. A survey conducted in 1943 recommended consolidation—based on vicinity—of Central, Gill Hill, Cool Spring, Plantersville, Lone Oak, Macedonia, Oak Grove, Trinity, Unity, Midway, Bethany, Traffic, Davis, Gary, Wattsboro, New Grove, Camp, Friendship, Rosebud, Asbury, Varick, West Hill, Pleasant Oak, and Mount Olive.[cccxli] No action was taken by the School Board.

Atlas Stokes Robinson continues to cherish the memories of her early school experiences at the Cool Spring School. As Robinson put it, "Our little school was always a special place to be. The number one priority was to get an education and misbehavior at school was not tolerated. If we misbehaved at school, the teacher would visit our homes to talk with the parents, and this would ensure that misbehavior or disrespect never happened again. Due to school consolidation, our beloved Cool Spring School closed in the late 1940s. The students were transferred to other schools like Thyne Institute in Chase City, Virginia; Lunenburg Training School and Lunenburg Elementary School in Victoria; and Traffic School in Rehoboth, Virginia."

Shirley Stokes Byrd, Robinson's sister, added to the conversation. Byrd said, "I also can recall my years at this school. My best memory is when our teacher had made plans to cook lunch for us and sometimes she would make a pot of beans to eat. On those days, I made sure to bring my plate—white with the bright red trim—and a utensil with me. It was understood that the first person who got to school had to make a fire and get water from a nearby spring or neighbor's well. We didn't have bus transportation so we walked through the woods to school about three miles. When the teacher started our lessons—many times—we had to sit quietly while she worked with the others in the class because there were many students in the school."

Neale wrote, "But the issue of school consolidation was tabled until after World War II. People were talking about consolidation of the schools, but others found it unfeasible. The problem is a debatable one . . . it is offering a number of headaches in this time of few tires and little gas. High school consolidation was postponed, but would resurface."[cccxlii]

In the spring of 1944, the School Board again discussed the possibility of a high school, centrally located, to accommodate the secondary student enrollment of the entire county. This would provide an enlarged educational offering for the pupils on the high school level.[cccxliii]

In November of 1945, the School Board went on record with a resolution at its regular meeting as favoring a consolidated high school for *all* white students of the county. There existed a present and urgent need for additional school facilities, and to meet this need a point on the Victoria-Kenbridge highway was established. The estimated cost of building and equipment, including land, was $230,000, and the money could be obtained either as a loan from the State Literary Fund or by a bond issue approved by a majority of the qualified voters.[cccxliv]

In September 1946, a consolidated high school was proposed. However, the proposal was tabled because the Board of Supervisors believed that too much money was involved; therefore, no action was taken at the time.[cccxlv] The School Board did move forward on the issue with the purchased of 14.5 acres of land located between Kenbridge and Victoria as the site for a new consolidated high school.

In the fall of 1947, with carefree summer days a memory, students trudged back to school on September 6 to face nine months of study. There were twenty schools for Negroes, including the Lunenburg Training School and Kenbridge Graded School. For whites, the high schools of Kenbridge and Victoria; and the four elementary schools—Lochleven, Meherrin, Fort Mitchell, and Kenilworth remained in operation. The other schools had closed.[cccxlvi] The five Negro schools of Mount Olive, Bethany, Macedonia, Cool Spring, and Gill Hill closed in the spring of 1948.

The following year, in 1949, the schools of Plantersville and West End closed. The elementary students were consolidated with Traffic School.[cccxlvii] The schools of Varick and Oak Grove closed in the late 1940s; and Mount Bethel is believed to have closed in the early 1950s. These students were transported to the Kenbridge Graded School; and all secondary students at these schools continued their education at the Lunenburg Training School. In the Victoria area, the schools of Pleasant Oak, Traffic, West Hill, and Lone Oak had closed by 1950, and these students—elementary and secondary—transferred to the Lunenburg Training School.

The closure of Pleasant Grove, Fort Mitchell, Kenilworth, and Traffic (white) in the late 1940s created the need for a new consolidated school in the area. In fall 1949, the West End Elementary School opened its doors to students in grades one through six. The seventh grade was added by 1960.

In June of 1954, a large delegation of Meherrin citizens requested that the School Board keep the Meherrin School opened because community life centered on the school. The Board had spent money to improve the building in recent years, but it was in the midst of consolidation and the

Meherrin School closed. In the fall, the students were transported to the school in Victoria.[cccxlviii]

By 1955, the four schools for whites were Victoria High (8-12), Victoria Elementary (1-7), Kenbridge High (8-12) and elementary level (1-7), West End Elementary (1-6), and Lochleven Elementary (1-7). The Lunenburg High (8-12), Lunenburg Elementary (1-7), Kenbridge Graded (1-7), and the frame schools of Asbury (grades 1-7), New Grove (grades 1-7), Camp (grades 4-7), and Unity (1-5) operated for black pupils. All other small county schools had closed.

The Camp School closed in the spring of 1960—some students were transferred to the Unity School and others enrolled at the Kenbridge Graded School. This created an overcrowded condition at Kenbridge. In an effort to alleviate this new population problem, the School Board authorized Superintendent Fears to rent the Blackwell Temple A.M.E. (African Methodist Episcopal) Zion and Saint Luke's Episcopal Churches as temporary classrooms in the fall of 1961. These churches were located in the neighborhood—across the street from the school.

Alvester Edmonds commented on his experience when some of the small schools in the area closed. Edmonds said, "I attended the Kenbridge Graded School from the first through seventh grade. In the early 1960s some of us had to attend class at a local church. I distinctly remember walking to Saint Luke's—about a hundred yards or so from our school. We were overcrowded and there wasn't enough room for all of us to attend class in the school building."[cccxlix]

However, as part of the School Board school building program in 1961, plans were underway for a fourteen-room addition at Kenbridge Graded School (also called the Kenbridge Negro Elementary School) to be ready for occupancy in the November. A loan of $200,000 for remodeling came from the State Literary Fund. The new brick building would house 500 pupils. As a result of the new addition, other small frame schools were closed.[cccl]

In December 1961, the citizens turned down a School Bond Issue to build two consolidated high schools for Lunenburg County—white and Negro—costing about $1.2 million. The vote (unofficial) was 820 for and 1374 against. The question was whether the County of Lunenburg was willing to contract a debt and issue bonds in the amount not to exceed $500,000 for more classrooms in five schools. There was a true need for upgrading of schools.

The schools of New Grove, Asbury, and Unity closed in the spring of 1962. Some of these students transferred to the Lunenburg Elementary School while others enrolled at the Kenbridge Graded School.

Again, on November 9, 1962, the voters defeated the Bond election by a vote of 889 against and 745 for. A bulletin which was published before the Bond Issue vote said, in part, "it will become necessary that the schools operate on a double shift or room be rented out of town"—if the proposed Bond Issue is defeated.[cccli]

There were no other school consolidations until the fall of 1969. Lunenburg operated the schools of Central Senior High, Lunenburg Junior High, Kenbridge Elementary, Victoria Elementary, West End Elementary, Kenbridge Primary, and Lunenburg Primary. School closing efforts culminated in dramatic gains in consolidation. The trend toward fewer schools and larger enrollments has continued to the present time.[ccclii]

CHAPTER 10
PUBLIC EDUCATION
ISSUE OF THE CENTURY

"Racially segregated schools are inherently unequal."[cccliii]
—United States Supreme Court

Did the decision of the United States Supreme Court in the *Brown* case impact public education?

You can bet it did! Beginning in the mid-1930s, the National Association for the Advancement of Colored People (NAACP) led by attorneys such as Charles Hamilton Houston and Thurgood Marshall launched a legal campaign of "equalization" challenging the material inequalities between black and white schools. In 1950, however, the national NAACP decided to stop funding the equalization suits in Virginia and other states in favor of attacking segregation on constitutional grounds. Civil rights attorney and activist Henry L. Marsh, III recalls that "the rest of the Southern States were sort of watching Virginia to see what would happen. We had the strongest group of civil rights and NAACP fighters of any state in the union because that's where they chose to make a stand."

In April 1951, a student strike led by Barbara Rose Johns protesting the poor quality of the black Moton High School in Prince Edward County resulted in Virginia's first direct legal challenge to school segregation—*Davis et al. v. County School Board of Prince Edward County.*[cccliv]

Virginia's argument in favor of segregation, made by Attorney General J. Lindsay Almond, Jr., prevailed in the federal trial court.[ccclv] In summer 1953, Senator A. Willis Robertson said, "Because of the splendid arguments presented to the Supreme Court last year by that great constitutional lawyer—John W. Davis, and several State Attorneys General, including J.

Lindsay Almond, Jr., of Virginia—I was confident that the Court would up-
hold State school segregation laws. Further arguments were needed before
the Court made its decision on school segregation. The Court asked
whether the framers of the Fourteenth Amendment believed Congress
could use it to abolish segregation or wanted the Courts to have that power
and whether the Court had the power to interpret the law to outlaw school
segregation." Robertson felt that those questions had been fully and ade-
quately answered by the arguments of Davis and the others who pointed
out that after the adoption of the Amendment Congress had passed a law
authorizing segregation in the District of Columbia and several states which
voted to ratify the Amendment passed school segregation laws. Even religious organizations which had sponsored the Fourteenth Amendment later
established segregated schools for Negroes in the South.

Robertson continued "Virginia and other southern states have done
everything within their financial power to comply with a previous decision
of the Supreme Court regarding 'equal facilities and opportunity for education' be made available for all, regardless of race. Colored leaders in Virginia and generally throughout the South realize that 90 percent or more
of the cost of public schools is paid by white people although in twenty Virginia counties and in some states there are as many colored pupils as there
are white. The concern appeared to be if white parents in the Southern
states should refuse to patronize non-segregated public schools and oppose
the appropriations of adequate funds for public schools because their children are attending private schools, the quality of public education will necessarily decrease and the loss will be suffered by white children of those
who cannot afford privately supported education, as well as by the colored
children. Human nature had not greatly changed since the days of Thomas
Jefferson when the rich planters of Virginia defeated his public school bill
because of an unwillingness to be taxed for the education of the masses."[ccclvi]
But, the fight was not over!

The Byrd Factor

The influence of Harry Flood Byrd, Sr., was far-reaching into political life
of Virginians. The Byrd Organization reigned supreme from the Shenan-
doah Valley to the Eastern Shore, from northern Piedmont to the North
Carolina border, and through vast tracts of rural Virginia. He was an over-

arching leader who drew critical support from white voters in counties with large African American populations. Columnist T. Coleman Andrews in *The Kenbridge-Victoria Dispatch* wrote, "Whenever a Virginia gubernatorial or senatorial election is held and won, as they inevitably are won by Byrd supporters . . .point to something called 'The Organization' or 'The Byrd Machine' and credit that mystical body with the victory. What controls Virginia, politically, is a community of interest. The great majority of Virginians shared the conservative views of Senator Byrd and reflects their convictions at the polls. It is as simple as that."[ccclvii]

Harry Byrd was born in 1887 in a state scarred by poverty. He gained prominence on the state political scene in 1923 when he led a fight against a proposed fifty-million-dollar bond issue for highway construction. Although many of the state's urban business and industrial leaders favored the bond, Virginia's farmers feared that their lands would bear the brunt of new state taxes, and they opposed all proposals for it.[ccclviii] The bond issue was decisively defeated in a popular referendum. Abhorrence of public debt and cash-drawer frugality were hallmarks of the Byrd Era in Virginia.[ccclix]

Byrd never neglected Virginia's farmers. He had championed the farmers' cause in 1923 by opposing the bond issue, thus gaining strong support in Southside Virginia. Byrd was governor from 1926 to 1930 and to his credit was more often termed a progressive, although he had long been a conservative. He and his administration are conceded to have been one of the most fruitful in Virginia's history. Under his *Program of Progress*, Byrd converted a million-dollar deficit into a surplus; sponsored strict legislation which made lynching a state offense and all members of a lynch mob subject to murder charges; implemented voting and tax reforms to attract new residents and industry to Virginia; abolished the state tax on land; and promoted rural electrification, conservation, and tourist trade.[ccclx] There was strong support of Byrd in the Southside region of Virginia—the word was Byrd. An advertisement to support Harry Flood Byrd for governor appeared in *The Victoria Dispatch* as follows:

A True Virginian Ever First in Mind
Harry Flood Byrd

Is a farmer and know their needs. He is a Newspaper Man and familiar with conditions all over Virginia. He is a statesman and

> *knows the Law situation and is a known champion of LESS*
> *TAXES, attention is invited to Mr. Byrd's State Labor record in*
> *all legislation favorable to the working man.*

Vote For Him For Governor

Election victories, however, did not resolve the problems confronting Virginia. William Munford Tuck was elected governor of Virginia in 1946 and remained until 1950. In January 1949, Governor Tuck asked a special session of the legislature for more money to meet an "acute emergency" in the state's school system, which had been documented by the 1944 Denny Commission on education. The Virginia Education Commission, headed by Denny, found the schools were poorly financed, overcrowded, and inadequately staffed. In Virginia, there were 1,500 one-room schools; more than 1,000 were deemed fire or health hazards and were labeled "unsuitable" for students. Conditions in black schools were particularly appalling; many had no indoor plumbing, central heating, electricity, or bus service. Shortly after his election in 1950, Governor John S. Battle carried out his campaign promise by recommending that seven million dollars in state aid be given to localities for school construction. The General Assembly approved his proposal. The legislators also approved $45 million in an attempt to deal with inadequate and crowded facilities, notably the unequal black schools.[ccclxi]

Support in Lunenburg

School desegregation would become the public education issue of the century. Several articles were printed in the local newspaper to keep the citizens of Lunenburg and others informed of the state's position on the subject. In 1951, an article that appeared on the front page of *The Kenbridge-Victoria Dispatch* stated, "Governor Battle reiterated his determination to enforce the state constitutional mandate for segregation of the races in the public schools of Virginia." Commenting on the petition filed with the Prince Edward County School Board for abolition of segregation in the county and Farmville public schools, the governor said, "The plain mandate of the Constitution of Virginia provides for segregation in the public schools. No state or local official can ignore this constitutional provision, and insofar as it is within my power, it will be enforced. I feel that we are making real progress in the education of both white and colored children in Virginia, and if at some future date some federal court should attempt to act aside this constitutional provision, such action would, in my opinion, do irreparable injury to the public school system, if not completely wreck it."[ccclxii]

For forty years or more, crowds from almost every county in Virginia faithfully supported Harry F. Byrd and the subsequent procession of Byrd loyalists to the governor's chair. Some of Byrd's strongest support rested in the Southside region of Virginia. The words "Byrd For President" were printed in a 1952 editorial by *The Farmville Herald*. The article stated, "The Automotive Trade Association of Virginia has adopted a resolution urging Virginia's Senior Senator Harry Flood Byrd to become a candidate for the nomination of President of the United States, assuring him the support of the Association, and further urging people interested in good government to write Senator Byrd to urge his candidacy."[ccclxiii]

Byrd had strong support in Lunenburg County because of the Organization's self-proclaimed record of honest government and support of farmers. The Lunenburg support was demonstrated, with the rest of the state, during the 1952 Democratic Primary poll results with 1,117 votes were cast for Harry F. Byrd and his opponent Francis Pickens Miller received a total of 600 (see Appendix C – Table 3: Voting by Precinct in Lunenburg County, 1952).[ccclxiv]

Thomas Bahnson Stanley ran against Theodore R. Dalton for governor of Virginia in the fall of 1953. Lunenburg voters overwhelmingly supported Stanley, with a vote 1,175 compared to 336 for Dalton (see Appendix D – Table 4: Lunenburg Votes by Precinct, 1953). Stanley was inaugurated as the sixty-seventh governor in January of 1954.[ccclxv]

As anticipated by the NAACP legal team, the Virginia courts ruled that the school facilities were unequal and should be equalized to meet the standard of "separate but equal" laid out in *Plessy v. Ferguson*. The case was appealed to the United States Supreme Court and combined with four other cases under *Brown v. Board of Education of Topeka, Kansas*. On Monday, May 17, 1954, the Court handed down its school desegregation decision. The Court declared unanimously that racial segregation in public education was unconstitutional. The Court set aside a Kansas statue permitting cities of more than 15,000 to maintain separate schools for blacks and whites and ruled instead that all segregation in public school is "inherently unequal" and that all blacks barred from attending public school with white pupils are denied equal protection of the law as guaranteed by the Fourteenth Amendment. The doctrine was extended to state supported colleges and universities in 1956.

Congressman John Bell Williams, a 41-year old Mississippi lawyer, serving in his seventh term in Congress, was elected in 1946 the youngest representative in his state's history. A vigorous advocate of "dual sovereignty," Williams coined the term "Black Monday" to describe the U. S. Supreme Court school decision.

Governor Stanley said that the Supreme Court decision called for "cool heads, calm study, and sound judgment." He promised to consult with "leaders of both races" in the state. The next day, May 18, Governor Stanley announced that he had modified his plans to call a conference of state leaders of both races. The meeting with "leaders of both races" was never held. The court's decision no longer seemed to him to require such immediate action. Subsequently, Stanley announced that he would appoint a study commission (no mention of "both races") and the present policies of segregation would remain in effect for the coming year. The state took a wait-and-see stance.[ccclxvi] Smith wrote, "It was Friday, May 21, that the Sheridan school board in Arkansas voted 5-0 to integrate twenty-one Negro students with six hundred whites in the upper grades. On the next day, the school board, having heard from some of the parents of the six hundred white students, changed their vote, 5-0 not to integrate the Negro students in the upper grades.

Some Southern states were sure that compliance was out of the question. Alabama, Mississippi, Georgia, South Carolina, and Louisiana felt that way. The Georgia legislature went so far to consider bills to abolish the Supreme Court and remove all Negroes from the state. The feeling in the Deep South was very strong. Other Southern states were sure that compliance was possible. These included Arkansas, Delaware, Maryland, Kentucky, Missouri, Oklahoma, West Virginia, and the District of Columbia. The doubtful states were North Carolina, which was already showing signs for a willingness to comply; Florida, which was probably going to waver between the two camps; Texas, which was cautious but not defiant; and Virginia. Of the states that might have been expected to supply a thrust of leadership in one direction or another, Virginia was the most difficult to read."[ccclxvii]

Plan for Virginia

In June 1954, five weeks after his moderate statement on the Supreme Court's decision, Governor Stanley declared: "I shall use every legal means at my command to continue segregated schools in Virginia"[ccclxviii] Massive resistance had not taken hold, but the spirit of noncompliance was floating around like a "ghost" in the night.

On August 30, 1954, Governor Stanley appointed a Legislative Commission on Public Education. Senator Garland Gray of Waverly, Virginia was selected the chairman. The Gray Commission was to recommend to the General Assembly the steps the state should take to deal with the school crisis resulting from the Court's decision. The plan developed by the Gray Commission attempted to prevent extensive school closings and at the same time to avoid compulsory integration. A tuition grant program was recommended to permit pupils to attend nonsectarian private schools and public schools outside of the locality in which they resided.[ccclxix]

The commission was filled with white politicians from "Black Belt" Virginia counties. The "Black Belt" in 1950 consisted of thirty-one contiguous Southside and tidewater counties where the percentage of Negroes in the population ranged from forty to eighty-one. South of the James River, fanning out toward the Piedmont and along the North Carolina border, lay the eighteen populous counties of the Black Belt. Lunenburg was identified as one of these counties because Negroes accounted for 43.9 percent of its total population of 11,692 in 1950.[ccclxx]

Although voters approved the tuition grant program, the plan was shelved during a period of massive resistance to the desegregation decision. However, its main provisions were revived later following the recommendations of the Perrow Commission during the administration of Governor J. Lindsey Almond, Jr.[ccclxxi]

A "Plan for Virginia" would be presented by the Defenders of State Sovereignty and Individual Liberties to the Gray Commission, deliberating on the problems raised by the court's decisions. The underlying premise of this plan was that the local option would permit some desegregation and provision of state tuition grants to students leaving desegregated schools to attend private segregated ones. This was massive resistance, as yet unnamed. The state was not quite ready for it yet, but the Defenders were paving the way.[ccclxxii]

On May 21, 1954, several months earlier, the *Kenbridge-Victoria Dispatch* printed an article by Senator Byrd on segregation. Byrd stated, "The unanimous decision of the Supreme Court to abolish segregation in public education is not only sweeping, but will bring implications and dangers of the greatest consequence. It is the most serious blow that has yet been struck against the rights of the states in a matter virtually affecting their authority and welfare. The decision will be deplored by millions of Americans, and, instead of promoting the education of our children. It is my belief that it will have the opposite effect in many areas of the country. In Virginia, we are facing now a crisis of the first magnitude."

Byrd continued, "The Supreme Court had reversed its previous decision directing "separate but equal" facilities for the education of both races. He believed the about-face decision of the Court was cruel, in that the Southern States, accepting the validity of the previous decision in recent years, had expended hundreds of millions of dollars for construction of new Negro school facilities to conform to the policy previously laid down by the Court. The Court's decision in the *Brown* case struck a serious blow against the rights of the states in a matter vitally affecting their "authority and welfare." [ccclxxiii]

Shortly following the establishment of the governor's commission on public education in August, an incorporated interest group would rise to wield great power in Virginia's desegregation politics. Bob Smith (1996) wrote, "It was in Blackstone, in neighboring Nottoway County, that the Defenders of State Sovereignty and Individual Liberties became a reality on October 8, 1954. Simply called the "Defenders," representatives from eighteen counties were at this meeting and what emerged was the framework of an organization which pledged to maintain states' rights, individual rights, and preserve segregation in the schools. [ccclxxiv]

There was no "middle ground" for the defenders who opposed the education of white and Negro children in the same school. Many of the people in Lunenburg County demonstrated strong resistance to school integration as well. On November 1, 1954, approximately two hundred citizens met at the Lunenburg County Court House and founded a local chapter of the Defenders. This organization became a member of the state organization, which had been founded nearly a month earlier. The Honorable J. Segar Gravatt, Jr., of Blackstone, spoke to the group and brought out the aims of the organization. The leaders pointed out, "Segregated schools were to the best interest of both the white and Negro races of our state and county, and that this conclusion would be presented to the Governor's Commission." The Lunenburg Defenders' membership committee worked diligently to build up its support base in the county.[ccclxxv]

The Executive Committee—of the Legislative Commission on Public Education selected by the governor—decided to hold its first, and what proved to be the only, public hearing on the Virginia public school issue in the Richmond Mosque auditorium on November 15, 1954. Senator Garland Gray said, "There had been some 140 requests for speaking time at the hearing. In the view of this, we decided to hold the hearing in the Mosque." The *Kenbridge-Victoria Dispatch* reported that R. Maclin Smith of Kenbridge, delegate member representing Lunenburg and Brunswick Counties, urgently requested citizens to attend the hearing. Smith stated, "It is my belief this move is well chosen since many from this county—Lunenburg—have expressed their desire to attend. There had been ten or more resolutions from governing bodies and other organizations of this county in opposition to the Supreme Court's decision in regard to the integration of public schools. I definitely agree with these resolutions and shall support them."[ccclxxvi]

There were three interest groups actively engaged in Virginia's politics of school desegregation. Their arrival on the scene is identified by the order in which each is listed.

The Virginia State Conference of the NAACP joined with the Negro students in attacking the more material effects of segregated public education at the professional and graduate levels in the early 1930s. The legal staff of the Virginia State Conference of the NAACP had prosecuted successfully one of the four state cases included in the Supreme Court decision.

The Defenders of Sovereignty and Individual Liberties organizations of those who desired to maintain "state rights," however, shared the attitude that the court's decisions would be the worst possible course of action for Virginia.

The Virginia Council on Human Rights provided white integrationists with those tenets to which they could subscribe, whose meetings they could attend, and whose propagandizing activities they could support financially and vocally.

. . .On to Interposition

A nationwide movement in the South would add fuel to Defenders' fire. In October of 1955, John U. Barr of New Orleans announced that leading citizens from ten Southern states had agreed to become an Advisory Committee for a proposed nation-wide organization to promote Constitutional government such as the preservation of the independence of the legislative, executive, and judicial departments; to support the preservation of the sovereign rights of several states and individual liberties; and to counteract the decisions of the federal courts and the United States Supreme Court, which wrongfully abrogated, modified, or amended that provision of the United States Constitution.

Barr explained that the proposed organization would be called "The Federation for Constitutional Government" and the advisory group would include representatives from Virginia—Hon. William M. Tuck, South Boston; Hon. Watkins M. Abbitt, Appomattox; William B. Cocke, Sussex; Hon. Collins Denny, Jr., Richmond; Hon. James S. Easley, South Boston; Manning Gasch, McLean; Hon. J. Segar Gravatt, Blackstone; C. F. Ratcliff, Norfolk; Col. James M. Thompson, Gaylord; and the Hon. E. Floyd Yates, Powhatan. Barr continued, "Recognizing the magnitude of our undertaking, we feel that success for a nation-wide movement would best be assured if present effort was concentrated in the development of a strong organization in the South, and then invite all patriotic individuals and organizations to join in a coordinated, united front movement for the preservation of America under a constitutional form of government."[ccclxxvii]

In November of 1955, the editor of the local newspaper printed an article from the *Farmville Herald* titled: "WHICH ROAD." The editor wrote, "The decision facing Virginia is critical. A principle is involved, namely, whether or not the sovereignty of a state and its' constitutionally guaranteed right to handle its domestic affairs can be nullified by a decision of the Supreme Court. If it can be, then change the Constitution and repeal the Tenth Amendment first. Make it constitutionally legal. In the meantime, stand steady upon the legal rights of the State and protect its sovereignty."[ccclxxviii]

Smith (1996) pointed out, "What the Defenders could not stand for was as important as what they could stand for. That is, violence would mean ruin for the movement. But violence was not the only enemy the Defenders saw on their right. The White Citizens Councils and other racist organizations were spewing forth the seedy literature of race hatred, playing on the uncounted fears of ignorant white Southerners. The material, quite naturally, poured into the Defenders offices."[ccclxxix]

Benjamin Muse (1961) mentioned, "The Ku Klux Klan was completely discredited by the Defenders; and the White Citizens Councils that were beginning to spring up in other parts of the South were treated with suspicion. And with some of the State's politicians aiding them, the Defenders realized that just one incident of *Klanism* in the community could be detrimental to the organization in the eyes of the proper Virginians they must count upon for support."[ccclxxx]

On December 2, 1955, Governor Stanley asked the General Assembly to begin the process of amending the State Constitution so that public funds may be used for educational purposes in non-sectarian private schools. Superintendents of Region One met in Farmville on December 12. They went on record in favor of the Limited Constitution Convention to amend Section 141 of the Constitution of Virginia because they believed this action is essential to the preservation of the Virginia Public School System. Later, the Lunenburg School Board at a called meeting on December 20, 1955 urged all citizens interested in the preservation and improvement of the public schools to vote for the convention to amend the State Constitution.[ccclxxxi]

Other leading state educators supported the amendment as well. They endorsed a vote for the constitutional convention referendum that would take place in early January 1956.[ccclxxxii]

Attorney General J. Lindsay Almond, Jr. made an impassioned plea for democracy. He said, "I have fought this battle since May, 1951, and but for that fight, but for the matchless gallantry, but for the immaculate sense of honor, but for the unwavering courage of Prince Edward County, your schools would have been integrated three years ago. Listen, my friends, the public school system was wrecked on May 17, 1954, by the Supreme Court of the United States and all we're trying to do is pick up the pieces and put 'em back together. On January 9, come light or dark, come sunshine or rain, come fire or brimstone, come hell or high water, go to the polls and unshackle yourselves from the manifold shackles placed upon your wrists, upon your judgment and the future of your children by a politically-minded Supreme Court."[ccclxxxiii] The first step in the direction for a change was a favorable vote on the proposed amendment to Section 141 of the Constitution.[ccclxxxiv]

The people of Virginia and Lunenburg County voted for the calling of a Convention to change the State Constitution so state money could be used by children to go to private schools. The constitutional convention was the first step toward enactment of the tuition grants plan proposed by the Gray Commission as the point in design against enforced mixing of white and Negro children. As identified in the Gray plan, cities and counties had a range of local options to integrate their schools—to keep them segregated on a nonracial basis, voluntary plans, or to close them completely.

In a public statement, Senator Byrd said, "I will cast my vote in favor of the calling of a limited constitutional convention. We can depend on the General Assembly to act with wisdom and high patriotism to meet the most serious crisis that has occurred since the War Between the States. Only very rarely in the long history of Virginia has a General Assembly been called upon to solve a problem of such magnitude and far-reaching consequences to future generations of Virginians. It is my firm opinion that enforced integration will destroy the public school system in large areas of Virginia. This would be catastrophe; young Virginians now being educated in public schools must not be handicapped by lack of adequate education." The January vote was overwhelmingly in favor of a constitutional amendment; and in Lunenburg it was 2,313 for and 196 against.[ccclxxxv]

Governor Stanley, who had marshaled most of the State's political and legislative leaders in an "all-out" campaign to put over the proposal, said, "The voter's decision will be of 'tremendous' help to the General Assembly in coping with school problems caused by the United States Supreme Court anti-segregation decisions." Stanley was grateful to the voters for their support. The resistance movement was beginning to take hold.[ccclxxxvi]

In 1956, the resolution of interposition had been introduced in the Senate on January 9 and in the House on January 27. With two minor and one relatively major exception, the resolutions were basically identical. Each had in its key paragraph the following quote: "And be it finally resolved, that until the question here asserted by the State of Virginia be settled by clear Constitutional amendments, we pledge our firm intention to take all appropriate measures honorably, legally and constitutionally available to us to resist this illegal encroachment upon our sovereign powers, and to urge upon our sister States, whose authority over their own most cherished powers may next be imperiled, their prompt and deliberate efforts to check this and further encroachment by the Supreme Court, through judicial legislation, upon the reserved powers of the States."[ccclxxxvii]

In early February 1956, United States Senator A. Willis Robertson offered a bill on school operations to the Congress. Senator Robertson said, "I believe thoughtful citizens throughout the nation are disturbed by the current trend of the Federal Government to assume jurisdiction over matters heretofore reserved to the States and by the attitude of the Supreme Court which has, in effect, claimed the right to become an unrestricted policy-making body." An additional reason for offering this resolution was the Senator's belief that only through such a declaration can members of the Negro race get an education on a par with the white race in certain areas of our nation. He continued, "Those who drafted the Federal Constitution in Philadelphia decided to leave to the States, among other things, full control of public education and that action was emphatically supported by ratification of the Tenth Amendment. When the Fourteenth Amendment was adopted, for the protection of those who had been slaves, no one in the Congress or in any of the States which ratified the Amendment suggested it was intended to take from the States their control over public education. I am proposing that the right be asserted by giving the States the choice of operation either desegregation schools or the separate-but-equal facilities which all previous decisions of the Supreme Court declared were permissible."[ccclxxxviii]

On Friday, February 24, 1956, a campaign opposing school desegregation mounted with an announcement made by Senator Harry F. Byrd, Sr., calling for "massive resistance" against *Brown*. Byrd said, "If we can organize the Southern States for massive resistance to this order [Supreme Court's decree in the School Segregation Cases] I think that in time the rest of the country will realize that racial integration is not going to be accepted in the South." That same Friday evening, the Lunenburg Chapter of the Defenders met at the Lunenburg Courthouse, 7:30 in the evening. William E. Maxey Jr., Secretary of the State Organization, was the guest speaker. Maxey had resigned as Commissioner of Revenue of Powhatan County to work for the organization when it was first organized. The Honorable R. Maclin Smith, president of the chapter and a member of the Virginia House of Delegates, had planned to be present as well. This meeting marked the beginning of the resistance movement in Lunenburg County.[ccclxxxix]

On Monday, March 12, 1956, a Declaration of Constitutional Principles was presented to Congress by State Senator Walter F. George of Georgia, and in the House of Representatives by Representative Howard W. Smith of Virginia. An excerpt follows: "This unwarranted exercise of power by the Court, contrary to the Constitution, is creating chaos and confusion in the States principally affected. It is destroying the amicable relations between the white and Negro races that have been created through 90 years of patient effort by the good people of both races. It has planted hatred and suspicion where there has been heretofore friendship and understanding. We decry the Supreme Court's encroachments on rights reserved to the States and to the people, contrary to established law and to the Constitution."

Representative Smith continued, "Though there has been no constitutional amendment or Act of Congress changing this established legal principal almost a century old, the Supreme Court of the United States, with no legal basis for such action, undertook to exercise their naked judicial power and substituted their personal political and social ideas for the established law of the land. We commend the motives of those States which have declared intention to resist forced integration by any lawful means. We pledge ourselves to use all lawful means to bring about a reversal of this decision which is contrary to the Constitution and to prevent the use of force in its implementation." The interposition resolution was passed by the Virginia General Assembly in March 1956. In addition to Virginia, at least forty-two prosegregation measures had been recorded for the first three months of the year in Alabama, Georgia, Mississippi and South Carolina.[cccxc] U. S. Senator Harry F. Byrd had helped to author the "Southern Manifesto," which called for opposition to the Supreme Court's *Brown v. Board of Education* decision.

CHAPTER 11
THE MASSIVE RESISTANCE MOVEMENT

"There's no middle ground, no compromise. We're either for integration or against it and I'm against it ... If you ever let them integrate anywhere the whole state will be integrated in a short time."[cccxci]

—William "Bill" Munford Tuck

Massive resistance—once like a "ghost" in the night—was now a reality with passage of the interposition resolution by the Virginia General Assembly. It was a "calling" card for those who wanted segregated schools. In January 1956, Dr. Dabney S. Lancaster, Director of the State Referendum Information Center, spoke of the Gray Plan. Dr. Lancaster said, "The Supreme Court, in its decision on May 17, said that no child should be denied admission to a school on the sole grounds of race. The Court did not say that integration should be enforced. If then we are not to have enforced integration, there must be some alternative. The Gray plan provided such an alternative. We believe in local self-government. The Gray plan allowed each city, county, and town the choice between full integration, partial or no integration. If full integration is desired, no constitutional change and no legislation are required. If partial integration is acceptable, the assignment plan will meet the need in most cases. If there is to be assurance that there will be no forced integration, tuition is needed in addition to the assignment plan."

An assignment plan permitted local school boards to assign pupils to schools where, in the judgment of the Board, they could progress to the best advantage. The Board could use any basis for assignment except the race of the student. Lancaster thought the plan would probably be acceptable in many of the sections of the state. Where the plan was not acceptable, a pupil could not be forced to attend an integrated school. Under these conditions, the pupil—through their parent—could apply for a tuition grant (state assisted) in the amount not to exceed the per capita cost of their education in the county or city school during the previous session. The grants would be available to white and Negro pupils. Lancaster stressed, "A favorable vote on January 9 will ensure Virginians of the opportunity to continue to provide educational opportunities for all the children of the Commonwealth."[cccxcii]

Public education was also impacted by a legislative resolution introduced in the mid-1950s. Gates (1962) wrote, "The House Joint Resolution [H.J.R] No. 97, introduced by Delegate Samuel E. Pope of 'Black Belt' Southampton County, resolved that it was a policy of Virginia that there would be no racially mixed athletic competition between public school teams or individual students while attending public schools. This statement of policy—not law—was passed by a voice vote in the house, and a vote of twenty-six to ten in the senate."[cccxciii]

L. Stanley Lambert and James Quinn would experience the consequences of this policy nine years later. Lambert wrote, "I was told by the basketball coach there was a district policy that we couldn't play on the team, and that he could not guarantee our safety during the games at rival schools." It is not clear whether the lack of opportunity to play on the sport teams was due to the time of enrollment or no protection at rival schools. Apparently, both scenarios were true.[cccxciv]

The Defenders and state leaders continued their attempt to defy the Court's decision on school desegregation. In July 1956, *The Kenbridge-Victoria Dispatch* reported: "With 12,000 members, the Defenders said they would back a series of legislative proposals to preserve complete separation of Negro and white students in public schools. What the Defenders want is a plan as ironclad as it could be to preserve complete racial segregation through the state. They propose to get it by withholding state funds from schools that may be integrated, by having the state withdraw its consent for school boards to be sued, and by having the state assume control of the schools which become involved in integration litigation. None of these proposals was included the recommendations from the Gray Commission" This plan was to preserve segregation by state law *everywhere* throughout the state.[cccxcv]

A series of articles printed in the local newspaper conveyed the sentiments of citizens in response to the Court's decision in the *Brown* case. Strong opinions and emotions ran high as many Lunenburgers found themselves in the midst of meetings and rallies held by blacks and whites.

Some of the strongest arguments against school desegregation emanated from church pastors. James F. Burks, pastor of Bayview Baptist Church in Norfolk, Virginia expressed his view of school desegregation. In an editorial printed in *The Kenbridge-Victoria Dispatch*, he wrote, "Disregarding the basic principle of segregation will ultimately lead to the mingling of the tides of life, a mongrelizing of the bloodstream of men, and will eventually weaken rather than strengthen America. High school students in Norfolk are already expressing their approval of mixed social activities and marriage. Once this begins, no power on earth can stop it. We had better be aware. If I were black, I would praise the Lord for it, and would not want to make myself anything to the contrary to what God made me to be. This is merely a clarion call to the old-fashioned fact of racial self-respect."[cccxcvi]

In August 1956, Governor Stanley took the next step in defiance against school desegregation when he convened a special session of the General Assembly to act on Massive Resistance legislation. The Stanley Plan—as it was called—created a state Pupil Placement Board to block assignment of black students to white schools using racial criteria. In Lunenburg County, strong support of the governor's position was demonstrated when the Board of Directors of the Lunenburg Chapter of the Defenders at a meeting in Victoria, Virginia drew up a resolution on August 23. The resolution stated: "The Lunenburg Chapter were unalterably opposed to integration of the races in the public schools of Virginia; The Lunenburg Chapter is proud to endorse the plan recently proposed by the Honorable Thomas B. Stanley, Governor of Virginia, to prevent integration of the races in the public schools of Virginia at any level or in any locality. The Representatives of Lunenburg County in the General Assembly of Virginia are hereby urged to support, work and vote for the plan proposed by Governor Stanley." The resolution was signed by Samuel H. Allen, president.[cccxcvii]

In September 1956, M. A. Hubbard, executive secretary of the Farm Bureau Federation of Virginia, testified during a public hearing of the special session of the General Assembly. He said, "The farmers have demanded that the movement toward integration be headed off. If leaders of the dominant race in Virginia could have seen any possible advantage in integration, we daresay that this would have been accomplished on a voluntary basis a long time ago. Our Negro leaders of vision can foresee full well the heartache, frustration, and smothered opportunity that would be the inevitable result of compulsory association. They know, too, that there can be no satisfaction for the members of their race resulting from enforced association which is purchased at the price of bitterness, social exile, and long lasting racial animosity." He went on to say, "These would be poor substitutes for the inter-racial understanding, cooperation, and mutual appreciation which have long characterized race relations in Virginia. Our fine upstanding Negro citizens are intelligent people, and we cannot believe that they willingly exchange the substance of interracial harmony for the mirage of social chaos masquerading as 'equal' opportunity." Hubbard concluded with the promise of full support of a vast majority of farmers in the Farm Bureau, who were strongly opposed to any integration in the public school system.[cccxcviii]

Lunenburg operated twelve schools in 1955-1956—five for whites—Kenbridge High/Elementary, Victoria High, Victoria Elementary, West End Elementary, and Lochleven; and seven for blacks—Lunenburg High, Lunenburg Elementary, Kenbridge Graded, New Grove, Camp, Asbury, and Unity. The Lochleven School closed at the end of the school year, and the children transferred to the school in Kenbridge.

The Lunenburg County School Board also made its resolution to endorse the 'segregated' school system on September 5, 1956. At its regular meeting, the Board adopted the resolution that: "This Board is satisfied that a continuance of the existing system of public schools in Lunenburg County is in the interest of all concerned, and that it meets the approval of the responsible citizens of the county. The Board resolved that they were:

1) opposed as a matter of principle and policy to any degree of mixing of the races in the public schools of the State of Virginia; 2) opposed to any legislation relating to the assignment of students or others which would directly or by implication recognize as valid the Supreme Court decision of May 17, 1954, relating to public schools; and 3) is of the firm belief that it would be impossible to operate a system of public schools, efficient or otherwise, in Lunenburg County, except on the basis of complete racial separation as at present. It was further resolved that copies of this resolution

be transmitted to the representative of Lunenburg County in the General Assembly of Virginia. The people of the county have acted deliberately, cautiously, and firmly. They stand adamantly against racial integration. They are willing to do their part in support of segregated schools. They will do without public schools, in preference to integrated schools."[cccxcix]

The school personnel for 1956-1957 had been selected and plans were in place for another school term. There were eleven schools in operation—Victoria High, Victoria Elementary, Kenbridge High/Elementary, West End Elementary, Lunenburg High, Lunenburg Elementary, Kenbridge Graded, and four small schools.

In February 1957, an article by *The Farmville Herald* was printed in *The Kenbridge-Victoria Dispatch*. The Herald's editor said, "From several sources we have heard recently this or that legislation must be passed to help Prince Edward County meet the school issue of integration brought about by the "Black Monday" decision of the Supreme Court of the United States. We would remind you that Prince Edward County is 'simply a symbol' for the State of Virginia in this situation. The fact that the people of this county through its Board of Supervisors stood steadfast against integration of schools last May 31, 1956 has saved the school systems of Virginia and allowed time for the Gray Commission Study to focus the attention of the people on the illegal decision of the Supreme Court."[cd]

In early 1957, the Defenders held their Third State Convention on March 22 and 23 at the Hotel Jefferson in Richmond. A large delegation from Lunenburg County was expected to attend to renew their faith that everyone in the United States hadn't given up to socialism, communism, and NAACPism. In early October 1957, the Lunenburg Defenders hosted a large crowd at the Victoria Community House to demonstrate their resistance to school desegregation. President Earl Adkins of Hells Corner presided. Mayors E. C. Glover, Jr., of Victoria, G. B. Bridgforth of Kenbridge, and James T. Waddill, Jr., former school superintendent, made a few remarks to the audience. Congressman Watkins M. Abbitt of the Fourth District was the featured speaker, and he was introduced by Judge Robert S. Weaver, Jr., of Victoria.[cdi]

On November 6, 1957, the members of the State Board of Directors of the Defenders met for their annual meeting in Richmond to elect officers for the ensuring year. The executive committee was composed of Robert B. Crawford, Farmville; E. Floyd Yates, Powhatan; William B.

Cocke, Jr., Sussex; J. Segar Gravatt, Blackstone; Collins Denny, Jr., Midlothian; J. J. Jewett, Chesterfield; Harvey E. White, Norfolk; Jack Rathbone, Arlington; R. J. Oglesby, Charlottesville; and Francis West of Martinsville. The Legal Committee of Ernest W. Goodrich, Surry, and J. J. Jewett, Chesterfield, was reappointed. The committee would prepare a program to present to the Legislative Committee prior to the next session of the General Assembly.[cdii] There was a meeting at the Victoria Community House on a Thursday evening in January of 1958 to hear Circuit Court Judge William Old of Chesterfield County. Judge Old was called the "Father of the Doctrine of Interposition" by the Defenders. Smith wrote, "A Virginia attorney named William Old produced a pamphlet on "interposition," the theory that a state may interpose its authority to render the Supreme County decision null and void. The Defenders, growing more powerful almost daily, gratefully adopted it as the true intellectual expression of the will to resist."[cdiii]

The question of non-resident tuition resurfaced in Lunenburg. The per pupil instructional cost for the 1957-58 school term was $205. The School Board, at its regular meeting on August 7, 1958, passed a resolution that required all children who were not residents of Lunenburg County to pay tuition to attend the schools of Lunenburg County. Three hundred dollars was charged for each child between the ages of six and eighteen, and tuition in the amount of two hundred dollars was charged for each pupil over twenty years of age. The resolution was made a year before the closing of public schools in Prince Edward County. Perhaps members of the School Board had contemplated a large number of children from neighboring Prince Edward enrolling in Lunenburg schools, particularly those near the county line.[cdiv]

In mid-February 1959 over 300 Southside Virginians—most of them Defenders—gathered on a Sunday afternoon to hear their officers give their viewpoints on what had been recent actions of Governor Almond and the State Legislature. The audience was exhorted to go home and tell their neighbors of the need for private schools and the need for renewed massive resistance. There were five resolutions unanimously passed at the meeting. Resolution #4 stated: "For the moment, Virginians should proceed upon the basis that, if their children are to receive an education, it must be furnished in independent schools, and in every locality our people should begin preparation for such schools."[cdv]

The "Heritage of Freedom" movement was gaining momentum in the fight for Constitutional Government. C. Benton Colner of Waynesboro, a businessman and former head of the Waynesboro Chamber of Commerce, was named the state chairman of the movement to be known as the "Bill of Rights Crusade." Since the operation of public schools was left for the state's counties and cities to decide, the "Bill of Rights Crusade"—a grass-roots organization—had garnered support from practically every county and city in Virginia for constitutional government. A mass meeting was planned for March 31, 1959 at the Capitol Square in Richmond, Virginia as the day of "freedom's greatest challenge to the forces of tyranny." Colner said, "The Crusade objectives would call upon all Virginians who would not compromise their constitutional rights to demonstrate this to their elected representatives and to Crusade for this objective. We are resolute in our intention to resist without compromise Federal usurpation of these rights under all circumstances and will call upon our representatives to interpose the sovereignty of the Commonwealth." School desegregation was a major issue, but not the only one.

An ad appeared in *The Kenbridge-Victoria Dispatch* for Lunenburg citizens who were interested in attending the Crusade mass meeting in Richmond. Tickets were available at local businesses in Victoria such as Dupriest & Williams, Vaughan's Super Market, and Nelson's (former Greyhound Bus Station) for $2.25 per person; and in Kenbridge at Southside Motor Company and Kenbridge Hardware & Equipment Co., for $2.00 per person. Four buses were used to carry Kenbridge and Victoria citizens, and many others drove their cars. Most business closed in both towns on March 31 in support of the Crusade. The governor was invited to attend, but sent regrets. Reportedly, about 90 percent of the 140 assemblymen did join the "Crusaders" and sat on the Capitol steps and listened.[cdvi]

Still, unwilling to admit they were losing the school desegregation battle, the Lunenburg Defenders called for a citizens' rally to be held at the Victoria Community House on November 19, 1959, at 8 P.M. The meeting included the Virginia Crusaders for Constitutional Government and other organizations. John W. Carter, a member of the Danville City Council, and the Honorable Frank P. Moncure of Stafford were scheduled to speak. Miles M. Austin, a local clergyman and president of the Lunenburg Chapter of the Defenders, said, "The time has come for a meeting at the summit, of all citizens who have not accepted the surrender of their constitutional rights. The Crusade brought thousands to the state capital in March and, through its speaker, pledged to continue the fight for "our rights and principles. This grassroots movement by the people has been endorsed by the Defenders and the Victoria meeting will bring together these two groups who have been carrying on the fight for Constitutional Government." The meeting was open to the Defenders, their families and friends, and to those like-minded citizens throughout Southside Virginia. Austin spoke strongly during the meeting for the constitutional rights of the state to decide if and how public schools should integrate.

One of the largest crowds had gathered. There were over 400 people in attendance, with Defenders from Prince Edward, Charlotte, Surry, Amelia, Nottoway, Dinwiddie, Chesterfield, Albemarle counties, and Lynchburg and Arlington, Virginia. Austin presided over the meeting with the Honorable R. Maclin Smith of Kenbridge, who introduced the county officials and a fellow member of the House of Delegates, Lou Irby of Blackstone. The Citizens Council of Brunswick and Lunenburg and the Crusaders were recognized and praised by Austin.

The Crusade leaders—Charles Carter, John Carter, and Ed Silverman—were introduced by Charlie Garden of Kenbridge. Ed Silverman introduced John Vance, who was state president of the Farmers Union, and Arthur Mahaney, a State Farmers Union representative. The Blackstone Lions Club, Blackstone JV, and the Farm Bureau were praised by Silverman for their support in the Crusade march. E. J. Oglesby of Albemarle County and professor at the University of Virginia told of the work being done in Charlottesville in the private school system there. Robert B. Crawford of Farmville, state president of the Defenders, introduced the speaker of the evening, John W. Carter of Danville. Carter was an attorney and member of the Danville Town Council. The newspaper report suggests that Carter gave one of the greatest speeches ever given in Lunenburg since the forefathers had gathered at the Lunenburg Court House in 1861 and declared Lunenburg County as the "Old Free State of Lunenburg." Carter said, "The governor [Almond] did nothing after closing the schools. He did not seek to open them under his supervision, nor did he call the legislature into session. He simply sat and did nothing but stake the entire massive resistance fight upon the validity of the tuition grant law. So, rather than fight with the weapons which had been provided him, the governor sat supinely by and on his motion placed the weakest aspects of the massive resistance laws in jeopardy through a test case, assuming the attitude that these were the only aspects of the massive resistance laws worthy of being put into effect by the chief executive."[cdvii]

Meanwhile, Governor Almond made but a few public statements. There were rumors in ever increasing intensity that Almond was going to abandon the massive resistance laws and compromise the constitutional rights of the Commonwealth and its citizens. In his closing remarks, Carter said, "While I have predicted that Mr. Almond will undertake to seize the leadership of the conservative element of the Democratic Party, I further predict that either Lieutenant Governor Stevens or Attorney General Harrison will seek the Democratic nomination for Governor—that the people of the State of Virginia will not forget these men but will remember that they broke and fled in the face of the enemy; and that these men will go down in defeat into political oblivion."[cdviii]

They Closed Schools

Dr. Davis Y Paschall served as state superintendent of public instruction from 1957-1960. He had broad experience in public school work and had held the position of director of elementary and special education. Paschall found the Commonwealth confronted with the closing of public schools in Virginia. Senator Byrd had hoped the state-wide policy of massive resistance would set the pattern for total resistance in the South to the Supreme Court. It was Byrd's response, which declared the ruling an unconstitutional attack on states' rights that set the tone for events to come. As the local desegregation suits worked their way through the federal courts in 1957 and 1958, two special committees of the General Assembly held hearings in each locality where there was a suit. Although the committees called the black plaintiffs to testify, few were intimated from withdrawing from their cases. Governor J. Lindsay Almond, Jr. had convinced white Virginians that they could have both continued segregation and stronger public schools.

On September 4, 1958, Almond divested superintendents of Virginia schools of their authority to desegregate their schools; he also advised that if they go against his order they would be found in violation of Virginia laws. Almond closed nine Virginia schools, locking out nearly thirteen thousand students. For the white majority, the terms of the debate changed: instead of segregation versus integration, now it was desegregation versus closed public schools. The attempt to substitute segregated private academies for the closed public schools was totally inadequate in the face of Norfolk's ten thousand displaced students, while in the smaller communities of Charlottesville and Front Royal, a sharp fight among whites ensued—pitting pro-public school parents against backers of the segregated private effort.

On December 6, 1958, white parents in Arlington, Norfolk, and other cities joined together to form the Virginia Committee for Public Schools. In addition to the middle-class parents in the school communities, Almond began to hear more influential voices of dissent about the school closings. Also, in December, twenty-nine of the state's leading businessmen told him that the crisis was adversely affecting Virginia's economy.

The collision with the federal courts had occurred when on January 19, 1959 both the Virginia Supreme Court of Appeals and the United States District Court struck down the massive resistance laws passed by the Virginia legislature in 1956; and the decision of Governor Almond to closed schools in Front Royal, Charlottesville, and Norfolk was overturned.[cdix] In early February 1959, Virginia was forced to operate public integrated schools by federal power; and Negro children attended the formally white schools in three Virginia communities.[cdx] The threads of the 'massive resistance' cord were unraveling and the Defenders could sense it!

Supporters of massive resistance expected a defiant last stand, but Almond surprised them. A new plan was formulated with Almond's appointment of a legislative commission headed by State Senator Mosby G. Perrow. Their program, called the Perrow Plan, left the burden of desegregation in place of massive resistance on the black parents with its "freedom of choice" concept, repealed the compulsory attendance law, and relied on the Pupil Placement Board, using ostensibly nonracial criteria, to keep desegregation to a minimum.[cdxi]

Also, in February, the legislature approved a repeal of the state's compulsory attendance law in favor of a "local option" statue, and a tuition grant program to make state funds available—approximately three million dollars—for children whose parents would satisfy the State Board of Education that there was no adequate public schools available for them to attend; and that the welfare of the children would be best served if they attended a nonsectarian school or public school in localities other than where they would normally attend. The grants would total two hundred and fifty dollars or the amount of the actual per pupil cost of operation in the locality in which the children reside or whichever is less. The instructional cost for 1958-59 was approximately $225. On August 9, 1965, the School Board reported that eight white students residing in the district were attending private school on a tuition-grant basis.

Massive Resistance by the state government was dead. The crisis was over, but resistance to operate integrated public schools had taken a stronghold in Prince Edward County. Smith wrote, "On June 2, 1959, the Board of Supervisors of Prince Edward County announced its intention not to appropriate money to operate public schools for the coming year. Behind this action in point of time lay the torn body of the politic of massive resistance." The public schools in Prince County closed between the years of 1959 and 1964.[cdxii]

The Prince Edward County children were not totally destitute of educational opportunity. For many African American students, schooling was provided with relatives in nearby communities or at makeshift schools in church basements. The *American Friends Service Committee* helped to line up homes for students whose parents consented to send them to integrated Northern public schools. During the Kennedy Administration, Free Schools held opening ceremonies on September 16, 1963 with assistance from the Prince Edward Free Schools Association. Four public school buildings—including formerly white Worsham High School—were utilized for approximately seventeen hundred Negro students. Smith wrote, "The job of rehabilitation attempted by the Free Schools, which operated for one year, could not reach the John Smiths, but it could and did reach just about other kind of educational causality—and they were plenty and varied a lot." The Free Schools closed at the end of the school year, and in September 1964 virtually the same student body moved into the re-established public school system in Prince Edward County.[cdxiii]

Rebecca Lee Randolph shared her experience when the schools in Prince Edward County had closed. Randolph said, "I was unable to attend school for two years due to the closing of the schools in Prince Edward County. We lived on the border of Prince Edward and Lunenburg Counties, therefore, we walked approximately two miles to meet a Lunenburg County bus. My two sisters, brother, and I were allowed to attend Lunenburg County schools from the fall 1961 through spring 1963. My sister, a senior, graduated from Lunenburg High School." Many of Prince Edward's disenfranchised students continued their education in Lunenburg although the School Board had approved non-resident tuition policy. Randolph did not return to Lunenburg in the fall of 1963, but enrolled in the Free Schools that had opened in Prince Edward County.

On May 25, 1964, the U. S. Supreme Court in *Griffin v. School Board of Prince Edward County* case ruled that Prince Edward County had violated the rights of students to an education and ordered the schools to reopen. NAACP lawyers Frank D. Reeves, Henry L. Marsh, III and Samuel W. Tucker were actively engaged in the litigation to force the reopening of the Prince Edward County school system on an integrated basis. Randolph was among the student body that returned to the re-established public school system when it opened in September 1964.[cdxiv]

Private Education

There were a few private schools in Lunenburg County prior to the turn of the twentieth century. Neale wrote, "Those with means educated their children at home or hired someone as a tutor to educate a group of children from several families. The larger plantations often had actual schools with a tutor who boarded there and sometimes distant children boarded. There are examples of these schools allowing some children of slaves to attend. Sue Leigh Smith held school in her father's home, "Laurel Branches," for both black and white children." Private schools in the early 1900s included the Flat Rock Academy (1907) and Mrs. Scott's Boarding School for Young Ladies in Hungry Town. The Rehoboth School was originally in the home of the teacher, Jennie Hamlin, but then moved to a granary at the property known as Lang's.[cdxv]

Beginning in the mid-1950s, after the U. S. Supreme Court's decision on school desegregation, private education based on ethnicity became an education option. The Lunenburg Chapter Defenders invited William J. Story to speak during a meeting at the Victoria Community House on March 5, 1959 at 7:30 P.M. Story was the Superintendent of South Norfolk Schools, and his topic was *Private Schools in Southside Virginia*. Although considered a segregationist, he had attracted much attention with his announcements that he favored assigning white children of parents who favor integration to Negro schools. This idea was readily accepted by segregationists who thought it would be fitting justice to those white persons who had not opposed integration. He said, "I asked the school board to assign to Negro schools those pupils whose parents have expressed a desire and 'willingness' for their children to attend integrated schools. And sending white pupils to Negro schools will give Negroes integration and 'makes everyone happy."[cdxvi]

In neighboring Prince Edward County, the Prince Edward Foundation offered an opportunity for private schools for Negroes, called Southside Schools. Following the announcement of the charter for Southside Schools, the Southside directors announced that letters would be sent to the parents of every Negro child in the county to determine who wanted education. By December 29, 1959, only one application was received. Smith wrote, "The next month, January 1960, Southside School announced that it was postponing its efforts on behalf of the Negro children of Prince Edward. With that announcement, for all practical purposes, the Southside Schools idea ceased to be a live option for the Negro children in Prince Edward."[cdxvii]

The Foundation had to be ready to provide private education for approximately fifteen hundred white children in the county. The private school initiatives were supported by private donations—in and out of the county—and tuition grants from the state and tax credits from the county. Cash and pledges tallied up to $163,213.36 toward a goal of $300,000 for the county drive. An announcement for the construction of the first unit of the campus-style plant came from the Foundation's President Blanton Hanbury. "We hope to have the first unit ready for use in September," the school leader said. C. W. Glenn, chairman of the building committee, reported that construction would begin as soon as architect, J. Henley Walker of Richmond, provided his committee with detailed drawings.[cdxviii] Prince Edward Academy (now Fuqua School) had become a prototype for the *all-white* private schools formed to protest school integration. Smith wrote that Blanton Hanbury remarked, "Private schools are here to stay, there's no question about it."[cdxix] The saga of the massive resistors' zeal for private, segregated education did not end in Prince Edward.

In the 1960s, the Blackstone Day School began its operation in Blackstone, Virginia. By March 1966, The Lunenburg-Nottoway Educational Foundation had contracted with the Payne Construction Company of Blackstone to build a new school. Kenston Forest School was the name selected for the school and teachers were being secured. In April, the Board of Directors of the Lunenburg-Nottoway Educational Foundation announced that students could enroll at the Blackstone Day School in

Blackstone, Virginia and at the American Legion Building in Kenbridge, Virginia.[cdxx]

In April 1966, The Kenbridge Day School Foundation also announced that sufficient underwriters had agreed to underwrite a minimum operating budget of $42,000 and the private day school would be in operation for 1966-67 beginning in September. Applications were being accepted for teaching positions and could be submitted to Kenbridge Day School address. The Kenbridge Day School and the Kenston Forest School in Nottoway County jointly provided transportation for students attending either school. Scholarships were also available at the Kenbridge Day School and were awarded based on academic achievement, citizenship, need, and recommendation of the applicant's current teacher.[cdxxi]

By May, patrons had secured for a building for the school from the American Legion to operate a grade school for grades one through seven. Some white parents chose to send their children to private schools such as Blackstone Day School, Brunswick Academy, Kenston Forest, South Hill Academy, and Prince Edward Academy (now Fuqua School), but a majority of Lunenburg's white pupils continued to attend public schools in the county.[cdxxii]

Marjorie B. Powers spoke candidly about her years as an educator. Powers said, "After graduating from Windsor High School in 1933, I attended State Teacher College (now Longwood University) in Farmville, Virginia. I only went two years, but took classes in the summer and at night. In 1935, I accepted a job at the Holland High School in Nansemond County, Virginia and remained there for nine years. In the meantime, I had met a young gentleman from Kenbridge, Virginia, and when he returned from service, we were married in 1944." In 1946, the couple moved to Kenbridge, where Powers taught students in the elementary department at the Kenbridge High School for twenty years.

When asked about school desegregation, Powers said, "Mr. Revere, principal, was always so modest and nice—nothing negative was ever spoken of integration—it was just a nice transition. In my opinion, there were no feelings of animosity. My reason for leaving public education was my desire to be a principal, and I had an opportunity to do so." In the fall of 1966, Powers ended her tenure as a public school teacher and took the position of headmistress at the Kenbridge Day School. She remained there until it closed in the mid-1970s; and many of the students enrolled at the Kenston Forest School in Blackstone, Virginia.[cdxxiii]

On January 23, 1969, a group of approximately 250 people met at the Veterans of Foreign War Hall in Victoria, Virginia, to establish a private school in the Victoria area. The officers elected were Dr. Clinton D. Griffin, president; Billy S. Smith, vice-president; H. E. McLaughlin, secretary; and Franklin Smith, treasurer. McLaughlin said, "There is much sentiment here favorable to the formation of a private school. I and other parents are convinced that a school with small classes and under local control could better educate their children." The guest speakers for the event were Charles T. Moses, Jr., of Appomattox, and Joseph H. Norman III of Enfield, North Carolina. Moses was one of the leaders in organizing the Robert E. Lee Academy in Appomattox in 1967, and would discuss some of the requirements and problems in establishing a school and how to approach them. Norman had helped to organize several private schools, including the Enfield Academy, a Christian School. He gave a step-by-step plan of the organizational procedure.[cdxxiv] There was no private school or academy established in the Victoria area although private education had become popular.

CHAPTER 12
CIVIL RIGHTS MOVEMENT AT HOME

The Civil Rights Movement of the 1950s, 1960s and 1970s was one phase of the African American struggle for freedom. It was Virginia that many of the most important legal landmarks of the civil rights movement originated. Irene Morgan brought the suit that desegregated interstate bus travel in 1946. Another Virginia case extended this prohibition against segregation to include interstate bus waiting rooms and restrooms. One of the five school desegregation lawsuits decided by the U. S. Supreme Court in 1954, resulted from the 1951 student strike at Moton High School in Farmville led by teenager Barbara R. Johns; The case of *Green v. School Board of New Kent County* (1968) became the most important school desegregation decision since 1954; and the Richard Perry Loving's case resulted in the overturning of seventeen states' laws banning interracial marriage.[cdxxv]

In the 1960s or sooner, the Lunenburg County Branch of the NAACP, members the of New Grove and First Baptist Churches, and other civil rights workers met at the NAACP Headquarters (Freedom House), Peoples Community Center, and in private homes to develop strategies and make plans to push for school desegregation. Both voter registration and community organization were already on the association's priority list—next was the public school situation.[cdxxvi]

The Jim Crow Life

Jim Crow laws, enacted after the Reconstruction period, were state and local laws in the United States that negatively influenced the daily lives of African Americans. These laws sanctioned the segregation of public transportation, public schools, and public places—restrooms, restaurants, and drinking fountains for whites and blacks. The United States military was also segregated.

Vanessa S. Walker (1996) wrote, "North Carolina went so far as to require the segregation of the textbooks used by black and white children." In many school systems, discrepancies were evident in the pupil-teacher ratio, length of school term, materials and resources, the supplemental services provided, and the expenditure per pupil in average daily attendance. Too often, the separate facilities for the African Americans were consistently inferior to those provided for their counterparts and contradicted the declaration of "equal" under oppressive Jim Crow laws.[cdxxvii]

Russell Lacy Callahan described what it was like to live under this regime. Callahan recalled, "Jim Crow was a most inconvenient and oppressive time. Many people had to go 'out of their way' to achieve what they wanted to do. When I went to eat in a local restaurant or store where food was served, I had to go to the back entrance because black people could not be served inside the business. A sign—'colored only'—was posted next to the door. It was the same for school transportation and textbooks—segregated and too often second-hand. That's the way it was—hard times. I know it was bad, but there was nothing I could do about it!"[cdxxviii] African Americans living with Jim Crow laws were denied many of the opportunities for economic advancement and the right to be treated with dignity and respect.

I began to think of my life experience with Jim Crow as Callahan shared his memories. Even now, I still have thoughts of growing up in my hometown—Victoria, Virginia—in the 1950s and 1960s. Pictures are permanently etched in my mind of walking into the doctor's office in town—as a young child with my mother—and sitting in the waiting area with the words in large, black, neatly written letters posted on each side of the office wall—*white* (sign on right) and *colored* (sign on left).

There are memories of the peering eyes of a salesperson when my mother was shopping and browsing through the merchandise. I've thought of times when the white clerk—seeming rather irritated—spoke to us in an unpleasant tone or was slow to respond when assistance was needed. I have revisited in my psyche the many times when my parents went to town to take care of business—both of them standing next to each other at the counter—and the clerk making eye contact and talking to my mother, but ignoring my dad who was the breadwinner of the family. Why? I've asked. Now, don't misunderstand me. Not every salesperson displayed this type of behavior. Nonetheless, this scene occurred so often that I still remember it!

There were questions in my mind: What prevented my siblings and I, and other black children in the community, from attending the schools located just a few blocks away from our homes? I don't remember being told by my parents about a rule or law that prevented me from going to those schools—just that I didn't go to school with white children. My awareness of racism became even more heightened on those school days as we waited at the bus stop and the buses with white children passed by. It was on those occasions—too numerous to count—that some of the children poked out their tongues, stuck up the middle finger or yelled racial slurs at us. Even today, I still remember—in elementary school—the old hand-me-down textbooks from the white schools with the names of strangers written on the inside cover and pages torn or missing. Yes, separate everything—including education! However, there were white children in the community whose parents allowed them to befriend us. I have fond memories of the Williams family that lived a block away.

I had mixed feelings about the time when schools were integrated in the fall of 1969. I was jubilant because it was my senior year, but also angry at times. The strong negative feeling was present because I felt ripped apart—as I believed—from a place of comfort and familiarity at Lunenburg High School. This was my school—the place where I had been since the eighth grade. There are memories of some casual conversations with a few of my white classmates at Central High, but for the most part I felt invisible and insignificant. Not just with those students, but estranged from the white faculty and staff members as well. Therefore, I was less talkative and not as outgoing. I found myself somewhat reserved and not willing to answer the teachers' questions aloud or read orally in class. But all was not lost. Hallelujah, it was June—graduation time! I was done with the "pity" party. I continued my education—received college degrees—and have experienced a successful career in public and higher education.[cdxxix]

The Lunenburg Community

Victoria, Virginia—with its three blocks of stores—was a "hub," as merchants called it, for about half of Lunenburg County's 12,500 people and some residents of surrounding counties. The area was nearly half Negro in the 1960s.[cdxxx]

In 1965, the Virginia Students' Civil Rights Committee (VSCRC), an interracial group of college students, participated in the *Virginia Summer Project* in several counties in Southside Virginia. The *Virginia Summer Project* involved anti-segregation protest, voter registration and organization work, and other civil rights activities in areas of historically high black populations. It was modeled after the *Freedom Summer Campaign of 1964* in Mississippi. Nathaniel Lee Hawthorne, Sr., member of the VSCRC and NAACP, along with other civil rights leaders, sponsored boycotts in Lunenburg. These activities were designed to rid the county of the segregation which not only permeated local businesses, but public education as well.

Civil rights workers—such as William "Bill" Monnie, white student activist Nan Grogan Orrock and others—had been in Lunenburg County since the early summer 1965, and this action concerned the town's white leaders. The VSCRC was stationed at the NAACP headquarters (Freedom House) located on Mecklenburg Avenue in Victoria, Virginia. This is where the NAACP leaders and civil rights activists spent time meeting and planning for their field work with voter registration, and preparing reports sent Hosea Williams in Atlanta, Georgia. Monnie wrote, "The summer of 1965 was an extremely active summer, particularly because of the passage of the 1965 Voting Rights Bill that empowered Negroes to register to vote and subsequently generated extreme opposition by the KKK. I was assigned to write weekly reports and send them to my supervisor, Hosea Williams, back in Atlanta, Georgia. He was the Director of the Southern Christian Leadership Conference (SCLC) Department of Voter Registration and Political Education, and responsible for supervising volunteers in the Summer of Community Organization and Political Education (SCOPE) units throughout the South."[cdxxxi]

The Washington Post reported, "The North Carolina Chapter of the United Klans of America had decided to stage its first invasion of Virginia, and some Lunenburg businesses posted the rally flyer announcement in their store windows. Many Negroes were angry and demanded that Victoria merchants denounce the Klan. There was no denunciation, and boycotts took place. William Henry Winston, of Kenbridge, had met with the Victoria town officials on the problem. Winston was quoted to say, "Oh, they [town leaders] criticize the civil rights workers, who are non-violent. But when, in the midst of the Klan uprising here, they did not speak up—then their silence must be taken as evidence of Klan sympathy."[cdxxxii]

Hawthorne remarked, "Caravans of Negro families could be seen—on a Saturday afternoon—pouring into neighboring Towns of Kenbridge and Crewe. The boycott was 'nearly 100 per cent effective,' and on one afternoon the number of clerks outnumbered shoppers in Victoria stores. White store merchants openly tried to counter the Negroes' boycott with a so-called 'buy-in' by Klan sympathizers from outside Victoria at stores that agreed to carry a poster advertising Klan rallies." In spite of this counter action by outsiders, the boycotts continued.

Negroes were further angered a couple of weeks earlier when a group of Negro civil rights workers were standing near the Freedom House when Hawthorne's car was fired upon by a carload of antagonists. A bystander was wounded.[cdxxxiii] The victim was Alfonza Webster Stokes—age twenty-one at the time. The Stokes' family home was across the street from the Freedom House; therefore, he had easy access to the building and the activities that took place there. Stokes recalled in an interview, "I don't remember a lot about the day or the time that this incident happened, but I do remember a close friend and several others were standing just outside of the Freedom House when a car moving at a slow pace passed us. With no indication of trouble, suddenly a gunshot blast rang out. With its white occupants, the car sped away, headed toward one of the local restaurants in the downtown area of Victoria. That's when I realized a bullet had grazed my upper right temple. I had on a hat, and I think that it saved me. I was immediately transported for medical attention to a local doctor in town and the incident was reported to the local police department. I suppose an investigation occurred, but as of this day no assailant was every found or prosecuted."[cdxxxiv]

During the summers of 1965 and 1966, VSCRC staff members had conducted "Freedom Schools" for Negro children in Lunenburg County. These schools were also conducted in Amelia, Nottoway, and Mecklenburg Counties in the summer of 1966. Negro history, art, music, outdoor recreation, reading, and field trips to local points of interest were taught in an atmosphere that encouraged children to question and think creatively.[cdxxxv]

Monnie (2015) wrote, "On August 3, 1965, there was a demonstration march to the Lunenburg County Courthouse by nearly 300 local citizens. The march was in support of the impending passage of the *Voting Rights Act of 1965* (August 6) and to protest the existence of the Poll Tax. The Poll Tax List listed the people who pay their Poll Taxes into colored and white sections and there was refusal to write the word "Mrs." before a Negro woman's name. The march was also intended to protest inadequate voter registration hours, but on July 31, 1965 the electoral board decided to grant adequate hours for voter registration just a few days before the demonstration. Grateful demonstrators displayed signs thanking the electoral board for granting adequate voter registration hours to the citizens. The march began at the First Baptist Church, 821 Lunenburg Avenue, in Victoria and continued to the Lunenburg courthouse where the marchers lined the streets for a short time and then proceeded to the Tussekiah Baptist Church nearby to end the demonstration with a song and prayer."

Carolyn Vera Callahan was an eighth grade student attending Lunenburg High School at the time. Callahan wrote: "In the fight for civil rights in the 1960s freedom rights organizers arrived in Lunenburg County, Virginia. African American residents from local and surrounding neighborhoods such as Victoria, Kenbridge, Blackstone, and Fort Mitchell, Virginia, were active participants in organized events. The march was led by the pastor of the First Baptist Church in Victoria.

Before the march began, a designated adult was responsible for recording names and other identifying information for all participants. Instructions were given by the leaders. Participants were provided with signs to carry. Songs would be sung along the route of the march. Most important, the leaders emphasized the march would be peaceful. Beginning at the church marchers walked 3.5 miles from Lunenburg Avenue to the Lunenburg County Court House on Route 49 South, the county seat. Marchers walked on the shoulder of the highways or, where present, on sidewalks. Along the route, songs sung included 'We Shall Overcome,' 'Ain't Gonna Let Nobody Turn Me Around,' 'We Shall Not Be Moved,' and 'Oh, Freedom.' As some cars drove past marchers, they slowed down and white passengers peered out their car windows. There was no disturbance. The march was successful and peaceful."[cdxxxvi]

The registrar's office was open on Saturday, August 21. There were 176 people registered. As Monnie puts it, "The floodgates of voter registration had opened! The most significant factor was the participation of the citizens of the county in getting their fellow citizens to register. This is an example of how ordinary citizens took responsibility for their own destiny and created their own 'historic' event."

In the spring of 1969, two Lunenburg High School juniors were strongly urged by Annie Holloway Holmes to apply for part-time employment at the Peebles Supermarket in Victoria, Virginia. This is believed to be the first time in the County's history that African American students had been employed by a major grocery business in the town. They were Shirley Robertson (Lee) of Victoria and Stanley "Stan" C. Lee of Kenbridge, Virginia.[cdxxxvii]

Stan Lee wrote, "The summer of 1968 was coming to a close and so was my job. I was working a summer job clocking forty-five hours per week and taking home thirty-five dollars per pay period. Somewhere between having a car, buying gasoline, clothes and dating, thirty-five dollars did not last long. I would have to wait until the next summer to make that amount of money. It was 1968 and I was starting my junior year at Lunenburg High School. During the year I talked to one of my friends who had a job working at the Peebles Supermarket in the town of Victoria. I was later contacted by Mrs. Annie Holloway Holmes, guidance counselor at Lunenburg High School, in reference to a position at Peebles. After talking with her and going over certain work expectations of the program, I was hired to work in the same grocery store with my friend. I was very happy about the news of a job! I did not know at the time getting the opportunity to work at this store was history in the making. This job gave me an opportunity to not have to spend another summer working in the tobacco fields or warehouses at below minimum wages. I started working at the store in the meat department. I worked with the department manager and another worker who was a good young man and taught me a lot. There were some older workers from other departments of the store that did not seem happy to see a young black man working where we had not worked before. Some of them would make rude comments and made sure I heard them. I did not let this discourage me or run me away. I was a good worker—I liked and needed this job. I stayed with the job for a while, but it was "goodbye" to Lunenburg High and "hello" to Central High School as a senior in the fall of 1969."[cdxxxviii]

Legally mandated racial separation was governmentally dismantled by the *Civil Rights Act of 1964*. As a result of the civil rights movement and the

Voting Rights Act of 1965, doors of opportunity were gradually opened to African Americans. Many of those who were domestic workers or share-croppers had gained employment in the public sector. This was as revolutionary in changing society as was the War for Independence in the eighteenth century and the Civil War in the nineteenth.

In *The Evening Star*, Nathaniel Lee Hawthorne outlined his hopes for his 10-year old son, Nathaniel Lee II this way: "I just hope the day my son goes job-hunting, he'll be free to get a job as a policeman, in a bank, or anywhere else he may want." However, Hawthorne, mindful of the numerous threats made on his life, said he is unsure whether he, himself, will live to see that day."[cdxxxix]

Freedom of School Choice

The passage of *Civil Rights Act* (1964) not only impacted society, but a significant change took place in the provision of public education. In compliance with this new legislation, the School Board submitted a plan of desegregation to the Commissioner of Education for acceptance. Compliance was in the form of a "freedom of school choice" plan. On May 7, 1965, the School Board voted unanimously to begin desegregation in the fall. The plan would be publicized in the local newspaper for two successive weeks prior to its implementation; and meetings held to prepare parents, pupils, staff and community for changes that were forthcoming.

The Board also authorized Superintendent Fears to write a letter acknowledging receipt of a petition for John H. Croslin, Sr., president of the Lunenburg Branch of the NAACP, R.F.D., Meherrin, Virginia, and to send him a copy of the Desegregation Plan adopted by the Board at the May meeting.[cdxl] The Board agreed: "We, the members of the board, realize that no country can long endure if it fails to respect and obey the law of the land. We also realize that obedience to the law is the basis for maintaining our freedom and human dignity . . . we will administer and operate our schools in such a manner that we will be in compliance with the aforementioned law. No person will be denied, excluded or discriminated against by this Board on the basis of race, color or national origin. It would not be practical to offer a freedom of choice to all grades in 1965-1966 due to over-crowding conditions in our present school buildings." Simply stated, the Board only offered this option to any child who would enter grade one, two, eight, or twelve during the school term. With the plan approved, the desegregation was set in motion. It was late summer when many parents were furnished the application form with instructions printed on the reverse side (see Appendix F – Application for Placement of Pupil in the Lunenburg County Schools).[cdxli]

Nathaniel Hawthorne, VSCRC volunteer, wrote Superintendent Fears to request a public meeting to explain how the form was to be completed. In a newspaper article, Fears stated that the form was simple to fill out and that they did not need explaining. Fears did hold meetings at various schools in the county. He claimed these meetings were only for the purpose of answering questions concerning the guidelines; however, he was the first superintendent in Southside area of Virginia to do so.[cdxlii] A pupil placement form had to be completed and returned to the superintendent's or school principal's office. Choice was mandatory if students planned to attend a school other than the one they would normally attend!

The submission of the application form resulted in the enrollment of sixteen African American students in the white schools in Lunenburg County. In Kenbridge—L. Stanley Lambert and James Quinn (grade 12); Bertram Callahan, Don Gray, Wendell Carter (grade 8); Ellen Hawthorne (grade 7); Nathaniel Hawthorne, Jr., (grade 5); Phillip Gee (grade 2); Phemie D. Hawthorne; and Madreana Freeman (grade 1). In Victoria—John R. Croslin, Bobbie A. Crane, Bessie M. Callahan (grade 12); Marcia Slaccum (grade 8); Msonga-Mbele Andre Parvenu; and Yyron Croslin (grade 1).[cdxliii]

Easter Smith Crowder remembered when the first time African American students enrolled at the white school in Victoria. Crowder said, "In 1965, I was a cafeteria worker when four African American students—two boys and two girls—were the first to enroll in the high school. These students were allowed to walk across the street together to come to the cafeteria for lunch each day—possibly to avoid any incident of teasing or taunting from the other students. I don't recall hearing of any problems from the cafeteria staff. The school closed in the spring of 1966, and I transferred to new Central High School."[cdxliv]

Margaret Cushwa Cocks, English teacher, spoke candidly of her experience when the first African American students came to Kenbridge High School. Cocks said, "Speaking of school desegregation, I remember two African American students in the senior class who enrolled in the fall of

1965. They were L. Stanley Lambert and James Quinn. Stanley was assigned to my English class because he was in the college-bound group. I remember him as an excellent student who could have been the valedictorian of any senior class. Of course, I knew about James Quinn, but he did not take any classes with me. Our principal wanted things to run smoothly and kept everyone on an even keel when the black students enrolled. Kenbridge High School closed at the end of the school year, and I transferred to Central High School where I remained as a librarian until retirement in 1975. I became acquainted with other African American students and faculty members. I have fond memories of students like Marcia Slacum, and staff members such as Carl H. Jones, guidance counselor; Chester L. Conyers, assistant principal; and especially, Joanna J. Bell, who was my counterpart at Lunenburg Junior High School. Throughout those years we (Bell and I) took several educational trips together; and she made sure that I was notified and invited to travel along. She also made all the arrangements, too!"[cdxlv]

The placement of pupils by the School Board in the 1966-67 and 1967-68 school terms was the same as 1965.[cdxlvi] Lunenburg continued to operate public schools under its local option—free school choice—plan until a "done" deal occurred in December of 1968.

CHAPTER 13
A "DONE" DEAL

*"We conclude that in the field of public education the doctrine of
'separate but equal' has no place."*[cdxlvii]

—Chief Justice Earl Warren

The Road to School Desegregation

James W. Thweatt was appointed Lunenburg's seventh superintendent of
Lunenburg County Public Schools in fall of 1967, succeeding Macon F.
Fears, who officially retired on November 1 of the same year. Thweatt had
been a vocational-agriculture teacher, and the principal of Victoria High
School (1962-1966) and Central High School (1966-1967). In February
1967, he was selected as the assistant superintendent. Thweatt, a native of
Prince George County, Virginia, was a graduate of Virginia Polytechnic Institute and the University of Virginia.[cdxlviii] He may be described as the "Man
of the Hour" because of his position in the midst of school desegregation.
How did he handle such an enormous task since there were pressure groups
on both sides? There were those for the mixing of races in the schools and
others against it.

In fall 1965, the racial characteristics of the school population were
1,675 white, 1,540 Negro, and other: "0." Sixteen African American students had enrolled at the white schools—Kenbridge (7 males and 3 females);
and Victoria (4 males and 2 females). Lunenburg operated two high schools

and five elementary schools— Lunenburg High School (grades 8-12), Central High School (grades 8-12), Kenbridge Elementary (grades 1-7), Kenbridge Graded School (grades 1-7), Lunenburg Elementary (grades 1-7), West End Elementary (grades 1-7), and Victoria Elementary (grades 1-7).

There were approximately 110 African American students enrolled at the newly consolidated Central High School by the fall of 1966. One African American male taught physical education (boys) at Central High School; and a female was employed as a librarian at the white schools in Kenbridge and Victoria. The "local option" plan—as implemented—supported segregation because no African American administrator had been assigned to a white school; and there was no white administrator, teacher or student associated with any black school in the county.[cdxlix]

The pressure was mounting for Lunenburg County to fully integrate its schools. Legal action was taken because members of the community were dissatisfied that the School Board continued to operate a dual school system. In August 1968, the NAACP filed suits in the Richmond and Norfolk District Courts asking for the elimination of alleged racial discrimination in the school systems of nine Virginia counties—Essex, Lunenburg, Dinwiddie, Northumberland, Lancaster, Caroline, Isle of Wight, Charlotte, and Pittsylvania. The United States District Court was also asked to order the nine counties to provide plans for the elimination of racial segregation in all facets of their respective school systems, including administrative personnel, teachers, clerical and custodial help, and transportation.[cdl]

On December 30, 1968, a decision was handed down by the United States District Court, Eastern District of Virginia-Richmond Division. It was the case of *Phemie D. Hawthorne, etc., et al, Plaintiffs v. County School Board of Lunenburg County et al, Defendants*, designated as Civil Action No. 5949-R. The Honorable Robert R. Merhige, Jr. gave the orders in the face of threats of a mass exodus of white pupils and teachers from the public schools. County officials believed that freedom of choice would work better than any more drastic method because if general racial mixing were forced in a school population heavily Negro, the white minority would flee the school system. Judge Merhige pointed out, "A failure in the program was that no white children had enrolled in the Negro schools." In Merhige's estimation, no effort had been made by the Lunenburg County School Board to eliminate its "dual" white and Negro school system. The local newspaper reported the judge said, "Lunenburg has assigned its teachers on a racially discriminatory basis, a practice that must be eliminated." His findings showed that no Negro teacher held a full-time position in a white school nor had any white teachers been assigned full-time to Negro schools. School officials pointed out four Negro teachers were teaching full-time in white schools and thus, created integration. Merhige also said, "The school system did, in actuality, operate a segregated system because no white administrator or teacher was assigned to, nor did any white pupil attend any Negro school."[cdli]

Claude Littleton Barnes, Jr., former member of the Lunenburg County Board of Supervisors, representing the Brown's Store District, was present in the courtroom. Barnes said, "We—county officials—school board members; county supervisors; and Sam H. Allen, legal counsel for the Board, attended a hearing before Judge Merhige in Richmond, Virginia to hear his decision about the Civil Rights suit filed against the school system. In my opinion, he [Judge Merhige] had made it very clear that school desegregation was a 'done' deal, and there was no need to waste time fighting it. So we traveled back to Lunenburg to develop a desegregation plan for the public schools here. The Lunenburg County School Board had thirty days to develop the plan."[cdlii]

On January 3, 1969, the School Board held a special meeting to discuss the Court's decision handed down on December 30 and to devise a desegregation plan. In general, the plan would completely eliminate the aspect of racial segregation or separation.[cdliii]

Another School Board meeting was held on January 21, 1969 A resolution was adopted to show good faith and intent to comply with the aforementioned judgment as follows: "Be it resolved that the proposed plan for the conversion of it school system to a unitary, desegregated system be submitted to the U. S. District Federal Court, Eastern District-Richmond Division in compliance with the judgment issued on the thirtieth day of December 1968 in the case designated as Civil Action N0. 5949-R." Finally, the fight for school desegregation in Lunenburg was over. Wait, not so fast! The Board—on the other hand—unanimously authorized its attorneys to take legal action to appeal the ruling in the *Hawthorne* case; and endeavor to obtain reversal of the Court's ruling.[cdliv]

The next month, February 12, 1969, Virginia's tuition-grant program was stuck down by a special three-judge federal court. However, the financial benefits lingered on until June 30. The court said that the state's tuition grant statutes "contravene the Constitution of the United States" because they permit a continuance of a segregated public school system.[cdlv]

In an effort to "flex" its legal muscles, and utilize the call of the last "rebel" yell of the "Old Free State of Lunenburg," county officials filed a notice of appeal in the ruling by Judge Merhige that ordered the School Board to abolish its freedom of choice pupil assignment system. The case was filed with United States Court of Appeals Fourth Circuit. County officials argued that if they were forced to abandon freedom of choice as a method of assigning pupils, the whites would leave. The school population was 1,567 Negro and 1,385 white. County officials contended that it was better to have some racial mixing in a "freedom of choice" system than to have an all-Negro system abandoned by white pupils. The case was argued on June 9, 1969; and a decision was rendered on July 11, 1969. The *Hawthorne* case was included with the case of *Angela Walker, etc., et al., Appellees, v. County School Board of Brunswick County, Virginia, et al., Appellants.* The attorneys in these cases were Emerson D. Baugh, Lawrenceville, Virginia; and Frederick T. Gray, Richmond, Virginia, (Williams, Mullen & Christian, Richmond, Virginia); and Samuel H. Allen, Kenbridge, Virginia, for appellants; and Henry L. Marsh III, Richmond, Virginia, (S. W. Tucker of Hill, Tucker & Marsh, Richmond, Virginia); Jack Greenberg, and James M. Nabrit III, New York City, for appellees. The Court agreed that black students were in a substantial majority but, freedom of choice had been a "one-way street."[cdlvi]

In affirming Merhige, the Court said, "Relatively little integration had occurred under freedom of school choice plan in Lunenburg, and that it— Lunenburg County—was not seriously urged by officials that the plan has not worked to eliminate racial discrimination or that it was likely to work in the foreseeable future." The Court also pointed out that in previous decisions by the United States Supreme Court had foreclosed consideration of those types of legal arguments. Lunenburg had lost its appeal case. It was as C. L. Barnes, Jr., said Judge Merhige had characterized it—"a done deal."[cdlvii]

School officials, although reluctant, had begun planning for the full school integration and assistance was needed. Segregated schools would no longer exist—they were like colorful flowers that had faded at summer's end—just a memory.

Getting Assistance with School Desegregation

With the inevitable looming, officials sought assistance to help with the integration of its school system. Bessie Chatmon Hopkins spoke of this time when school personnel needed to work together. Hopkins said, "On the eve of school desegregation, Edith Davis Jones and I were selected by Margaret L. Collier, principal, to serve as representatives from the Kenbridge Graded School on a county-wide school committee to devise a plan for the integration of students and faculty. There were representatives from the other county schools including Galvin L. Jenkins and Annie H. Holmes from Lunenburg High School. I'm not sure about the names of the white teachers and administrators who attended the meeting. The meeting was held in the library at one of the schools in the county. There were tense moments as school representatives—black and white—sat across the room facing each other. Superintendent Thweatt selected a chairperson. He wanted to ensure that the task would be accomplished; therefore, he emphasized the need for us to work together as a 'coordinated' group to get the job done. I must admit, however, working through the process of developing a plan—with faculty and staff members that I had not worked with before—was not an easy one."[cdlviii]

School officials contacted the Curry School of Education at the University of Virginia in Charlottesville, Virginia to get assistance with implementing the desegregation plan; and to know what minefields to avoid. The Consultative Resource Center (CRC) for School Desegregation provided that link. It ran on federal grant money from 1967 to 1980 as a little-publicized effort in how to bring people together.

In the *Daily Progress* article, "Noticing Their Efforts," Bob Gibson interviewed Dr. James "Jim" Bash. Dr. Bash was one of the two former directors of the CRC, a former principal at schools in Bristol, Pittsylvania County, and Farmville, Virginia. Bash recalled, "The center was invited by many superintendents across the state to carry on 'desegregation seminars' for teachers and school administrators, and staff members. The CRC staff traveled all over the state doing that—putting black students and white students together from formerly segregated schools was uncharted territory. It was pioneering and involved seeking cross-cultural understanding among groups not accustomed to thinking of, speaking to or acting around each other as equals. So much of the hidden agenda was in the kind of language you use. Certain uses of language strike minorities hard. Black people know it. They feel it. They have to. They know things and feel things that nobody else does. An example of language that blacks and whites discussed was the use of words such as 'you people.'"[cdlix]

Dr. Howard "Hank" W. Allen was appointed assistant director with Dr. Bash. Later, Allen succeeded Bash to become the first African American director of the CRC from 1973 to 1980. Dr. Allen had a successful seventeen-year career teaching and coaching basketball in Danville, Virginia before his employment at CRC. He spoke of his experience during school desegregation era. Dr. Allen said, "School desegregation wasn't easy by any means. There were good moments and bad moments, but we had to work with the bad and good. And that's what we tried to do. Our staff worked with cafeteria workers, custodians, bus drivers, and everyone who was employed in the school system who worked with these problems—and we talked about them. There were different levels to deal with and it wasn't easy. In the beginning, many of the participants in the training sessions were very much against school desegregation, but at times they came back to say to us, 'We enjoyed that— we needed that—we're glad to be part of it.' But, as time went on, they knew what they were doing was the right thing to do."[cdlx]

Equality and Opportunity Arrives!

Following the Court's ruling, "pairing" was a method used to achieve a more equitable distribution of the students, faculty, and staff. "Paring" meant that two nearby schools were grouped—one providing instruction for the lower grades, and the other for the upper grades. A desegregation plan for Lunenburg schools was finalized—taking into account the geographical zone, capacity of the building, distance of student's residence from school, and convenience of bus transportation to school. The plan follows:

- The name of the Lunenburg Elementary School changed to Lunenburg Primary—to house students in grades one through three that had attended the Victoria Elementary and Lunenburg Elementary.

- Victoria Elementary School—to house students in grades four through seven from the schools of Victoria Elementary and Lunenburg Elementary.

- The name of the Kenbridge Graded School changed to Kenbridge Primary School—to house students in grades one through three from the schools of Kenbridge Graded and Kenbridge Elementary.

- Kenbridge Elementary School—to house students in grades four through seven from the schools of Kenbridge Graded and Kenbridge Elementary.

- West End Elementary School would house students in grades one through six. Students in grade seven would transfer to Victoria Elementary.

- The name of Lunenburg High School was changed to Lunenburg Junior High School housing all students in grades eight and nine.

- Central High School became a senior high school housing all students in grades ten through twelve.

All teachers were assigned to provide the needed professional staff at each grade level and subject area for which he/she was qualified, and no teacher would be released on the basis of race, color, or national origin. If it was necessary to demote or release any teacher, it would be done on the basis of enrollment, professional competence and qualifications, or immorality. In February 1969, a survey was conducted to determine the number of the teachers that intended to return to school system in the fall. School Superintendent Thweatt provided to the School Board results of the survey that indicated seventy-four of 78 white, and sixty-four of 68 African American faculty members intended to return. One may be inclined to ask: Did Lunenburg really experience "teacher flight" as a result of public school desegregation? The results of the survey seem to suggest that the answer to this question is *NO*. The mass exodus of teachers from the school system did not occur with ninety-four percent of them planning to return to the classroom.[cdlxi]

Racially speaking, little change had occurred in the assignment of central office personnel, teachers, building-level administrative and support staff prior to 1969.[cdlxii] This trend would change as a result of the Court's ruling in July 1969, but inequality is noted:

School Board Central Office
James W. Thweatt, Division Superintendent
John H. Wells, Director of Instruction

Haywood R. Watkins, Sr., Coordinator of Federal Projects[cdlxiii]
Louise T. Gatling, Deputy-Clerk and Secretary to the School Board
Stella B. Oakes, Secretary

Central High School

John H. Hoppe, Jr., Principal
Chester L. Conyers, Assistant Principal/Coach/Physical Education[cdlxiv]
Louise K. Ozlin, Guidance
Carl H. Jones, History/Guidance[cdlxv]
Margaret C. Cocks, Librarian
30 Teachers (9 African Americans, 21 white)

Lunenburg Junior High School

Galvin L. Jenkins, Principal
D. Barry Carnes, Assistant Principal/Physical Education (Boys)
Annie H. Holmes, Guidance
Virginia McLaughlin, English/Guidance
Joanna J. Bell, Librarian
21 Teachers (10 African Americans; 11 whites)

Kenbridge Elementary School

J. C. Potts, Principal
Allen S. Bridgforth, Assistant Principal/7th grade teacher[cdlxvi]
Evelyn Glenn, Librarian
Louise Ripberger, Special*
16 Teachers (6 African Americans; 10 white)

Victoria Elementary School

John T. Young, Principal
Isaiah G. Hopkins, Assistant Principal/7th grade teacher[cdlxvii]
Jacqueline S. Haskins, Librarian[cdlxviii]
18 Teachers (5 African Americans; 13 white)

West End Elementary School

William K. Hammack, Principal/6th grade teacher
Bessie R. Callahan, library aide[cdlxix]
5 Teachers (1 African American; 4 white)

Kenbridge Primary School
Rhoecus L. Cousins, Principal
Elizabeth Robertson, Librarian
LaNelle Shields, Special*
9 Teachers (5 African Americans; 4 white)

Lunenburg Primary School
Franklin D. Warren, Principal
Barbara Williams, Special*
Edith S. Washington, Special*
Angeline Lea, Special*[cdlxx]
12 Teachers (6 African Americans; 6 white)

In September 1969, John H. Hoppe, principal of Central Senior High School, wrote an open letter to the citizens of Lunenburg County that was printed in *The Kenbridge-Victoria Dispatch*. An excerpt reads, "I wish to use this means to express the gratitude and thanks to the faculty and student body of Central Senior High, and to all the citizens of Lunenburg County for the cooperation and support we have received in this past week of opening school. You have a reason to have confidence in your young people enrolled in Central Senior for the poise and general good judgment that they have shown during these hectic opening days when forty-eight hours needed to be crammed into twenty-four. With your support we will have a successful 1969-1970 school year."[cdlxxi]

Thweatt, "Man of the Hour," resigned his position as the school superintendent in August of 1970. Someone said, "Thweatt had been a 'buffer' between the principals, teachers, and parents since he became superintendent of Schools. We are sure the pressure has been great, and the county will miss his guidance during the coming years; however, we hope any new administrator appointed can do as well or better for the county." Thweatt accepted a position with the State Department of Education as Supervisor of School Plant Surveys.[cdlxxii]

CHAPTER 14
HALLOWED GROUNDS

Public education in Lunenburg County evolved steadily—over a centennial period—from one-room log cabins in 1870 to modern brick facilities by 1970. The towns of Kenbridge (1908) and Victoria (1909) began to develop their own flavor and commercial offerings to the residents, and public education was included. In the early 1900s, brick schools were constructed in the towns, with an ever-increasing number of the small frame schools erected throughout the countryside. Many of the original schoolhouses and buildings continued to be used by school system well into the mid-twentieth century.

Presently, there are approximately twenty-five schools and school-related buildings still standing on their original sites. They are Central High, Fort Mitchell, Hite, Kenbridge Elementary, Kenbridge High (now Kenbridge Community Center), Kenbridge High Gymnasium, Kenilworth, Lochleven, Lunenburg High, Lunenburg Elementary, Oak Grove, Plantersville, Reedy (Negro), Robertson, Rosebud, Rubermont, Board of Education Office (now Lunenburg County Alternative Education Center), Lunenburg County School Board Annex, Snead, Traffic (Negro), Unity, Victoria Elementary, Victoria High, West End Elementary, and Woodrow. None of these buildings are used by the school system except Central High, Kenbridge Elementary, Victoria Elementary, and the former Board of Education Office. The former Kenbridge High and gymnasium; Lunenburg Elementary; Lunenburg High and its home economics cottage, vocational-agriculture shop, and cannery; and the small schools of Fort Mitchell, Hite, Kenilworth, Lochleven, Lone Oak, New Grove, Oak Grove, Plantersville, Reedy, Robertson, Rosebud, Rubermont, Snead, Traffic, Unity, and Woodrow are owned by a public or private entity. Another former building is the one-room frame structure on Eighth Street in Victoria, Virginia across from the street from the Lunenburg County Alternative Education Center. The former Lunenburg County School Bus Garage was abandoned and demolished.

This section provides a historical sketch of some schools and school-related buildings.

ELEMENTARY SCHOOLS

Dundas Graded School

The Dundas Graded School was located on Fairview Road near the former Virginian railroad in Dundas, Virginia. The school site is approximately seven miles east of Kenbridge, Virginia in the Lochleven District. The Dundas Graded School, constructed in the early 1920s, housed students in grades one through seven, with classes doubled up. Students who wanted to continue their education at the secondary level were transported to Lochleven School or Kenbridge High School.[cdlxxiii]

In 1930s, there were two teachers—Virginia Lee Bacon and Beulah Rainey and approximately sixty-four students at the school. Tom Epper Wilkinson was the principal and he taught students in grades six and seven.[cdlxxiv] Others who taught there included Iva Perkins, Thelma Goodwyn, Elizabeth C. Davis, Louise Hawthorne, Irene Inge, Nannie Potts, Virginia Malone, Beulah Vaughan, Daisy Edmonds, and Alice G. Ferguson.

In June of 1941, when the school was on the verge of closing because of low enrollment, a delegation from Dundas asked the board not to do away with the school. Superintendent Crittenden stated that he could see no way to keep the school open. The school closed at the of the 1941-42 school year; and the children were transported to the nearest area schools. The Dundas School—privately owned—was dismantled in 2016.[cdlxxv]

Fort Mitchell School

The Fort Mitchell School was constructed sometime in the early 1920s. This school in located in the southwestern part of the Lunenburg County about thirty yards from Fort Mitchell Drive in the Rehoboth District. Teachers included W. S. Morton, Martha Townsend, Glenna Ward, Ruth Carter, Lucy Tisdale, Mildred Shelton, Maude Shelton, M. H. McGrew, Janice Stockton, Ruth Townsend, Macon F. Fears, and Mildred F. Shaw. The Fort Mitchell School closed in the spring of 1949. In the fall, the elementary students were assigned to the newly constructed West End Elementary School and high school students were transferred to the Victoria High School.

The school was later sold to the Woodman of the World, and the name "Woodman Hall" was adopted. Today, Woodman Hall still is a center for community activities such fish fries, stews, and meetings.[cdlxxvi]

Hite School

After the Hollydale School at this site was destroyed by fire in the 1880s, a small, frame building with decorative eaves was constructed as its replacement. The Hite School, now unoccupied, is situated in a patch of woods on the east side of South Hill Road (#138) between St. John's Church Road (#612) and Hinkle Road (#611.)[cdlxxvii]

Kenbridge Elementary School

Public education began in a one-room log cabin first in Kenbridge, Virginia (formally Tinkling). The cabin was soon replaced by a frame school built on Church Hill, near Olive Branch Methodist Church, at a cost of $1,200. In 1906, three rooms were added to the structure; and it was said to be the first school building in the county with more than one room. There were three teachers—one for each grade. The teachers were Mr. Warriner, Mamie G. Blackwell, and Emma Hethorn—one of them serving as principal for elementary education. There was a divergence of opinion as to who the principal was that first year. Teachers for the next year were Coleman B. Ransom, Mamie G. Blackwell, and Natalie Neblett. Neblett later became the wife of Ransom. Frank Bedinger, Mary L. Bridgeforth, and Mamie G. Blackwell were teachers during the third school year just after the Town of Kenbridge, Virginia was founded in 1908.

In 1910, the staff changed, and the school was moved to a site on Sixth Avenue where an eight-room building was constructed. The school remained at that location for approximately twelve years until a new three-story brick school was constructed on Fifth Avenue. It was occupied in December 1922. The elementary department was located on the lower floor of the Kenbridge High School building, and housed students in grade one through seven. In 1951, two wings were added to the building which provided additional space.[cdlxxviii]

In fall 1965, five black students enrolled at the school. The high school department closed in the spring of 1966, and all high school students were transferred to Central High School in Victoria, Virginia. The name of Kenbridge High was changed to Kenbridge Elementary when the school was fully integrated in the fall of 1969. The school housed students in grades four through seven and was "paired" with the Kenbridge Graded School (now Kenbridge Elementary School). Rhoecus Leburn "R.L." Cousins, who had been the principal of the Lunenburg Elementary School for three years, took the helm as the principal of the Kenbridge Primary School (formally Kenbridge Graded School).[cdlxxix]

James C. Potts—who had taught agriculture, general business, and driver education (1948-1966) at Kenbridge High School—was appointed principal. Allen S. Bridgeforth was the first African American to serve as the assistant principal. Potts remained at Kenbridge Elementary until his retirement in 1986. The school building was closed in later years and the students consolidated with Kenbridge Primary School. The name of the school was changed to Kenbridge Elementary, housing students from kindergarten to fifth grade.[cdlxxx]

Kenilworth School

The Kenilworth School served white children in the Rehoboth District for many years. This schoolhouse is located approximately ten miles southwest of Victoria, Virginia and stands just about fifteen yards from the Ontario Road. Other former teachers at Kenilworth were Rainey Moses, Evelyn Nolley, and Garland Spencer.

N. Harvey Jeter spoke of his school days at Kenilworth. Jeter said, "My mother, Annie Thelma Harding, attended this school the first year it opened in 1909, and the school provided for elementary and secondary instruction. My teacher was Berta L. Hardy. We only had two classrooms for students from the first through seventh grades when I went to this school. Back then, we didn't have indoor plumbing and there was no water fountain. Therefore, two students had to go to a nearby spring and bring water for us to drink. We used a potbelly wood stove for heat in the winter. The stove was made of cast iron with sand box in front to protect the floor from hot coals that fell from the stove. Hugh Shelton drove a bus that he owned so we could attend school; and he transported students back and forth to Victoria High School."[cdlxxxi]

The Kenilworth School closed in the spring of 1949 when the new West End Elementary School was opened in the fall of the same year. Jeter still has fond memories of this old schoolhouse although it is in poor condition with broken windows, and a dilapidated front porch. The Kenilworth schoolhouse is used by its owner as a storage place for rolled hay.

Lunenburg Elementary School

In the early 1920s, an elementary education was offered as part of the Lunenburg Training School curriculum. The school was located approximately two miles east of Victoria, Virginia on Highway 40 (K-V Road). It is believed that a four-room, frame school was completed sometime in 1918 with one room was used for elementary education. The location of the school was suitable to accommodate Negro children living in the Victoria area. Later, additional frame buildings were constructed on the site. The principal had oversight of the elementary and secondary departments. Eventually, the school became overcrowded as the small schools of Davis, Lone Oak, Pleasant Oak, Traffic, Nutbush, Plantersville, and Union Central closed.[cdlxxxii]

In 1954, a new brick building was constructed on the site across the street (now School Road) from former Lunenburg High School. The school—Lunenburg Elementary School—was considered a modern facility at the time with twelve classrooms, large hallways, an administrative office, a library, a clinic room, custodian's closets, and a cafeteria which dubbed as the auditorium. A steam boiler and electrical heating was used to warm the building. However, there were still several frame structures on the site with a potbelly stove that used coal and wood to heat the classroom.

The teachers were Carl H. Jones, Rudolph V. Doswell, Geraldine Jones, Mary E. Stokes, Versie L. Taylor, Nancy Morse, Edith P. Irby, Pearl V. Davis, Lelia M. Williams, Alice Jackson, Myrtle Smith, Mattie Marable, Bernice Jeffreys, and Ruby Ragsdale.

In fall 1959, Sherman C. Vaughan was appointed the assistant principal; and he taught seventh grade. William W. Craighead, principal of the Lunenburg High School, also had oversight of the elementary school. An education was offered in grades one to seven with the exchange of classes beginning in grade seven. The core curriculum consisted of arithmetic, science, reading, language arts, spelling, and social studies. Students who successfully completed grade seven were promoted to eighth grade; and had an opportunity to participate in a graduation exercise before moving on to the Lunenburg High School.

The students had to walk back and forth from the brick schools to frame buildings for classes until the late 1960s. Communication was challenging because the frame buildings did not have a public address system or electronic bell installed. Vaughan ended his tenure in Lunenburg County the spring of 1965.[cdlxxxiii]

In the fall, Rhoecus Leburn Cousins succeeded Sherman C. Vaughan as principal of Lunenburg Elementary. Four new classrooms—electrically heated—were added; and two electrically-equipped, pre-constructed frame buildings were installed on the west side of the school near the playground. These buildings housed the remedial programs—mathematics and reading—offered through Title I funds.[cdlxxxiv]

The name Lunenburg Elementary was changed to Lunenburg Primary School in the fall of 1969 a part of the school desegregation plan. The school housed students in grades one through three. Franklin "Frank" D. Warren was named the principal of the school. Warren had been the assistant principal and athletic director at Central High School prior to his new position as principal. The school closed as the Lunenburg Primary in the early 2000s when the middle school concept was implemented; and re-opened as the Lunenburg Middle School, housing students in grades six. In later years, due to the school's age and deteriorating condition, a new middle school was constructed on Tomlinson Road in Victoria, Virginia, housing students in grades six through eight. Currently, the former Lunenburg Elementary School building is privately owned.[cdlxxxv]

Oak Grove School

In January 1920 Peter B. Winn and his wife, Edmonia Winn, gave two acres of land—for $45 dollars—to construct the Oak Grove Baptist Church, church cemetery, and a school next to the church for colored children in the vicinity. The site on which the school is located did not provide adequate space for a playground. The front yard of the church was used for play during recess. School materials and supplies were limited. Thomas Ross Irby, a 1970 graduate of Central High School, stated that his grandfather, Peter B. Winn, was one of the school's founders and the school was privately owned.[cdlxxxvi]

It is believed that the first teacher was Anna F. Holcomb. The teachers taught first through seventh grades. Students had to walk to school a radius of up to four miles. The school league paid the teachers' salary and assumed all responsibility for the school. Other teachers in 1920s and 1930s were Nanny Lassiter, Rebecca Steward and Wynona Bell. In the 1940s, Elizabeth T. Wood, Adele Bragg and Otis Winn Dixon continued in the role as teachers. The last teacher/principal was Ethel Watkins when the school closed in the late 1940s. The children were assigned to the Kenbridge Graded School.

The Oak Grove School still stands on its original site in the Brown's Store District of Lunenburg County, approximately 3.5 miles north of Kenbridge, Virginia. Plans are underway to preserve the school building.[cdlxxxvii]

Plantersville School

The Plantersville School is located southwestern area of Lunenburg County on Plantersville Road in the Rehoboth District. It is believed this school was built in the late 1920s. Presently in extremely poor condition, this schoolhouse with a tin roof once provided a place for African American children to receive their education.

Elloise Marable Callahan was student at the school. Callahan said, "The people of the Plantersville community purchased two acres of land from Jim and Mattie Townson who had a store in Plantersville. The school patrons named the new one-room frame building—Plantersville School. The school housed students in grades one through seven. Some of the teachers were Rosa C. Marable, Viola Rolett, and Jasper Davenport.

In those days, transportation was very limited; therefore, the building was used for many other activities such as food sales to raise funds, Sunday school classes and meetings, quartet singing, as well as other programs presented by the school children and organizations in the community. With no modern conveniences, a nearby stream was our source of drinking water for the teacher and the children. The boys would usually be assigned to get water in a pail and bring it back to the school. There was no bus transportation; therefore, we walked several miles to and from school each day."[cdlxxxviii]

By 1950, the Plantersville School had closed due to low enrollment. Another student reported that she and others were transferred to other schools to complete their education—Traffic School (grades one through seven), and those in high school attended Lunenburg in Victoria, Virginia.[cdlxxxix]

Robertson School

The Robertson School is one of the oldest frame buildings still standing. It is believed to among the first schools constructed in the late 1800s for white children in the community. The school closed around 1915 or 1916; and the students were transported to the Woodrow School. This former schoolhouse—in extremely poor condition—is located on Moore's Ordinary Road in the Brown's Store District, approximately five miles, northeast of Kenbridge, Virginia.

The school was named after Jack Robertson, a farmer who owned the school and surrounding land. Charles E. Welborn, property owner, commented, "In 1995, I spoke to a gentleman about this building. He was about eighty-four years of age and a former student at the Robertson School. He confirmed the structure as the Robertson School, and said that it had been built on four acres of land near the Jonesboro Road." This school's only door faces away from the road with one window in the rear. The chimney was located on the left side of the building. The use of a potbelly stove as a heat source and the architecture of this building are typical of most rural schools during the late 1800s and early 1900s.[cdxc]

Rosebud School

The Rosebud School—in poor condition—is located on Fairview Road approximately six miles east of Kenbridge, Virginia on private property. This is the second schoolhouse constructed for African American children in Dundas, Virginia. The first school was constructed in 1902. It was through the efforts of Robert Morse—one of the most prosperous citizens in the community—that the movement for a school was instituted. The patrons purchased one acre of land and erected a one-room frame school. Bettie Hardy, the first teacher, was paid by the School Board. In 1912, the site was deeded to the school board.[cdxci]

Nellie M. Morse was appointed the teacher in 1937. By the mid-1940s, Mabel Bridgeforth served as principal and teacher in grades one through seven. Bridgeforth was followed by LaNelle Shields, who taught at Rosebud until it closed in the spring of 1953.[cdxcii] The Dundas School is privately owned.

The Snead School was constructed in the early 1920s. Today, it still stands on private property and is maintained by its owner.

The Snead School is located approximately four miles south of Kenbridge, Virginia, on Snead Store Road in the Brown's Store District. About 1921 or 1922, white families in the Snead community became concerned about not having a school located somewhere close by. On January 1, 1924, George C. Snead, and his wife, Violet Love Snead, deeded the land for the construction of the school. Daisy Snead Love was the first teacher, and there were about twenty-nine students who attended the first year. Most of them walked to school. In June of 1926, F. O. Love was appointed teacher at the school. The school term of 1927-28 was the last and some of the children were transported to the school in Kenbridge while others enrolled in the nearby Nonintervention School.[cdxciii]

Unity School
The Unity School was established in 1873 through the united efforts of Robert Harris, Joseph Gee, Banister Lee, and William Crawley. Unity was a two-room; frame structure located approximately eight or ten miles south of Kenbridge, Virginia. The school was named after Unity Church, which was erected on the same site. The first teacher was Charlie Hepburn, and the second teacher was Hannie Almond from New

York. Roosevelt Green and Brenda Harris were the teachers in the early 1930s.[cdxciv]

The first Unity School was destroyed by fire, and in the early 1940s, a new—sixty-foot-by-twenty-four-foot—two-room building was constructed by Archer Morrison. Morrison was a local carpenter and husband of Lucy Hinton Morrison. The latter schoolhouse is located on Craig Mill Road, approximately four miles south of Kenbridge, Virginia, in the Brown's Store District of Lunenburg County. The school and its property are owned by Lewis Carl Reese. Reese said, "I remember walking many days three or four miles to attend the first Unity School—rain or shine—because there was no bus to ride to school. On cold, frosty days we had to keep fire in the pot-belly stove that used wood and coal. Of course, our restroom facility was an outdoor building. I went to school at the Lunenburg Training School in 1936 after my seventh grade year at Unity."[cdxcv]

In 1937, the school was deeded to the School Board for public support and Nancy Morse was appointed the teacher.[cdxcvi] Morse was followed by Hilda B. Hawkins in the early 1940s. By 1947, Bertha Sapp was the teacher for grades one through three, and Carolyn Billups was the principal and teacher in grades four through seven. Sapp was followed by Viola B. Brydie, but Billups remained principal and teacher at Unity into the early 1950s. Beatrice Garland replaced Brydie as teacher, and in 1955, Billups transferred to the Kenbridge Graded School while Garland remained at Unity as the principal and teacher until spring of 1959. In fall 1959, Viola B. Brydie returned to the school for one year to teach in grades one through five. By fall 1960, Brydie had transferred to another county school; and she was replaced by Ananias Washington—principal and teacher in grades four through seven. Washington was joined by Elizabeth C. Jones, teacher in grades one through three. Both Washington and Jones remained at Unity until it closed in the spring of 1962.[cdxcvii]

Early Mason Reese—former student at Unity School and retired farmer—spoke of how his father came to possess the school building and its property. Reese recalled, "When the school was no longer used by the School Board to educate children, my father, James Early Reese, offered the highest bid of $2,000 for the school building with two acres of land during a public auction in the early 1960s."[cdxcviii] Now, in poor condition, the Unity School is used as a storage building for farm use.

Victoria Elementary School

In 1895, the first schoolhouse for white children in Victoria, Virginia, was a little one-room building just south of the former railroad bridge with the wife of James T. Waddill, Sr., as teacher. In 1902, a larger building was constructed on the Waddill's property, and two additional rooms were added in 1907—creating a three-room school. S. W. Curtis was the principal of the new school. The industrious people of the booming railroad town felt better facilities were needed for the ever-enlarging population. They wanted an elementary and high school education to be available for their children.

In 1912, elementary education was reorganized; and the grade school would be housed in the first high school building. The classes grew in size. Soon after the World War I, Victoria found itself in need of still a larger school. In the 1920s, another three-story building was constructed next door to the original 1912 school and it would provide space for the high school students.[cdxcix] The principal of the high school had oversight of elementary education.

The construction of a new elementary school—across the street from the high school—was included in the $600,000 Bond Issue for school construction passed by voters in February, 1948. The contract was awarded to the Mottley Construction Company of Farmville, Virginia with the low bid of $112,257. In 1950, a more modern building became part of the Victoria High School complex. Located on what had been originally designated as the Town Square, this new facility had eight new classrooms and a large, more efficient cafeteria than the old cafeteria that had been located for many years in the basement of the first old high school building.

In 1965, two African American male students enrolled in the first grade at the Victoria Elementary School during freedom of school choice. They were Yyron Croslin (younger brother of John Croslin) and Msonga-Mbele Andre Parvenu. There were no African American females who enrolled.

In the fall of 1966, following the closing of the Victoria High School, John L. Young was named the principal. Young had been principal of the West End Elementary School for two years before his new assignment at Victoria.[d] Darlene Marshall (Biggers), an African American female, was employed as a librarian at the Victoria and Kenbridge Elementary Schools. Isaiah G. Hopkins became the first African American assistant principal and a seventh grade teacher there in the fall of 1969.[di]

The present-day Victoria Elementary School that dates from 1950 has been renovated and enlarged to include a modern library and gymnasium. The school was fully integrated in 1969, and houses students from kindergarten to grade five.[dii]

West End Elementary School

The West End Elementary School was located in the southwestern area of the county on Ontario Road in the Rehoboth District. It was occupied in the fall of 1949 when Kenilworth, Fort Mitchell, and other small white schools in the area closed. W. N. Pound was the first principal. There were six grades—one through five with one teacher in each grade; and the principal taught six grade students. Pound left West End in the spring of 1953.[diii]

In the fall, C. E. Damon succeeded Pound as principal and teacher.[div] Damon left West End after only one year. Robert West replaced Damon in the fall of 1954.[dv] By 1959, Franklin B. Hilltzheimer had been selected as the school's leader; and a seventh grade class was added. Following Hiltzheimer, John T. Young was appointed principal in August 1964.[dvi]

Glada Jarvis Dunnavant talked about her years as an educator in Lunenburg County and tenure at the West End Elementary School. Dunnavant said, "I was born in Lunenburg County and I've lived here all my life. After graduating from James Madison College in 1946, I taught first graders in the elementary department at Kenbridge High School for three years. I left teaching for a while to raise a family; and returned sometime after to continue teaching second grade students at Victoria Elementary School. I was assigned to the West End Elementary School on the eve of school desegregation in 1964. We had grades one through seven and there was one teacher for each grade. The principal also taught our seventh grade students. Extracurricular activities for the students included the 4-H Club, a Student Cooperative Association, Student Safety Patrol, and a school newspaper staff." She seemed to have enjoyed talking about the four sets of twins at West End. Dunnavant chuckled when she said, "We [the other teachers and I] enjoyed watching the children during their playtime at recess; and when they got all dressed-up for Halloween."

She continued, "There were no black students at West End when I began teaching there in 1964 or when the free school choice plan was implemented in the fall of 1965. However, a few black students enrolled in 1966; and by fall 1969 all the public schools were desegregated. I was assigned to another school within the next few years, and I retired in 1985 after twenty-three years in public education."[dvii]

During the 1965-66 school term, there were approximately 125 pupils; one school secretary—Anne T. Bailey; two cafeteria workers— Ethel Watts, Lucille Harding; one custodian—Bessie Crump; and four bus drivers— Robert Adams, Albert Watts, Ben Beck, and Morris Beck at West End. By fall 1966, the School Board had transferred John T. Young to the Victoria Elementary School; and Gladys W. Dodson replaced Young as principal.[dviii]

Bessie Reese Callahan spent time at the West End Elementary School. Callahan said, "In spring 1966, I was notified by Superintendent Fears that in the fall I would be transferred from Kenbridge Graded School to the West End Elementary School where I would be assigned as an aide in the library. There were no African American students attending this school when I arrived there. The next year I was reassigned as receptionist in the school's main office. I remember that a female student named Gloria J. Barksdale was the only black student enrolled in the first grade. Later, a few more students enrolled there. West End was a good place to work, and I remained there for a number of years."

Gracie Saunders spoke about her daughter attending the West End School. She said, "My daughter did not enroll in the all-black Lunenburg Elementary School in the fall of 1966. The superintendent had assured me that she would be safe at the West End, which was closer to our home. As it turned out, she was befriended by two white students in her first grade class—Linda Kunath (Brooks) and Wanda Bailey (Barnes). The trio has remained friends to this day.[dix]

William K. Hammack succeeded Gladys Dobson. Hammack was the principal at West End when the school was fully integrated in 1969.[dx]

Frances Price Wilson, a former student at the West End School, remembers when the school desegregation took place in the county. Wilson wrote, "I attended West End Elementary School from grade one through six. I remember thinking how brave the black students were to come into a traditionally white school. School life for them was not easy. They were proud and strong and stayed true to their commitment. Little did I know that in just a couple of years, I would be attending eighth grade at Lunenburg Junior High School (formerly Lunenburg High School—the all-black high school)."[dxi]

Today, the West End Elementary School is privately owned.

HIGH SCHOOLS

Central High School

The discussion of a single high school for the county began in the late 1930s. In November 1938, a large crowd of school patrons gathered during the Victoria Parent-Teacher Association meeting to hear Superintendent Crittenden discuss the results of a survey conducted by the State Planning Board. Among the recommendations made was the discontinuance of the high school at Kenbridge and Lochleven and establishment of a high school at Victoria. By fall 1942, the high school at Lochleven had consolidated with Kenbridge High.

The subject of a centrally located high school resurfaced in 1945 when the School Board resolved to build a consolidated high school for white children. A committee from the State Department of Education—composed of Dr. Fred H. Alexander, Director of Secondary Education; C. K. Holsinger, Superintendent of Henrico County Schools; L. Carper, Superintendent of Allegheny County Schools; D. J. Howard, State Director of Agricultural Education; and W. I. Dixon, State Director of Buildings and Grounds—made a survey of Lunenburg County to determine a site for the proposed school. A letter from the committee was presented to the School Board. After much discussion, the Board authorized Fears to investigate the feasible sites, and this proposed program of consolidation would be presented to the public to solicit its opinion.[dxii]

In March 1947, a delegation of five men from the Kenbridge Chamber of Commerce appeared before the Board with a request for either additional school buildings in Kenbridge, or a consolidated high school.[dxiii]

The voters of Lunenburg County voted in favor of a $1,300,000 Bond Issue to improve the school system on March 19, 1964. The Board of Supervisors granted the School Board permission to employ an architect and purchase a site for the construction of a consolidated high school in the county.[dxiv]

Central High School as pictured in the Yearbook, 1966

In fall 1966, Central High School, "Home of the Chargers," opened its doors after the high schools of Kenbridge and Victoria had closed. The school is conveniently located on Highway 40 (K-V Road) east of Victoria, Virginia. The school housed students in grades eight through twelve from 1966 to 1969. Macon F. Fears, superintendent since 1943, had oversight of the construction of the school and its operation during freedom of school choice. Lunenburg County maintained the two high schools— Central High of Lunenburg and Lunenburg High.[dxv]

James W. Thweatt was appointed the first principal. Franklin "Frank" D. Warren was selected as the assistant principal.[dxvi] In February 1967, John H. Hoppe, Jr., was appointed to replace Thweatt as principal. Hoppe held the position of Supervisor of Instruction for two years before his appointment as principal.[dxvii] In July, Thweatt was appointed the assistant superintendent of Lunenburg County Public Schools; and officially became superintendent when Fears retired on November 1, 1967.[dxviii]

Public school desegregation officially took place on Tuesday, September 8, 1969.[dxix]

Central High was reorganized as a senior high school housing students in grades ten through twelve. Chester L. Conyers replaced Warren as the assistant principal. He was the first African American school administrator assigned there. Conyers had been the physical education teacher for boys and coach at Lunenburg High School.[dxx]

There were approximately twenty-two white and twelve black teachers. The number of black students had more than doubled to 257 of the 566 students enrolled in grades ten through twelve (see Appendix E – Table 5: Lunenburg County Public Schools Enrollment, Fall 1969).[dxxi]

This was the first time that all high school students in the county had to learn to work together. A statement—by the members of the 1969-1970 senior class—was printed in the 1969-1970 *Sword and Shield*—the school's yearbook. The statement and class motto offer tribute to the trailblazers and unsung heroes of the Lunenburg County Public Schools. It simply states:

> *PROBLEMS . . . Segregation in an integrated school, prejudice, distrust, lack of school spirit threaten Chargers during the year of change; CHANGES . . . A year of change, an end of an era, a beginning of another, and two peoples divided by ignorance and fear learn together, and learn acceptance of one another; IS RESLOVED BY WORKING TOGETHER . . . But in classes, in sports, in activities, the problems received solutions; the problems of a new situation are resolved by a united effort.*

CLASS MOTTO:
WE COME TO LEARN TO WORK TOGETHER;
WE LEAVE TO WORK IN PEACE.[dxxii]

School leaders, staff members, and the students did their best to create a smooth transition from segregation to full integration within the school. Still, some personnel seemed uneasy in handling social and extracurricular activities such as the prom, club membership, and homecoming. For example, the selection of a high school homecoming queen by popular vote of the student body was a tradition. Prior to this time, each high school—Central and Lunenburg—had its own criteria for the selection of the homecoming queen and the court participants. In October 1969, Central High School had its first integrated homecoming court with no homecoming queen selected that year. It is believed that the decision made to present a homecoming court of princesses only and escorts was an attempt to avoid any hint of racism during one the most social events of the school year. Apparently, there were no major problems or complaints regarding the decision. The school would provide an opportunity—through popular vote—for the selection of a homecoming queen; and in later years, queens of African American descent were selected.[dxxiii]

In June of 1970, the first fully integrated senior class graduated. What a historic moment for Lunenburg County!

Kenbridge High School

The first Kenbridge High School opened its doors shortly after Kenbridge, Virginia was founded in 1908. A new eight-room brick building was erected on the corner of Sixth Avenue and South Decatur Avenue, a block from Broad Street. Paul S. Blandford was the first principal. He had been the principal and a teacher at the Ledbetter School just before his arrival at Kenbridge.[dxxiv] The newspaper reported, "The student body of 1912 was the first to attend the new school building. By 1913, the school went to tenth grade, and then in 1914 to the eleventh. Some students, as a result, graduated twice and received two diplomas. If a teacher was absent, one of the tenth or eleventh grade students would take the class." The senior class roll of 1915 included eight members—William A. Almand, Edward G. Bailey, Allie Mae Dickerson, Amelia Stuart Hatchette, Eula Leora Inge, Orpha Elizabeth Kelly, Ratling J. Parrish, and Jesse R. Skinner. The principal was J. J. Kelly, Jr.[dxxv]

In September 1922, the student body relocated to a new three-story brick building erected on Fifth Avenue. The school housed the elementary department on the lower level; and secondary students—grades one through twelve—were located on the second and third floors. There was a library, cafeteria, administrative office, and a spacious auditorium. The school was heated by a coal-burning furnace until it was remodeled in later years. In May 1923, the first graduation class included Frank Reeves Gee, Harris Gee, Andrew Lee Lewis, Bernard Saunders, Louise Bell, Mary Brooks, Mary Etheridge, Lois Dickerson, Madeline Gary, Sally Hardy, Willie Hazelwood, Mable Ragsdale, Odell Snead, and Gladys Snead.[dxxvi]

George Luther Walker, the first principal at the newly constructed high school, created and implemented the "five-point" child health program because he wanted the children to develop and maintain good health habits. The program later brought him some statewide notoriety.[dxxvii]

In the 1930s, a home economic cottage was constructed. Located on the west side of the school building, it was completely furnished with a living room, dining room, bedroom, kitchen, bath, and small hallway. A frame building was constructed for agriculture classes, and by 1941, a vocational shop building was erected at the school site. In the 1960s these buildings were no longer needed, and eventually dismantled.

Edward Gwaltney Chatmon was the custodian at Kenbridge High from 1939 until his retirement in 1965. Bessie Chatmon Hopkins said, "My father loved his job and served as a role model at school and in the community."[dxxviii] In 1965, Herbert Maddox, Jr., succeeded Chatmon. "Byer,"—as he was so lovingly called—continued as the school's custodian throughout the freedom of school choice and desegregation years. Maddox retired in the 1980s after fifteen years of service at Kenbridge High School.

In fall 1965, five African American students enrolled in Kenbridge High for the first time in the school's history. There were L. Stanley Lambert and James Quinn—seniors—graduated in 1966; and Bertram Callahan, Wendell Carter, and Don Gray—eighth graders—enrolled at Central High School in the fall of 1966.[dxxix]

Helen W. Buchanan provided insight into her teaching career in the elementary department at the Kenbridge High School. Buchanan said, "In 1934, I graduated from Westhampton College in Richmond, Virginia, with a degree in English education. I taught in the Pittsylvania County Public Schools—1934 to 1939—and married O. M. Buchanan on October 9, 1937. We moved to Kenbridge, Virginia, in 1939; however, I did not begin teaching seventh grade at the Kenbridge High School until the fall of 1957. In fall 1963, I was assigned to teach fourth grade students.

In my opinion, school integration was really difficult for both the teachers and students in 1965. I never doubted my skills as a teacher, but I had never taught a black child before. However, my fears were alleviated when Haywood R. Watkins, Sr. talked to me about my skills as a teacher and the love I had for children. And the argument for me was settled at that point!"

With full retirement looming, Buchannan semi-retired, but continued to teach part-time beginning in the spring of 1977. She completely retired from public education in spring of 1979.[dxxx]

The high school department at Kenbridge High closed at the end of the 1965-1966 school year with James Hall "Jim" Revere was principal, and Don W. Deaton, assistant principal. Some members of the faculty and staff were Edith Hite, G. Shirley Potts, James C. Potts, Lois Marshall, Elizabeth H. Little, Anna T. Coleman, Louise K. Ozlin, Helen S. Potts, Margaret C. Cocks, Eleanor W. Bell, Virginia L. Tisdale, Alice J. Predgo, Mary Hawthorne, Margaret W. Irby, Celia Sosa Snead, Dorothy M. Matthews, Catherine Murdoch, and Bessie D. Atkinson. There were seven cafeteria workers—three white and four African Americans. Other principals were Lee Morton, Ashton Ozlin, and Frank Spindler.[dxxxi] The former Kenbridge High School sat vacant for years following the remodeling of the nearby Kenbridge Elementary School. The high school building has been remodeled and is now the Kenbridge Community Center that houses the Kenbridge Town Hall, Kenbridge Police Department, and other community organizations and local businesses.

Lochleven School

The Lochleven School is located about fifty yards from Highway 138 (South Hill Road) in the Lochleven District approximately ten miles south of Kenbridge, Virginia. Agnes Wilson gave five acres of land, and the School Board bought two additional acres. The school was established in 1921 when the people in that district said that they would build a six-room school if the School Board "would help form an accredited high school." The board agreed to furnish teachers if the building was completed by September. The patrons donated to the school fund raising from a day's wages up to five hundred dollars. With the building plans furnished by the State Board of Education, Lochleven School was completed for the fall opening. Enrollment on the first day was so large that extra rooms were needed. Later, a library, laboratory, music room, and an auditorium were added because of the funds raised by the community league.

The first principal, Lucy Davis, handed diplomas to eleven graduates in 1922. She was succeeded by J. F. Kennedy—principal from 1922 to 1924; and J. T. Waddill, Jr. succeeded Kennedy in 1924. In September 1925, Jim Hall Revere was named the principal; and by fall 1933, school officials boasted that 175 pupils had enrolled.

In May 1935, J. T. Waddill, Jr., division superintendent and former principal of the school, presented 14 diplomas to members of the senior class.

In 1947, Lucille I. Tuner became principal and seventh grade teacher. Others teachers were Ashton Ozlin, C. N. Thompson, Sarah Inge, Mabel Powers, India Thompson, Mattie Evans, R. T. Clark, Harriet Bacon, Willie

Hazelwood, Juliet Mann, Marion Jett, Edna Birdsong, Lucille Ingram, Sarah H. Thompson, Hettie Rudd, Hallie Cage, Mary L. Hawthorne, Mary Barnes, and Catherine Murdoch.[dxxxii]

Claude Littleton Barnes, Jr. began his education at the Lochleven school in 1927. Barnes commented, "I remember the first Lochleven School as a small, one-room building with no modern conveniences. My aunt, Mary Barnes, taught at the school in the 1930s; and she volunteered to transport neighborhood children in her car to and from school. The most distinguishing feature about her car was that it would only start with a turn of the 'crank' located in the front grille just below the hood. I'm not sure of the model, but I know that old 'crank' caused a mishap or two!" Barnes chuckled as he shared a story about his aunt's car. He continued, "One day my cousin was trying to start the car and the crank suddenly kicked back. He ended up with a broken arm. More rooms were later added to the school because there were so many children. We didn't have a gym; therefore, all of our basketball games were played on dirt floors in the Old Farmer's Warehouse in Kenbridge, Virginia. My last year at Lochleven was 1939."[dxxxiii]

In 1935, Jim Revere left Lunenburg to return to his native Middlesex County, and taught there for two years. In 1937, he returned to Lochleven and was principal until 1940 when he was appointed principal of Kenbridge High School.[dxxxiv]

The Lochleven School senior class consolidated with the seniors at Kenbridge High School in the fall of 1942. In 1943, the School Board had authorized Superintendent Fears to close the high school department and transport all secondary pupils to the Kenbridge High School.[dxxxv] By fall 1944, all eighth grade students were transferred to Kenbridge because of a small enrollment.[dxxxvi] However, the elementary department remained opened serving students in grades one to seven.

Elsie M. Almand was as student at the Lochleven School. Almand reported, "Mack D. Moore became principal and teacher of grades six and seven of the Lochleven Elementary School in the fall of 1949. He remained at Lochleven until he joined the United States Army in 1950."[dxxxvii]

Moore was succeeded by Donovan Hill as principal; and Hill was followed by T. W. Stafford Jr., in 1953.[dxxxviii] Beginning in the fall of 1956, H. K. Magnusson was appointed Lochleven's new principal. There were three teachers; and Magnusson also taught students in grades six and seven. The

Lochleven School closed in the spring of 1957; and the children were transported to the school in Kenbridge in the fall.[dxxxix]

The Lochleven School served as a polling station, and was once designated as a post office. The school—privately owned—stills stands on its original site, but in poor condition.[dxl]

Lunenburg High School

Lunenburg High School was organized as Lunenburg Training School sometime in the early 1900s. The Negro's place in Southern society seemed—to most Southerners—to demand what was loosely held to be vocational training, and thus, the word "training" was included in the name of the school. This belief provided a "legitimate" excuse to neglect expensive Negro high school construction in many cases.[dxli]

The Lunenburg County School Board promised to furnish half of the material if the patrons would buy the land, furnish the labor, and the remaining material for construction of a building. A league of citizens secured ten acres of land from the Staples' estate on Route 40 (now K-V Road) in the Plymouth District approximately two miles east of the Victoria, Victoria. Reportedly, as a result of insufficient funds in the hands of the School Board, Carney Love and Augustus Stokes, two Negro citizens, signed a seven hundred dollar note to make up the deficiency for the construction of an adequate building for education.

A three-room frame building was completed, but it had no modern conveniences such as electricity, running water and indoor restrooms. The school offered two years of work on the secondary level under the supervision of Wilford Seldon Clark, the first principal. Clark proved to be a very capable and efficient worker. The teachers were Lucille C. Overby, Wilnette Brown, and E. Pearl Evans; and later, Elizabeth J. Cradle, Ada Jenkins, and Reps A. Hinton joined the faculty.

The supervisor was Lucy M. Morrison.[dxlii] In the 1923 *Lunenburg School Life newsletter*, Morrison wrote, "Overlooking the heights at Victoria across on the other side of the railroad is the beautiful location of our training school. Messrs. Jones and Lewis, two of our white friends of Victoria, gave us two acres of land and we bought eight more acres, and on this plot the school board has built a lovely three-room building. Plans were underway for the construction of a five-room building with an auditorium to accommodate the children from different sections of the county. The students would receive a second grade certificate."[dxliii] The frame building was constructed for the cost of $4,900; and financed with contributions from African Americans ($1,400), White ($100), Public ($2,500), and Rosenwald Fund ($900). The wooden folded doors—which partitioned two classrooms—could be opened into a larger space to accommodate students during school assemblies. The heat source was a potbelly stove that burned wood or coal. The wood and coal storage room was located in the first room on the right of the hallway. Teachers were responsible for making the fire when a custodian was not available.

By 1924, the elementary department was established as the enrollment increased; and three-room frame building was erected next to the rear of the larger five-room structure.[dxliv]

In September 1926, Miss Shelton and Lelia Morgan Williams were employed as teachers for the training school. Principal Clark was on leave during the school term of 1928-1929 for further study. He returned the following year—in 1929—and remained at the training school until June 1931. In Clark's absence, Bessie Morris was appointed to serve as principal.[dxlv]

Kenneth P. Evans succeeded Clark as principal in September 1931, and the school made rapid progress. Evans worked very hard to get Lunenburg Training on the state accreditation list. The height of the development of Lunenburg Training School was reached when the school was accredited in 1933.[dxlvi] The first school song, "Hike Along Lunenburg, Hike Along," was created by Evans.[dxlvii] The principal had oversight of the elementary curriculum as well. The school operated under the seven-four plan—elementary (grades1-7) and secondary (grades 8-11)—that allowed the pupil to graduate upon the completion of the eleventh grade.[dxlviii]

The teachers for 1937-1938 were Richard Pegram, Maudell Bracie, Elizabeth J. Cradle, Lucille Overby, Lelia Williams, and Dorothy L. Young. Students who participated in the elementary program and successfully completed the course of study were awarded a certificate in the spring of 1938. This academic certificate signified that the students were ready to continue studies at the secondary level and take courses leading to college or enroll in classes that offered home economics, vocational and agriculture education.

In spring 1943, Evans' strong leadership would once again be demonstrated when he submitted a letter to the School Board to request 250 chairs for the school and materials for a library table. However, the Board left the task of securing these badly needed supplies to Superintendent Fears and Roscoe Carden, school trustee.[dxlix]

Joanna Jackson Bell was employed as the first librarian by the fall of 1944. Bell said, "There was no system of library studies in place when I came to the "training" school. It was important to me for the children to have access to lots of reading materials—especially books. There was someone to assist me in getting the library organized, and it was great to see the program develop! Initially, we had a small reading area, but a larger library was available when the Lunenburg Elementary School was constructed in 1954. The library was shared by both the elementary and high school students. In 1966, another library was included in the new addition to the existing Lunenburg High School. It was more spacious with storage rooms for audio-visual equipment and resources, and lots of shelves for books, and reference materials compared to what we began with."[dl]

The next great development in secondary education took place when the school began to operate under the seven-five plan.[dli] In June 1945, the School Board approved the eighth grade as a part of high school program. Beginning in the fall, students had to complete twelve years of education— seven years in the elementary grades; and five years at the high school level. Two teachers—Elloise Marable Callahan and Annie Holloway Holmes— were hired to teach the eighth-grade level students. Callahan and Holmes each had approximately 54 students in their homeroom and taught most of the subjects. Discipline problems were minimal. Students were easy to manage and learning was evident. The eighth grade was an exploratory grade; and it provided a time of transition between the elementary grade and the grade in which actual secondary instruction began. Pupils moving from the elementary level had an opportunity to review thoroughly the fundamental subjects and adjust themselves to high school work.[dlii] Five years earlier, however, in June 1940 the School Board had adopted a resolution to install the eighth grade in schools the of Kenbridge, Lochleven, and Victoria to begin in the fall. The eighth grade—part of the grammar school—had no effect the number of units necessary in order for a pupil to graduate from the high schools. The subjects included English, civics, social hygiene, arithmetic, spelling, and history.[dliii]

The core of activities at Lunenburg included boys' and girls' clubs, a junior and senior league, a glee club or chorus, and athletics. The school had an activity period in the daily schedule which offered a splendid opportunity to guide the pupils in choosing their proper vocations. By this time, the training school was a center of cultural life for the Negro population in the county.[dliv]

In August 1945, the School Board approved the purchase of an outdoor fountain for the school at the approximate cost of ninety dollars, provided the school would pay two-thirds of the cost.[dlv] Unlike the rural schools—where water was secured for drinking from a nearby spring or neighbor's well—children in the towns had the "luxury" (if you can call it that) of a water fountain in their school. Many students remember when they tried to get a quick sip of water on those hot, humid school days and there was only a trickle of water from the fountain and sometimes it didn't work at all. This 1945 water fountain still stands proudly at the former Lunenburg High site. Years later, indoor fountains were installed when water lines from the town of Victoria were connected to Lunenburg High and Lunenburg Elementary.

Lunenburg had organized a guidance committee by the fall of 1946. This committee assisted pupils in solving problems, making adjustments, choosing a vocation and provided individual counseling. Most of the guidance was in the form of group assistance because of the lack of time and space. Each pupil was assigned a teacher of the student's choice for individual guidance. The guidance organization was characterized by teachers who were interested in the pupils, adequate records, a good filing system, occupational information on each pupil's interest, and a follow-up study of the graduates. Three years later, the school's guidance committee had begun to hold its regular meetings in the patron's home to interpret the schools' program. The daily schedule had a fifteen-minute period devoted to home room guidance; and the principal and assistant principal had one hour each daily to counsel pupils with individual problems. A full time guidance counselor would be needed to make the program adequate.

In 1947, the State Evaluation Committee (SEC) conducted an audited of the school site. It found that the existing building which housed the Lunenburg Training School plant was not suited to the development of a comprehensive high school program. The site needed an increase of at least fifteen acres. The committee recommended the erection of a new high school plant on the site of the Lunenburg Training School. The population and enrollment trends indicated that the building should be planned to house five hundred and fifty Negro high school pupils.

As a result of the SEC recommendations, the School Board erected and equipped a modern agriculture shop in 1948; and to build two new brick facilities on the site with the addition of five acres of land. These schools were Lunenburg High (1951); and the Lunenburg Elementary (1954).[dlvi]

Many continued to refer to the new secondary facility as the 'training' school although the school's name changed to Lunenburg High School. In fact, the three African American seniors—Bessie M. Callahan, Bobbie A. Crane, and John R. Croslin—were identified in the Victoria High School yearbook, *The Panther*, as transfers from Lunenburg Training School in 1965.

Unfortunately, the new school construction was not sufficient for the increase enrollment, and the frame buildings on the site continued to be used for sixteen more years. These frame buildings had electricity, but still had no running water, indoor plumbing, and air-conditioning.

In February 1952, a fire destroyed the school's frame kitchen. Due to a lack of water connection to the town, the fire truck had to pump water from a creek, as it only had a capacity of 250 gallons. The Kenbridge and South Hill fire departments responded to the scene, and the three companies concentrated on the two other wooden buildings where classrooms were located. The estimated loss was about eight thousand dollars. The building was not replaced with only three months remaining in the school year.[dlvii] Cora Berkley had been the manager of the school's kitchen for many years, and Irene Glasgow (Young) provided assistance. Plans were already underway to include a new cafeteria when the elementary school—Lunenburg Elementary—was constructed across the street from Lunenburg High.

In fall 1952, Charles S. Marshall was appointed assistant principal. Oscar Wood served as assistant principal in 1953, 1956, 1957, and 1958. Charles Matthew Jones was appointed assistant principal in 1954 and 1955. Principal Evans retired in 1955; and William Waddell Craighead, agricultural teacher at Lunenburg since of 1941, succeeded Evans in the fall of 1955. There were thirty-six teachers, two custodians, three cafeteria workers, eighteen bus drivers, and a large working Parent-Teacher Association.[dlviii]

In spring 1956, funds were no longer made available to the School Board to support the 'Jeanes' supervisory program. Clara A. Morse returned to the classroom as an English and dramatics teacher in the fall.[dlix]

In fall 1959, Annie H. Holmes was appointed the assistant principal; and in next year, she was assigned as guidance counselor at the school. She was expected to fulfill her responsibilities in this new position in addition to the job of assistant principal and history teacher.[dlx]

The school's first student handbook was printed in 1960. The members of the committee were Pauline Maddux Drummond, proofreader; Lillian Holloway, typist; James Allen Smith, Jr. and Galvin L. Jenkins, resource persons. The handbook included a historical sketch of school and other important information for the students.[dlxi] The committee members concluded the historical sketch with this statement, "Much had been done in those days of uncertainty, strife, and confusion with the greatest task of school desegregation which lay ahead."[dlxii] One may ask, "Why this statement?" Perhaps these educators were keenly aware of the changes being made in public education as a result of the landmark decision of United States Supreme Court in the *Brown* case or maybe, they were trying to find a reasonable explanation of the School Board's reaction or inaction to this ruling.

The teachers put their best effort forward to educate the children in spite of the conditions, and they demonstrated a high spirit and pride in their school. A new school song had replaced "Hike Along Lunenburg." The song, simply named "Alma Mater," was composed by—Annie Holloway Holmes, Pauline Maddux Drummond, Pearl Hines Lynch, Ruth W. Duke. When asked about the purpose for composing a new school song, Holmes replied, "We wanted a song to reflect the academic culture of our school and the pride we had as educators teaching the students at our Alma Mater—Lunenburg High School."[dlxiii]

Alma Mater
(Tune: O Solo Mío)
Hail Thee Fair Lunenburg, Our Dear Alma Mater
Our Praise we give to Thee, For all Thy loyalty.
Thy teaching we shall heed, and our watchword service be;
May we forever give Thy name the honor.
Refrain:
We'll always honor Thee, Tho far away
We'll always hail Thee, both night and day,
We'll work, We'll fight to win
When duty calls us, we shall obey.
Though years may come and go, and we wander far from Thee;
We'll hold Thy Banner high, of colors white and blue

We'll stand for purity, and we'll strive to swell Thy fame,
We'll e'er be true and praise Thy name forever.

This song was performed at nearly every formal occasion, and especially, during the exciting homecoming games with rival football teams notably—Luther H. Foster High School (Nottoway County); James Solomon Russell High School (Brunswick County) in Lawrenceville, Virginia; West End High School and East End High School (Mecklenburg County).

Craighead ended his tenure as the principal at Lunenburg High in June of 1961.

By the fall, Galvin Lewis Jenkins had been appointed principal of Lunenburg High School. Prior to Jenkins' appointment, he had been an agriculture and vocational instructor for eleven years at the school. Carl

Galvin L. Jenkins

Hardy Jones was appointed the assistant principal; and in addition to his administrative assignment, Jones would later be appointed a guidance counselor.

In spring 1962, all small schools for Negroes had closed; and this created overcrowded conditions at Lunenburg High, Lunenburg Elementary, and Kenbridge Graded.

The students at Lunenburg High participated in new extra-curricular activities as the school's programs progressed. A 1962 article in *The Kenbridge-Victoria Dispatch* stated, "For the first time in the history of Lunenburg High School, a corps of majorettes was organized. Members of the group were Mamie King, Elmertis Tisdale, Virginia Bagley, Joyce Winkler, Theresa Young, Rosa Hawthorne, and Mary Douglas with Carolyn Thomas as head majorette. This group made its first appearance on November 1, 1962 at the Homecoming game where they performed during half time. Their performance was lauded by everyone. The majorettes were dressed in uniforms of white felt trimmed in gold made by the Home Economics Department. Staff directors were B. L. Hamilton, Ella L. Fowlkes, and R. D. McKenzie. The organization of the majorette corps was the first step in plans for starting a band at the school.[dlxiv]

The creation of the majorette's corps and band helped to generate community spirit, increase school pride, and provide an opportunity for students to participate in non-academic activities. The "Blue Devil" mascot and school colors of white and royal blue have never been retired. They continue to be used by Lunenburg Middle School to this day.

By fall 1963, Annie H. Holmes was appointed as the guidance counselor at Lunenburg High School. After seventeen years—following the recommendation in 1947 for a guidance counselor at the school—the students now had access to full-time school guidance services.

A Continuing Education Program was also offered at the schools—Lunenburg High and Lunenburg Elementary—to all persons of Lunenburg County. The purpose of this was to enrich the adult offerings at the school; to improve the educational level of adults and dropouts who had many problems of adjusting to the fast-moving activities; to help adults learn how to make the most of what they have; to use their own abilities and resources; to raise moral, physical, and cultural standards; and to help adults become better citizens. Courses were offered in foreign language, English, mathematics, furniture making, bricklaying, typing, shorthand, bookkeeping, office machines, small gasoline motors, welding, electricity, dressmaking, first aid, health and home nursing, band, piano, art, reading, writing, arithmetic, spelling, and social science.

Members of the school community felt strongly about adult education. This belief was supported by a quote in a public notice that read, "We think that our school should have a Program of Continuing Education as an integral part of the educational activities of our school. We believe strongly in education for children and youth, but we think that H. G. Wells was right when he said, 'It is not education for children that can save the world from destruction. It is the education of adults.'"[dlxv]

On October 17, 1963, the School Board, through Superintendent Fears, requested permission from the County Board of Supervisors to borrow $400,000 for permanent school construction to expand the school at the Lunenburg High School site. The Mottley Construction Company of Farmville, Virginia, contracted the project at the high school and expansion of the elementary school for $476,000. The request was tabled by the Board of Supervisors until a future meeting, to give the members a chance to think it over. Over the years, there had been talk of new construction, renovations and modernization of the schools. Three bond issues for school improvements had been voted down by the citizens of the county.[dlxvi]

The frame buildings on Lunenburg's campus were seen by the county officials during an annual school tour prior to the annual budget session in December of 1963. The group included members of the Board of Supervisors; School Board members; Superintendent Fears; the Honorable R. Macklin Smith, member of the House of Delegates; W. R. Moore, Clerk of Court; and Sam H. Allen, Commonwealth Attorney. Some members of the group had seen the fairly new brick buildings in the front, but had never taken time to observe the frame buildings in the rear. What they saw was hard to believe still existed in Lunenburg County! There were classrooms with potbelly stoves, large cracks around the doors and windows and small ones in the floors. One supervisor said, "I didn't realize the need was as great as it is."[dlxvii] These building continued to be used as classrooms until schools desegregated in 1969.

On March 10, 1964, the voters of Lunenburg County passed the School Bond. Superintendent Fears hoped that all work at the Lunenburg High School would be completed by the fall of 1965. Additional space was added to the existing building including an auditorium-gymnasium, library, home economics and commercial departments, shop, laboratory and six classrooms.[dlxviii]

In May, members of the class of 1966 were the first to conduct their commencement exercise in the new gymtorium.[dlxix] Basketball games and other school-related activities were held at the Peoples Community Center (now a modern facility) located at the corner of Tidewater Avenue and West Seventh Street in Victoria, Virginia.

From the halls of the Lunenburg High School and Lunenburg Training School have come persons from all walks of life and professions—educators, civic and community leaders, judges, ministers, professors, attorneys, business-owners, professional athletes, architects, authors, doctors, and other prominent citizens. This school is still beloved by many that graced its hallway!

In 1969, the name of Lunenburg High changed to Lunenburg Junior High as part of the school desegregation plan. The school housed all county students in grades eight and nine. Donald Barry Carnes was the first white administrator assigned to the school in the fall of 1969. Carnes said, "I came to Lunenburg County in 1966 when Central Senior High School opened. I taught science [grades eight and nine], and coached football, girls' basketball, and track. I was approached by the Superintendent about a transfer to the Lunenburg Junior High School—formally the all-black county high school. I accepted the position of an assistant principal and taught physical education to the boys, and continued to coach football, girls' basketball, and track at Central High School."[dlxx]

Galvin L. Jenkins continued his leadership as the principal at the junior high school. After twenty years, he retired in June of 1980. Mildred Jenkins said, "Every now and then I get tears in eyes as I view the poor condition of our beloved school from across the street—the place where my husband, Galvin L. Jenkins, served as principal for many years."[dlxxi]

In subsequent years, the middle school concept was implemented, and the name of the Lunenburg Junior High School changed to the Lunenburg Middle School—housing students in grades six through eight. The Lunenburg High School building still stands, but is no longer under the School Board's control.

Victoria High School

The education of its children was one of the first and chief concerns of the town leaders and school patrons in Victoria, Virginia. Pulley wrote, "We find them—founding fathers—requesting the Circuit Court to call an election on March 21, 1911, for the purpose of approving the issuance of bonds for a high school building. The election was called and the bond issue approved. A brick building was promptly erected and was ready for occupancy when the school term opened in the fall of 1912." The Victoria High School had two chimneys with a copula centered on top of the building. The school opened with a principal and four teachers. The high school principal had of the oversight of the entire school including the grammar school program. Soon thereafter, the first cafeteria was opened in the basement of the school.[dlxxii]

Victoria High School had its first graduating class in 1913. The entire class consisted of two Waddill brothers; and members of the second graduating class of 1915 were Marian Flippo and Meredith Fowlkes. The classes grew larger, and in 1922, a second large brick building was constructed on Lee Avenue adjacent to the earlier one to provide space for the high school grades. It featured a large study hall in the center surrounded by eight classrooms, an auditorium and stage on the lower floor that could double as a gymnasium because of the wooden floor. The first building completed in 1912 also housed the grade school children. In later years, the roof of this building was remodeled and cupola removed.

On September 11, 1924, *The Lunenburg Call*'s lead story was "Victoria School Open Today with Competent Staff of Tutors on Hand." J. M. Tignor was principal; and Leigh C. Whaley, the assistant principal. Tignor expected a record number of students to enroll. Athletics and instrumental music would be featured during the school year. There were seventeen teachers— three high school, and fourteen in the lower grades.[dlxxiii]

A school song was composed and for Victoria High, and the panther was its mascot.

"The Panther FIGHT Song"
I'm Panther born and Panther bred
and when I die I'll be Panther dead
So Rah, Rah for Panthers…Panthers

> *Rah, Rah for Panthers, Panthers...*
> *Rah, Rah for Panthers*
> *Rah, Rah, Rah!*

There were two Negro custodians at the school from the 1920s through early 1940s. One was named "Shorty" and the other called "Buster." No last names were listed for these gentlemen. However, a photo of the pair is archived at the former school by the Victoria High School Preservation Foundation, Inc.^{dlxxiv}

In 1928, the high school was remodeled. Changes were made to the exterior of the building. Two more classrooms were added and the floor plan was reconfigured to allow for a library and the principal's office in the center of what had been the large central study hall. The auditorium floor was replaced with concrete, sloping toward the stage for better viewing of performances.

The first annual Health Parade at the school was held in May 1929. The children had been checked to determine if their eyesight, hearing, teeth, weight and height were up to the standards. The "five-point" state banner was given to Victoria High for the most improved children in the county schools that year.^{dlxxv}

In the early 1930s—during the Depression years—C. J. Abbitt and J. H. Abbitt sold soup, hot dogs, and few other items to the children at lunch in the back of the auditorium. Richard Lee Kirby spoke of his elementary school days in the first school building. Kirby said, "The cafeteria was located in the basement of the school and it was basically a 'bread and soup' line. There wasn't a lot of food served back then."^{dlxxvi}

In 1935, the agricultural and home economics programs were made available as part of President Roosevelt's "New Deal." The building for these classes was located just down the hill from the high school.

In early January 1943, the Pleasant Grove School and all of its contents were destroyed by fire. The children were transported to the Victoria School, and classes were conducted in the in the auditorium for a short period of time. However, arrangements were made to have them transition into classrooms where their teachers—Elizabeth Hart (grades one to three); and Iva Perkins (grades four through seven) could continue to teach—just as it had been at their former school.^{dlxxvii}

Willie Robertson was employed as the janitor of the school with a pay of forty-five dollars per month in 1943.^{dlxxviii} Richard L. Kirby spoke kindly of Arthur James Pennington who had replaced Robertson. Kirby said, "Pennington became the janitor at Victoria High when I was a teacher at the school in the mid-1940s; and he was there for many years even into the 1950s."[dlxxix]

In fall 1965, African American students enrolled in the Victoria High School for the first time in the school's history. They were Bobbie A. Crane, John R. Croslin, and Bessie Mae Callahan—all seniors; and Marcia A. Slacum—an eighth grader.[dlxxx] Easter S. Crowder said, "I fully aware that some black students were going to enroll in the white schools; and I wasn't surprised when a few of them came to Victoria."[dlxxxi]

Marcia Slacum (Greene) of Meherrin, Virginia had left the Lunenburg Elementary School to enroll in Victoria High in 1965. When the new consolidated Central High School opened in the fall of 1966—following the closure of Victoria High—Marcia was among the 110 black students who enrolled there. She was also a member of the senior class when schools desegregated in the fall of 1969.

Joanna Jackson Bell spoke candidly of Marcia's experience as the only black student in the eighth grade at the Victoria High School. Bell said, "Marcia, my niece, resided in our home, and began her primary education at the Saint Matthews Lutheran Parochial School in Meherrin, Virginia. Later, she enrolled in Lunenburg Elementary School, where she remained until the end of seventh grade. The next year fall—in 1965—Marcia wanted attend the all-white school in Victoria and we supported her decision. She had talked with her grandmother, Rahab Doswell Jackson, about riding the bus and attending the new school. There were no reports of trouble at school, but riding the school bus with only white children was difficult. It was not pleasant for Marcia to sit on the seat segregated from the other children! There were stares and inappropriate words said to Marcia from the other children although some of them were her neighbors and they knew her. In spite of the difficult circumstances, Marcia continued to ride the bus and was never privately transported to the high school.[dlxxxii]

N. Harvey Jeter shared his thoughts about the atmosphere at Victoria High School during this period. Jeter said, "In my opinion, the years of free school choice and school desegregation went rather smoothly. My principal handled the situation well, and we didn't seem to have any problems with the new students. I specifically remember Marcia Slacum as an outstanding student."[dlxxxiii]

Victoria's later two principals—William R. Buttons, Jr., and James W. Thweatt—inspired the school educationally and athletically during their terms. In the second semester of 1966, Thweatt became the principal of Central High School. Robert Currie Elkins became the last principal of Victoria High, serving the remainder of the school year. Among the last faculty and staff members in the spring of 1966 were Helen M. Barnes, Douglas O. Bryant, John W. Daugherty, Evelyn H. Glenn, John H. Griffith, Ella S. Harrell, Charlie J. Hudson, Mary B. Jefferson, Nathaniel H. Jeter, Ola E. Jones, Roger K. Maier, Virginia N. McLaughlin, Thomas A. Palmore, Roberta C. Rickers, Mildred F. Shaw, Bernard W. Shinault, Celia S. Snead, Esther L. Wellons, Arline W. Winn, and Shirley Underwood (Hagg).[dlxxxiv]

The memory of Victoria High School will always remain in the heart of every graduate. Superintendent Macon F. Fears handed sixty-nine diplomas to members of the senior class at the commencement exercises. John Croslin was the first and only African American to graduate from Victoria High School. In spring 1966, Victoria High School closed its doors for the last time. Neither Bessie M. Callahan nor Bobbie A. Crane marched with their classmates. Fortunately, Callahan returned to Lunenburg High School in summer of 1966 and graduated; and Crane enrolled at Central High School in the fall of 1966 and completed his high school work there in 1967.

In September of 1966, under the leadership of Superintendent Macon Fears, the school building became part of the Victoria Elementary School complex—housing students in grades four through seven.

The Victoria High School principals were C. E. Koonz, W. G. Coleman, George Bowman, Hal J. Meredith, J. M. Tignor, Leigh C. Whaley, Davis Y. Paschall, H. L. "Butch" Blanton, William R. Button, Jr., James W. Thweatt, and Robert C. Elkins. Anne C. Hamlett and Stephen S. Israel wrote, "Beloved Victoria High School stands tall today safeguarding its collection of school and area memorabilia. The Victoria High School many years of service will not be forgotten." In an effort to preserve these memories, the Victoria High School Alumni Association has met annually since the spring 1982 to provide fellowship for former schoolmates and teachers at a school reunion dinner-dance. The former school has been rejuvenated into a public building by the Victoria High School Preservation Foundation Incorporation, with the Harry A. Wellons Auditorium providing a meeting place for the community. The original 1912 high school structure—that had been used for storage for several years—was eventually dismantled.[dlxxxv]

OTHER SCHOOL BUILDINGS

Kenbridge High School Gymnasium

Constructed in 1955, the gymnasium was part of Kenbridge High School's education program. It still stands on Fifth Avenue next door to the Kenbridge Community Center (formally Kenbridge High School). The sight of the gymnasium continues to bring back wonderful memories for many of the teachers, parents, and students who walked through its doors when various sport activities and other programs were held there. The building has been upgraded in recent years to include a paved parking lot. The present-day facility and grounds continues to be used as a recreation area—a place where citizens can enjoy community and cultural activities.

Lunenburg County Board of Education

In the spring of 1935, the Marshalltown School building was moved at the request of the School Board to 1615 Eighth Street in Victoria, Virginia. The building was converted into a combination vocational and agricultural building. The labor to move the building was supplied by the Federal Emergency Relief Administration, and the cost of new materials was paid out of the funds supplied by this agency and the State Agricultural and Home Economics Departments.[dlxxxvi]

This former School Board of Education office is presently the location of the Lunenberg County Alternative School Center.

The first School Board Central Office was located on Main Street in Victoria, Virginia. By the fall of 1967, the office was relocated to occupy the vocational and agriculture building following the closing of Victoria High School. The building was refurbished to include a board room, reception area, and office space for the staff. Offices were available for the assistant superintendent, director of instruction, clerk, coordinator of federal programs, and a private entrance to the superintendent's office. The textbook and instructional materials room was on the lower level of the building; and space was also available for the storage of janitorial; and other school materials and maintenance supplies.[dlxxxvii] Later, the Lunenburg Board of Education relocated to its present location at 1009 Main Street in Kenbridge, Virginia.

Lunenburg County School Board Annex

The School Board Annex is located at 1703 Marshall Street in Victoria, Virginia. This cinderblock building was originally a part of the Victoria High School site located northeast of the athletic field. The building served as the site of the Community Canning Center supported by the School Board beginning in the 1940s. There were four canneries in the county, one at each high school: Lochleven, Victoria, Kenbridge, and Lunenburg Training School. Later, a canning center operated at the West End Elementary School. Neale wrote, "One day a week the canning went toward school lunches."[dlxxxviii]

The center was frequently used by the citizens. L. E. Kent, agricultural teacher at the Victoria High School, who was in charge of the canning program said, "It [the cannery] has been much widely accepted by the public than he had anticipated for the first year." The School Board had approved the purchase of the necessary cans for preserving any food products donated to the school cafeteria, and anyone having a surplus for this purpose would be provided the necessary cans free of charge.[dlxxxix]

In June 1959, the School Board announced that the Community Canning Center located at the schools of West End, Kenbridge, and Lunenburg High would continue to operate. Some centers still operated into the 1960s. But the school canneries at Lochleven and Victoria would close because of the decrease in the number of products processed, the continued increase in the cost of operation, and the cost of repairing and replacing equipment.[dxc]

In later years, the School Board converted the cannery at Victoria into an annex office building for administrative and office staff. The special education director, school psychologist, supervisor of instruction, and the clerical staff were located there. The annex also served as a place for administrative staff meetings, staff training and workshops, and other school-related activities. The annex building closed when school employees were relocated to the former School Board Office on Eight Street in Victoria.

Home Economics Cottage at Lunenburg Training/ Lunenburg High School

In 1931, K. P. Evans and the school league raised money to build a five-room home economics cottage at Lunenburg Training School. Two rooms were used as living space for Evans and his wife. This building was equipped by the citizens with a contribution of $300 from the county toward the construction of the cottage.

Betty D. Jones was employed as the home economics teacher during the school term of 1944-1945. In fall 1945, the classes were taught by Agnes Jackson. In the early 1950s, Elizabeth Cain Jones was appointed home economics teacher, and classes conducted in the cottage.[dxci] In the late 1960s, the home economics cottage was sold and relocated. It has been remodeled into a private residence located on K-V Road in Victoria, Virginia.[dxcii]

Cannery at Lunenburg Training School

In January of 1944, a letter was submitted to the School Board by K. P. Evans, principal, stating that the patrons of the Lunenburg Training School wanted a Community Canning Center to be operated at their school. The Board agreed if it could be done with federal aid.[dxciii] The funding was approved and cinderblock building was constructed at the school site to begin operation in 1945. This center was described by Superintendent Fears as the 'most modern of its kind.'

Mary Locust Baker recalled going with her mother to the cannery located at Lunenburg. Baker said, "We had to get the food ready before taking it to the canning center. We prepared food such as beef, pork, and sweet potatoes that needed to be canned. When we entered the center, there was a long table to place the meat or vegetables so that it could be cut into smaller pieces for processing. As a young child, I was fascinated—to watch up close—how the machines processed the food, seal the can, and stamp the name of the contents on the outside."[dxciv] Cora Berkley supervised the cannery operation for many years. Elizabeth Cain Jones, home economics teacher, used her knowledge of food preparation to assist patrons with the processing and preservation of vegetables, meats, and fruit such as apples, which were often used to make applesauce. Daisy C. Jones' eyes brightened when she spoke of her experiences at the Community Canning Center located on Lunenburg's campus. Jones said, "I remember when the cannery was in operation, and the people—both black and white—brought fresh food to be canned for the winter. The equipment was electrical and automated. It was amazing to watch how the food traveled travel along the processing path, and there were a lot of peelings left, too!"[dxcv]

All community canning centers sponsored by the School Board had closed by the late 1960s. In fall 1969, the cannery at Lunenburg High was converted into a classroom; and later used for the masonry classes when Lunenburg became a junior high school. This building, in extremely poor condition, will probably be dismantled.

CHAPTER 15
IN THEIR OWN WORDS

This section contains personal reflections and recollections.

Bessie Reese Callahan spoke of her elementary school days. Callahan said, "I started first grade at the two-room Unity School in 1939. We had grades one through four on one side of the building, and the fifth through seventh grade on the other side. A large wooden partition in the center of the building was opened when we needed an auditorium. The school had ten large windows on the front of the building for natural light, but there were no windows in the rear or on the sides. Two front doors allowed students to go directly to their grade level. The teachers were Myrtle Cralle Smith, Mary Bernice Cralle Jeffreys, and one male teacher—William McFarland 'Mack' Jennings. We attended school from September to May. I thought of May Day as our special day because we participated in the various outdoor activities. It was always a thrill to win the baseball game when we played the team from Camp School!"[dxcvi]

L. Stanley Lambert had attended segregated schools in Lunenburg County from the first to eleventh grade. He had transferred from Lunenburg High to Kenbridge High in the fall of 1965. Lambert wrote, "I enrolled in Kenbridge High School as a college-bound student. My reasons were—better facilities and challenging academic courses in Latin and chemistry were offered there. My father was concerned with my decision to leave Lunenburg High, but my mother wanted me to go to the all-white school. I rode the school bus, but was transported privately from time to time.

This was my senior year and I only needed two courses to graduate—English was required, but I also took business, chemistry and Latin. I experienced little support from my Latin teacher—in a course that was made more difficult than it actually was. My other teachers were fine and treated me like any other student. When I asked questions, they answered them and assisted me with other classroom problems. I struggled with chemistry, but my teacher eagerly assisted me whenever I asked. After that class, I did not want to see chemistry again, but minored in the subject at college.

As I recall, the most unfortunate issues I faced were the fact that James Quinn and I—as athletes—were not allowed to play on the school's athletic team; and going to lunch with my classmates, but often eating alone. However, there was a classmate who made it his business to sit and talk with me from time to time. Other white male students who did not agree with our attending school with them and they let their disagreement be known with negative remarks. That made the environment tense at times, but bearable whenever another student or teacher intervened. Revere, our principal, kept a close eye on situations to ensure that we would not have problems at school and was aware of those instances. He would often tell me who the troublemakers were and ask me not to become involved in the nonsense. Revere reminded me that he disciplined equally, and would not hesitate to do what he had to do. The highlights that year were graduating from Kenbridge High and being accepted to college. And yes, I attended the senior prom! Unfortunately, the high school closed at the end of the school year."

Lambert received an undergraduate degree in biology from Virginia Commonwealth University in Richmond, Virginia; completed some graduate work in pharmacology; and entered a PhD program in Environmental Engineering.[dxcvii]

Edward A. Almand spoke of his first grade year at the Dundas Graded School. Almand said, "In 1941, there were four students in my class with two or three grades taught in the same classroom. My family and I lived about a mile from school in the small community of Dundas. We would walk to school on the paved road or scamper down the tracks of the Virginia Railroad line located near the school. There was a potbelly stove in the school that was used to heat the building. It almost always burned coal. Coal was easy to get in those days because of the railroad line through Dundas. On most days, my lunch consisted of a homemade biscuit that my mother had made and a baked sweet potato from the garden on our farm." Almand chuckled when he talked about the games some of the students played during recess time. He continued, "There wasn't a lot of entertainment at school in those days so we created our own games for fun. The 'dog and fox' game was similar to hide-and-seek—one of us would pretend to be a dog trying to catch the foxes. After allowing time for the fox to hide—usually in a nearby tree or behind the school—the dog would run all over the schoolyard trying desperately to catch all the foxes. Recess was the best time of the day—except for lunchtime, of course. Iva Perkins became my teacher when she transferred from the Pleasant Grove School to Dundas. She was a good teacher and strong disciplinarian."[dxcviii]

Mildred H. Jenkins was employed by the Lunenburg County School Board when she began her teaching career in elementary education in September 1952. Jenkins experienced firsthand the poor condition of the frame building in which she was assigned. Jenkins said, "I was so excited about my first day at school because I would get an opportunity to shape young minds, and provide relief for two other first grade teachers—Bernice Cralle Jeffreys and Ruby Ragsdale—who had 120 pupils on their rosters. I still remember the day Clara A. Morse, our supervisor, accompanied forty little eager pupils to my class located just up the hill from the new brick high school. In my building, there were five rooms with tall windows, and a large folding wooden partition between two classrooms that could be opened for assemblies or other activities. High school classes were held in the other two rooms. The teachers were Carl H. Jones and Rudolph V. Doswell. Coal was stored in the smaller room. Coal was often used in the potbelly stove to heat the building. There was privy near the building; and an outdoor water fountain that rarely worked. Water fountains were installed in the new building. My first teaching assignment in a frame building was a culture shock! I had moved from a school district—Southampton County—with modern brick schools for Negroes. In 1954, the new brick elementary school was constructed and I was assigned there."[dxcix]

Shirley Underwood Haag talked about her experience when the free school choice was implemented in the county. Haag said, "In 1939, I moved to Lunenburg County when I married Ralph Underwood. On July 1, 1962, I was employed as the secretary for the principal at Victoria High School;

and my husband supervised the school maintenance program and made repairs to many of the rural one-, and two-room schoolhouses and other school buildings.

In fall 1965 the first African American students enrolled at the school. I didn't hear of any incidences or problems with the students. The principal talked with us about the school integration issue, and said that we—as members of the Victoria High School faculty and staff—should respond in a positive manner. In my opinion, our principal should be given much credit for the way he handled this situation. Victoria High School closed in the spring of 1966; and I was assigned as the principal's secretary at Central High School in the fall. I retired on June 28, 1987 after twenty-five years of service."dc

Margaret Cushwa Cocks was a former English teacher and retired school librarian. Cocks provided a vivid description and insight into the field of education during her tenure as an educator. Cocks said, "I had taught two years in Powhatan County, Virginia prior to coming to Lunenburg. I was hired by Powhatan County School Board to take the place of a young woman who was planning to marry a lawyer. Of course, young ladies were not hired to teach if they were married, and at the time I was unmarried. I was contacted by a school official who asked two questions before giving me my first job: 'Do you ride in the rumble seat of the car?' and 'Do you smoke?' Back then, if you were unmarried, rode in a rumble seat and smoked cigarettes, you were considered to have a 'loose' lifestyle. I thought they were very unusual questions; however, my answer to both questions was 'no.'"

When Cocks came to Lunenburg County in the late 1930s, she resided in a boarding house on Fifth Avenue in the Kenbridge, Virginia. Superintendent J. T. Waddill, Jr. hired her to teach English at Kenbridge High School, where her classroom was located in the first floor near the cafeteria. The elementary classrooms were located on the lower floor, and high school classes were usually held on the second and third floors. She added, "There was also a cannery located on the school campus. I remember people bringing their produce to be canned there. The food was placed in a large tub, and it had to go through the process of being pasteurized before the canning took place."

"Speaking of school desegregation," Cocks continued, "I remember two African American students in the senior class who came to Kenbridge

High in the fall of 1965. They were Stanley Lambert and James Quinn. Lambert was assigned to my class because he was in the college-bound group. I remember Stanley as an excellent student who could have been the valedictorian of any senior class. Of course, I knew of James Quinn, but he was not assigned to any of my classes. When these students enrolled at Kenbridge, our principal wanted things to run smoothly and kept everyone on an even keel.

Kenbridge High School closed in the spring of that school year; and by fall 1966, the students in grades eight through twelve were transferred to the new consolidated Central High School. I was assigned there as well. During this time, I became acquainted with African American students and faculty members. I continued to cherish fond memories of students like Marcia Slacum and others; and staff members—Carl H. Jones, guidance counselor; and Chester L. Conyers, assistant principal. There are special thoughts of Joanna J. Bell, who was my counterpart at Lunenburg Junior High School. We—Bell and I—took several educational trips together throughout those years. She made sure that I was notified and invited to travel along and made all the arrangements as well." Cocks retired in 1975.[dci]

William "Bill" Monnie recalled his days as a civil rights worker in Lunenburg County during the summers of 1965 and 1966. Monnie wrote, "When I was in Lunenburg County—Southside Virginia—the primary focus for Hawthorne and I was community organization and voter registration. The 1965 Voting Rights Act energized and empowered the Civil Rights Movement in ways few of us anticipated; and in the space of a few short weeks, hundreds of Negro voters were registered in Lunenburg County, Virginia—where previously very few were able to do so.

Nathaniel Hawthorne, Sr., was my friend, father figure, and hero; and he had a lifelong impact upon the person I became. I can still vividly recall his pursed lips, [jutting] challenging chin, and hearty guffaw as well as his wise counsel. But most profoundly, I remember his loving nature that he first bestowed upon his wife and his children, and then extended to all he touched with his presence. All, except those who opposed him—with them he was a quiet, but fierce fighter.

There was Wayne Ghee. This gentle man would never address me by any name other than 'Mr. Bill 'regardless of my protestations. He took me into his home as his guest—as it turned out—with a high degree of risk to his own personal safety. During 1966 when I lived in his home, he nightly lit the potbelly stove in my bedroom and on weekends served me a breakfast of eggs and ham—ham that was freshly sliced from the leg quarters hanging in his smoke house. I learned later that Wayne was instrumental in protecting me from the Klan when they parked their trucks outside my bedroom window on the first floor of his house. Wayne informed me that he had his shotgun 'trained' on the Klansmen from a second story window whenever they showed up on many nights. He did not share this information with me until I was about to leave his home and return to my family in Massachusetts. He said he did not want me to worry.

Walter Scott Maddux was instrumental in the formation of a group known as the "Lunenburg Brothers." This group sent armed guards to Wayne Ghee's home to protect us when the Klan was actively planning to assassinate Hawthorne, Grogan and myself."[dcii]

Roberta Coldiron Rickers was employed as a fourth grade teacher at the Victoria Elementary School in October of 1962. She transitioned from the Hampton City School District to Lunenburg County. She had received a phone call from Lunenburg's school superintendent to offer her a job because there were more than enough students to open another classroom. Rickers reminisced about her former teaching years. She said, "I remember my first year teaching assignment in a small one-room, frame building located down the hill from the Victoria High School directly across the street from the School Board office on Eighth Street. The building had a wood floor, a small window on each side, and a potbelly stove that was used to keep us warm on those cold days. The students had to walk to the cafeteria located in the school on the hill each day for lunch; and recess was held in an area next to the football field across the street from our classroom.

The next school year, in 1963, I was assigned to teach English at the high school with a caseload of two hundred and eight students. I remember when the first African American students enrolled in Victoria High School in the fall of 1965. One student—Bessie Mae Callahan—was assigned to my class. She was a polite, but very shy student and did not speak openly in class when questions were asked. Back then, students were graded academically according to three factors—one-third on oral presentation; one-third on written assignments and homework; and one-third classroom participation. The school closed in the spring and the students were transferred to Central High. I did not return to teach in the public school in the fall because of health reasons. Later, I inquired about a possible position as a speech and drama teacher at Central, but there was nothing being offered. I accepted the position as a fourth grade teacher at the Kenbridge Day School in the fall of 1966. Now, I had less than one hundred students per day, and I never again returned to the public school."[dciii]

Ellen Hawthorne Wright is the oldest child of Nathaniel Lee Hawthorne's children. Wright and her brother, Nathaniel Lee Hawthorne Jr., spoke candidly about their school experience when they enrolled in elementary department at Kenbridge High School. Wright said, "My father, Nathaniel Lee 'Thomas' Hawthorne, Sr., decided that we would enroll at Kenbridge in the fall of 1965 when freedom of school choice was first started. I was unhappy about having to go to the 'white' school because I didn't know anyone in my class. There are things that stand out in my mind about that year—the fact that I felt very much alone and afraid each and every day; and I hated recess time because no one would play with me, and I often stood crying and alone in hallway next to my classroom. My brother, Nathaniel, saw me once and asked me about it when we got home. I said, 'Nobody wants to play with me at school.' I also did not like lunch time. Eating alone every day was awful. One day a white boy poured vinegar on me. I believe it was an intentional act. My clothes reeked with that strong smelled the rest of the day. Resentment and anger began to build and developed into a hatred for the school.

My experiences attending school at Kenbridge had a strong impact on the type of person that I am today. I am very much an introvert and loner. I tried to get good grades in school because I wanted to prove to the 'white people' that I was not dumb. I always thought that if I was smart, that they would be friends with me. This was not the case. I thought that things would get better, but they did not. There were still problems—I was black and my father was known as Hawthorne—the civil rights man!

As we continued in school, it seemed as if things were getting better with each passing year. When schools fully integrated in fall 1969, we didn't face the same problems as much. Many of the same white students who had expressed displeasure about us attending their school in Kenbridge continued with us to Lunenburg Junior High and then to Central Senior High.

I spent a lot of time helping in the main office and in the library when I got to high school. This meant that I did not have to interact much with other students. I felt that I did not fit in with the white kids or the black kids. I now know how important it was for us to do what we did—to put an end to segregation in the school system."

In a crackly voice and with a painful look on her face, Wright continued, "In 1965, we didn't understand why we had to go to the white school. But over the years, we've come to realize—following our dad's instructions—that we helped to open the doors of equal educational opportunities in the schools of Lunenburg County. Don't get us wrong—attending an all-white school was not a walk in the park nor was it a pleasant experience to be made to feel like you don't belong. As youngsters, it was hard to understand why we had to endure so much ridicule from some of the other children at school, and yes, some teachers, too!"

It is difficult for the Hawthorne children to talk about their school days even to this day. Wright concluded, "We felt rejected for being black at a white school and for being the children of Nathaniel L. Hawthorne, Sr. We now understand why our father insisted that we attend the Kenbridge Elementary School, and he supported us when we enrolled." Hawthorne youngest child, Phemie D. Hawthorne, and others were named in the NAACP civil rights case against Lunenburg County Public Schools in August 1968. She was enrolled in third grade at when the case was decided by the Court."[dciv] Wright is a business manager in Student Health Services at Virginia Commonwealth University in Richmond, Virginia.

Zella Reese Gray had attended the Kenbridge Graded School from the first to sixth grade before enrolling at Kenbridge Elementary School in the fall of 1966 during freedom of school choice. She wrote, "Imagine a world of sharing, laughter, friendship and playmates—then imagine a world of staring, silence and isolation because of the color of your skin. I left an environment of inclusion and entered an environment of exclusion. I lost the child I was—friendly, talkative, and outgoing to become scared, self-conscious and defensive. Again, it was all because of the color of my skin! The two white kids at my new school who attempted to talk to me were ridiculed by some classmates.

When Dr. King was killed some of my seventh grade classmates snickered and acted as if it was a happy day. However, I specifically remember my white teacher—with tears in her eyes—explaining the significance of Dr. King's life and death. She expressed dismay at the students' attitude. I remember receiving less than positive reactions and acceptance during my elementary and junior high school years. Surely this would end at the high school, so I thought. I remember when I went to the home economics class at Central High School. Students were often partnered during the class to complete assignments. When a white classmate was asked to name her partner, she replied, 'that nigger.' The word 'nigger' used during those times cut to the core. She said it with such disdain—like nothing else worse could have happened. I don't know whether she knew I heard her or cared that I heard her. I was not bold enough to confront her. Bus rides were no picnic either with the loud negative comments from the other children. I just wanted the ride to be over."[dcv]

Anne C. Hamlett taught U.S. Government and History at Central High School of Lunenburg from 1966 to 1978. Hamlett wrote, "In the 1966-67 school session, when I had returned to the county to become a charter faculty member at Central High School after teaching for a year at Thomas Jefferson High School in Richmond, I had already seen Lunenburg County and its two white high schools come through one transition, perhaps more traumatic in many ways than desegregation because of the intense rivalry between the two schools and the two towns of Victoria and Kenbridge. I taught primarily seniors that year who had come together from the county's two competitive white high schools. Although these students had been forced at the beginning of their senior year to leave the schools that they loved, that transition had been reasonably easy, and I trusted that the transition to full integration could also be made smoothly.

In compliance with court-ordered desegregation, the administrative staff of Lunenburg County Public Schools very wisely called upon the Consultative Resource Center of School Desegregation, created by the Curry School of Education at the University of Virginia, to assist the local system with the transition to full integration. The Resource Center promoted 'sensitivity training' at the local level throughout the state on how to bring people of the two races together. Many school systems in Virginia utilized the research that had been done by the Center to bring about peaceful change. Representatives of the Center made trips from Charlottesville to Lunenburg in the spring of 1969 to hold seminars for principals and two representatives from each of the black and the white schools in the county.

When Federal District Court Judge Robert R. Merhige, Jr., ruled during the second semester of the 1968-1969 school year that 'freedom of choice' was no longer acceptable and that all public school systems must prepare a plan for school desegregation, most people associated with the Lunenburg Public Schools were not surprised. It certainly had been only a matter of time before full integration of schools would come to Lunenburg County, for in 1954, more than a decade earlier, the Supreme Court of the United States had ruled against school segregation in the case of *Brown v. the Board of Education of Topeka, Kansas.*

In a small county like Lunenburg, the lives of members of both races were often intertwined even before the schools desegregated. The idea of people of both races getting along with one another was not foreign to me. In my family, we had friends in the African American community. My father, a Ford automobile dealer in Kenbridge, had African American customers, as well as trusted African American employees. My husband had grown up on Mecklenburg Avenue in Victoria and played with childhood African American friends, his contemporaries who lived in the vicinity of Victoria Roller Mills, his father's place of business on Tidewater Avenue.

During the opening days of faculty meetings that launched the 1969-70 school year, those of us who were in the spring seminars were entrusted with sharing what we had learned in our earlier sessions from representatives of the Center. The emphasis was on understanding cultural differences, overcoming stereotypes, and avoiding what might be interpreted as hurtful language.

Representatives from Lunenburg High School were Annie H. Holmes, guidance counselor, and John Reavis, who taught in the Business Department there. Galvin L. Jenkins, who was serving at that time as principal of Lunenburg High School, was also a member of the group." Hamlett and another white teacher served as representatives from Central High School. Hamlett continued, "I became good friends with both Mrs. Holmes and Mr. Reavis during these meetings. I respected them as very knowledgeable and compassionate individuals who impressed me with their kindness and good humor. Those friendships made in 1969 lasted over the years; well beyond those long-ago meetings. Mrs. Holmes and I embrace when today we occasionally see one another. Mr. Reavis died much too early in life. I visited him in the South Hill hospital when he was so very ill in the intensive care unit there. I mourned the loss of this good man, who had also become friends with my husband during the time that my husband was on the Lunenburg School Board in the 1980s and into the early 1990s. My husband also became good friends with Mrs. Holmes' husband, Mr. James J. Holmes, who served on the Prince Edward County School Board during my husband's tenure on the Lunenburg Board.

I had developed the philosophy during those early years of teaching that students would attempt to live up to the level of the teacher's expectations of them. If students were treated with respect, I felt that they would act in a respectable manner. I held out high expectations in conduct and in academics for all of my students—regardless of race—and generally they conformed to those expectations. As a result, I had no disciplinary problems in my classroom from the onset of full integration. The transition throughout the entire school went extremely well. In retrospect, I believe that I had been more concerned previously about the difficulties that must have been faced by the very small minority of African American students who attended the white schools under 'freedom of choice' during the first three years that I taught in the county than I was about the ability of both races to integrate completely. I have been delighted by the successes of former students from both races who have come through the public school system in Lunenburg County.

Furthermore, I am proud that both students and faculty in Lunenburg made the transition from segregation to integration in a positive manner. After all, we are all humans—regardless of race—and have more in common than any differences that have separated us."[dcvi]

Msonga-Mbele Andre Parvenu recounted his experience as a first grader at the Victoria Elementary School under free school choice in the fall of 1965. Parvenu wrote, "One of my first remembrances in this lifetime is that as a young child, six years of age, attending the Voter Rights March of 1965 from Victoria, Virginia, to the Lunenburg County Courthouse. I had no idea of the magnitude of this event, nor of the eventual impact that it would have on my life. I also remember my Aunt Lorraine and Uncle Charlie Hatchett taking me religiously on Sunday mornings to the Pleasant Oak Baptist Church. My Aunt Lorraine was a dedicated member and served on the Usher Board for a number of years. I recall spending long hours at church on Sundays, sometimes in a hot sweaty suit and sometimes with aching feet from the tight shoes I'd have on; but it was all so very well worth it, just to have an opportunity to internalize at such a young age the old 'Negro Hymns and Spirituals' that would remain with me for many years to come.

While on a fixed retirement income, my aunt managed to save enough money to purchase a brand new set of World Book Encyclopedias, the most recent 1964 edition, with the accompanying Child Craft children's collection. What an enormous investment, $400, which in 1964 must have seemed more like $4,000. She knew exactly what she was doing. Following church service on Sundays, I recall a steady parade of neighbors, friends, and relatives stopping by my aunt's house to read various segments of the encyclopedia to me, explaining what the contents meant—while often exchanging vegetables or fruit preserves in Mason and Ball jars for one of my Aunt's famous lemon meringue or sweet potato pies. They were preparing me for something, a future, which I was not aware of at the time. As the African saying goes, 'It takes a village to raise a child.' In this case, two villages—Victoria and Kenbridge—came together to raise this child at the onset of the school desegregation, and I am eternally grateful.

One day during the summer of 1965, my Aunt took me to the 5 & 10 Cent store in town. I would often see the white customers stare at me, sometimes pointing and whispering, 'That's that lil' colored boy that's 'bout to inna' grate our school system!' At another time, a local photo-journalist caught me by surprise and snapped a picture of me with a bright blinding light flashing in my face. I never found out who that person was or whatever became of that photo. But quite clearly, word was out that I was the little colored boy that would be one of the first 'Negro' students chosen to integrate Victoria Elementary School.

Finally, the fall of 1965 had arrived! My first year at the Victoria Elementary School was not at all an easy one. At the age of 6, I experienced the good, the bad, and the ugly—all at the same time. The majority of the white people lived in very nice houses near the center of town, and for decades the little yellow school bus would make its rounds along a relatively tight and convenient circle. When I was accepted at the school, the school bus was required to take a drastic detour about four or five miles east down the Poor House Road, where some of the black people lived. This took a considerable amount of time and became increasingly problematic during inclement weather—heavy rains, snow, sleet, hail, etc.

As the only black child aboard the bus, I experienced many unpleasant moments during my daily ride to and from school. I attribute much of this to the racist teachings of the parents—not necessarily to the young white students aboard the bus. I also recall having unpleasant experiences on the playground during recess. For those who don't know this, the playground can be a very dangerous place. I would often get dropped hard off of the see-saw and then laughed at. The monkey bars were an absolute 'no play' zone.

Instead of playing games or trying to make friends during lunch time, I would often retreat to the library—just a small room in the main school building—and read the only books available that reminded me of the world closest to what I knew. The only books available at the time were *Little Black Sambo*. Then there was also *Curious George*. I read them over and over several times. But these unpleasant experiences were far outnumbered by the fond memories I had in the classroom. My first grade teacher took a special 'liking' to me. Her name was Louise H. Hardy and she was a very kind lady. I knew such fundamentals as the complete alphabet, addition and multiplication tables, etc. Whenever the rest of the class was 'stumped,' the teacher would always call on me to provide the correct answer. The time that the 'village' had invested in me had proven to be well-spent. I was well ahead of my class, and no one in town would dare claim that Black students were not as smart as whites. No white parent, of any child in that classroom at least, could claim that a black child was inferior in intelligence. I credit this to those who volunteered to tutor me during my early childhood years. Even to this day, I proudly proclaim that, 'I stand on the shoulders of those who have walked before me.'

Indeed, a mind is a terrible thing to waste. That's why it is so critically important for us today to successfully train a child, and in turn, train this nation, to be a more peaceful and harmonious place, with social and economic justice at the forefront. The future is truly in our hands. There may be some difficult days ahead, but I believe that by working together, and by properly educating our youth, we will see it through. We—as a people— shall survive the best and the worst of times. That's my story and I'm sticking to it!"

Parvenu and his family left Lunenburg County sometime after the school year was over, and relocated outside of the State. Presently, he is a city planner for the City of Los Angeles and serves as a state commissioner for the California State Citizen's Redistricting Commission. Parvenu was one of only 14 candidates selected from a pool exceeding 35,000 applications statewide. He concluded, "I attribute all of the little success that I may have to the time and attention I received from my neighbors, family and friends I was blessed to have in my life as a young child growing up in Victoria, Virginia."[dcvii]

Violet Johnson Harris had attended segregated schools from the first to eleventh grade. She said, "I did not want to go to Central High School, but my father told me I had to go to get a better education and of course, I did as I was told. It was my last year in school and I wanted to make it my best. There were about 110 African American students enrolled at the school; and unfortunately, only two of us in the senior class. I attended classes— English, government, and distributive education—in the morning, and worked on a job in the community the rest of the school day. I was only at school for half the day and that made me happy." When asked why this was a happy time for her—a look of sadness appeared on Harris' face. She replied, "The time I was away from school helped me to cope with the verbal harassment I received from some of the white students there. I distinctly remember when two white female classmates attempted to rescue me a time or two. They tried to discourage the students from calling me names and other such things. I felt isolation and alone as I experienced negative words said to and about me. There were times when doors were closed in my face as I was about to enter the classroom. I don't know if it was accidentally or intentional. Some things that I experienced in school are difficult to forget. I had never been aware of racism until I came to Central High School because people in my community knew and respected each other."[dcviii]

Stanley C. Lee is a retired City of Richmond police officer from Chesterfield County, Virginia. Lee wrote, "The school year of 1969-70 was the first year that there would be only one public high school in Lunenburg County. Once again, I found myself being part of an historic event. I was a bit nervous and wondered what this change would bring—coming from the all-black Lunenburg High School and now attending a predominantly white school in my senior year. There were lots of questions—will my teachers be different? Will the black and white students get along in this totally new situation? I later discovered this was an experience I was proud to be a part of. I met new people and made new friends. We got to learn more about each other, our differences and the things in common. We changed things.

The only negative experience I recall is that one of my white teachers could not or would not enunciate the word 'Negro' correctly. I heard her say 'Nigras' many times as she taught with the word 'Negro' clearly printed on the page. I found it difficult to walk into that class and sit for a lesson the whole time. However, the school year of 1969-1970 at Central High School was exciting because we were seniors! I commend all of the students and teachers who were a part of school desegregation. But the graduating class of 1970, the starters of history in a new time for the county, did a remarkable job in working together. We made it through without incident, and with knowledge of a different kind. I am so proud that I was a part of this changing time."[dcix]

Frances Price Wilson wrote, "In the summer prior to attending Lunenburg Junior High school, fear of the unknown caused me great anxiety. Some of the adults in our district were also fearful. Their advice and comments as they tried to prepare us for attending the former all-black Lunenburg High scared us. In contrast, my parents assured me that all would go well and that I should remember to always be respectful to the other students, and especially, the adults in my new school, whether black or white. My mother drove a school bus, so she made sure that I understood the importance of respecting all people. Ironically, it was the other adults—outside of the school—that seemed to have the biggest problem with integration; not the students. I remember coming through the doors of the school and wondering if I would make it through the day—just as the majority of the other students may have been thinking. Meeting and bonding with many wonderful people like Helen Johnson Hendrick helped me realize that we—the students (black and white) were just that kids—going to school and growing up. The wonderful secretaries in the office, Ella L. Fowlkes and Minnie Y. Gordon, were the most loving and caring ladies in the school. These ladies gave many students a sense of peace and belonging during that first pivotal year and in the years after. I look back at those times of uncertainty, and feel thankful for having been part of history and blessed for the many friendships I made thanks to—the integration of Lunenburg County Public Schools. As a result of this relationship, I have proudly spent my entire working career in this school system." In the fall of 1969, all students—grades eight and nine—attended the newly named Lunenburg Junior High School.[dcx]

Howard "Hank" W. Allen spoke of the role that the Consultative Resource Center for School Desegregation played in assisting school divisions to fully integrate public education. Dr. Allen said, "There were twenty-seven centers located throughout the United States to help desegregate our schools, which was started with the funds granted in 1967 to the center at the University of Virginia. Our primary responsibility was to assist certain districts in Virginia, Maryland, West Virginia, and in Washington, D.C. in the process of desegregating their public schools. We began working with small school districts, but could not go into any district unless we were invited, and when we had completed the work, it would not be publicized.

The university did not publicize the Center's work, which was controversial among many white Virginians who were not keen on desegregated schools and who thought black teachers lacked the innate ability to teach white students. Our work focused on workshops during the summer and training sessions in the winter to help black and white teachers come together to try and solve some anticipated problems. We did not work with students—only adults in the school system. The idea was to train the adults to work with each other, and in turn, the adults could work with the students. And that wasn't easy! Some people did not understand what school desegregation really meant—even those who were taking training sessions—a lot of them did not believe in it. They did not want it. They were participating because the superintendent told them they had to be there, so they came to the training sessions. Many of these people turned out to be some of our best supports years later. They saw what we were doing—and knew it had to be done. But it was not long that black students had no or few role models in desegregated schools.

Many white Virginians simply did not accept black teachers educating their children, and generations of black teachers started to disappear from public schools. White teachers had to learn to teach black students, for whom many may have had lower expectations. There were no classes that I took in college that afforded me the opportunity to look inside of people, and understand why people thought the way they did, and how fearful some people are of this process of race relations. It was delicate—very delicate—and we had to be careful. We were careful as much as we could be, but we still had to talk about it. For example, several questions come to mind: *Who will be president of the senior class? Who will be the captains of your teams?* Other very delicate questions were *What about the junior/senior prom? How do you do that? What kind of music would you have?*

Decisions had to be made. There were all kinds of problems to solve—and the issue that caused the greatest problems in the schools, especially in high schools, was student activities. Dr. Allen continued, "In the black and white schools, there were cheering squads, but they were different. When the black students went to the white schools, usually a white person would be selected to direct the squad, and the white person excluded black kids." They had to solve this problem, too. And there were many, many problems that needed to be addressed."[dcxi] Unfortunately, Dr. Allen died just a few months following the interview.

Phillip Gee was among the five African American students who initially enrolled in the elementary department at Kenbridge High School. Gee wrote, "When I began the second grade in 1965, it was the first time I attended the Kenbridge School under the free school choice. I believe there were four other African Americans there at the time. I do not specially recall who the other students were because they were in other grades. Surprisingly, my second grade teacher's name was Mrs. Gee (not related). I recall that she treated me with total respect and do not recall having any issues with other students or staff members. I believe that my grandfather, Robert Millard Gee, worked at the school on the custodial staff of Kenbridge or with the county school system in some capacity. I do recall Mrs. Gee saying—on occasion—that if I were to do something wrong, she'd tell my grandfather.

A larger question might be—'Knowing what I know today, would I have gone to Kenbridge in the second grade or not—or would I have sent my children there?' The answer is clearly a Big Yes! I believe that starting at Kenbridge at such an early age helped me to gain a better understanding and greater appreciation of diversity. The world is faced with many challenges and having a deeper appreciation for the differences in people—racial, socioeconomic, gender, education, etc.—has helped to mature me in life in numerous ways. I always stressed to my children the old saying 'It is not what's on the outside, but what's in the inside.' God created us all uniquely equal."

Gee's educational experience and interaction with his white classmates appear to be better than the treatment received by other African American schoolmates. A possible reason may be that children in upper grades were keenly aware of issues surrounding integration and more willing to express their feelings more openly than younger children.[dcxii]

Claude Swanson Thompson shared memories of his elementary days at the Fort Mitchell School. Born in Fort Mitchell, Virginia, in 1921, Thompson lived on his family's farm just a few miles from the school. Fort Mitchell School was a three-room, frame building. He believes his father may have helped with the school's construction. Thompson said, "I started school in the first grade when I was eight years old and went as far as the sixth grade. I knew all the teachers who taught at the school, and all of my siblings attended the Fort Mitchell School.

Macon Fears, Ruth Townsend, and Nettie Smith were the teachers at the time. Fears resided in Ruth Townsend's boarding house, and they would walk to school together. Fears and Townsend later married. Glenda Wall would fill in on a part-time basis at the end of the school year. Nettie Smith was my first grade teacher, and in later years, Bertie R. Yeatts and Mildred Shaw joined the staff. Shaw lived nearly about two and a half miles from where I grew up, and I remember working on her farm many times. She was a wonderful teacher, but strict. Teachers could spank you with a 'switch' as a form of discipline. They kept order in the school—nothing went on out of the ordinary except a fist fight or two.

One room in the school was used to house the first and second grade; another room for the third to fifth grade; and in the back room, Macon Fears taught children the sixth to eleventh grade. My oldest brother graduated there in the eleventh grade. There was an old shed in the back where we kept our wood, and someone from the community would bring a load of wood on their truck. We had old iron heaters—one in each room—that got so hot at times it would run us out of the room! The heaters were about four feet with a flat top and fat round center. There was an opening where the ashes were taken out. They were called 'potbelly' stoves. When I was about ten years old, I served as the school's fireman. It was Superintendent Crittenden who got me the job of starting the fire in the stoves so it would be warm when the students got to school. I was paid one dollar per month.

We walked to and from school each day because we didn't have any buses when I first started to school, but eventually one of our neighbors purchased a small private bus to run from the Fort Mitchell School to the in Victoria, Virginia.

There weren't a lot of materials in the school, but we had a set of 'Baby Ray' reading books. Our parents had to buy the history, geography, arithmetic, and spelling books from the School Board office in Victoria. The books were ordered and someone from the office would bring them to the school and sell them there. The school term wasn't long. We started in September, and we got out the middle of April. Nearly everybody farmed in the community, and the children had to get out and work on the farm during the planting and harvesting season. In the fall, we didn't start school until the tobacco was ready for the market.

There was no cafeteria in the school. Our lunch consisted of a biscuit and with a piece of meat on it. Sometimes, we didn't carry any lunch at all—we'd just eat when we got back home after school. We had to carry water about one quarter of a mile from a neighbor's well. Each teacher had a bucket in their room, and everyone drank out of the bucket with little paper cups—fingers and all. The cups made from paper folded to hold the water. It worked well. During recess time, our baseball equipment was homemade. We managed to get a ball from somewhere and an old wooden board was used as a bat. Recess was three times a day—ten minutes in the morning—five or ten minutes after lunch; and a short recess—ten or fifteen minutes in the afternoon. In the wintertime, there were wet places around the school and we'd do a lot of skating when the water would freeze into a solid sheet of ice. What a good time we had!"

The school closed in the spring of 1949. Students promoted to the secondary level were transported to the high school in Victoria, Virginia; while the elementary students were assigned to the new West End Elementary School. Thompson concluded, "Mr. Spencer, another neighbor, bought his own bus; and at eighteen years of age, I was allowed to drive the bus part-time to the school in Victoria."[dcxiii]

Marjorie B. Powers shared her memories of teaching in Lunenburg County. Powers moved to Kenbridge, Virginia in February of 1946. She began teaching students in the sixth grade at the Kenbridge High School and remained there for many years until the school closed in the spring of 1966. In the fall, Powers was appointed headmistress of the Kenbridge Day School.

Powers taught sixth graders in the morning, and worked in the office in the afternoon of each day. She was responsible for ordering textbooks and supplies available through the public school system. She said, "The curriculum mirrored the public school—and since I had been in the public school all those years—I just copied what I'd ever done before and it worked well. My one purpose was to see a child learn—that was the highlight of my career—to teach a child how to write, read, and think. And above all of that, I always had devotions and they had to learn some Bible. They couldn't pass sixth grade if they didn't know the books of the Bible, and students learned much scripture.

The students learned to be good citizens, to love each other, serve their country, and do something for mankind. I taught many quotations that would come through life and I enjoyed every minute of it. If I could relive my life, I'd be a teacher again. I always wanted to be one, so teaching was the thrill of my life! I remember we had a small number of children, but every child that I taught I can say was there for a good purpose, and we had small classes and gave a lot of individual attention."

The day school offered activities and programs such as devotion, music, art, school pageant, May Day, field day, and special guests were invited to speak to the students from time to time. The students took field trips, too. When the first seventh grade students graduated, they had been to fourteen different places of interest throughout the state. Powers chuckled when she said, "We didn't have a cafeteria, but we did all right. The Tastee Freeze—local fast-food business—would allow us to order there on Fridays, and students didn't have to bring lunch that day. That was a real treat! Sometime parents would bring hot dogs, and we would have 'hot dog' day. So, we just coped with it and learned that you could do with a lot less and make a little less do.

I think the students got a broad education just like they would have received in the public school. Some of the best students I have taught came out of the Kenbridge Day School—they became lawyers, doctors, and so forth, so I think we gave them a good start. I really enjoyed my ten years at the day school. Over the years, many of my former students have come to visit me. Recently, two students that I taught at Holland High School in 1938—a doctor from Richmond and a Commonwealth attorney from Emporia visited my home in Kenbridge, Virginia."

Powers remained headmistress of the Kenbridge Day School until she retired in 1976 because of her husband's health. This private school closed and merged with the Blackstone Day School that later became the Kenston Forest School in Blackstone, Virginia.[dcxiv]

APPENDIX A

TABLE 1: UNIFORM EXAMINATION
FOR TEACHERS' CERTIFICATES, 1900

SAMPLE EXAMINATION QUESTIONS

CONTENT	WHITE TEACHERS	COLORED TEACHERS
Reading	What are the grammatical pauses?	What is phonetic analysis?
Spelling	What is (a) prefix? (b) A suffix? (c) Give five examples of each.	(a) What is a syllable (b) a trisyllable? (c) How should such a word as indigestible be classified?
Arithmetic	Find the L.C.M. of 2⅝ , 3⁵⁄₁₆ , and 3²⁷⁄₄₀.	Find the L.C.M. of 15, 26, 78 and 90. (b) Find the G.C.D of 144, 264, and 540.
Grammar	What is an adverbial object? Give an example.	(a) What are auxiliary verbs? Name three. (b) Name two verbs that may be used as either independent or auxiliary verbs.
Geography	Define longitude	Define latitude.
American History	Name the European nations that made explorations and planted settlements in North America, and name the regions settled by each.	(a) What were the objects of De Soto's expedition? (b) What regions did he traverse? (c) What became of De Soto?
Civic Government	(a) Who is the highest executive officer of this state? (b) By whom is he elected? (c) For what term?	(a) Name the several forms of government. (b) To which does the United States belong? (c) What is the object of government?
Physiology and Hygiene	Name the bones which make up the trunk.	Describe the spinal column.
Theory and Practice of Teaching	Name three subjects that should be included in a course for the professional training of teachers.	(1) Do you regard teaching as your profession? (2) Should the teacher be expected to make definite plans for each day's work outside of school hours? Give your reasons for the answer.

Source: Virginia School Report, Biennial Report of the Superintendent of Public Instruction of the Commonwealth of Virginia, Richmond, Virginia, 1900, 82-91.

APPENDIX B

TABLE 2: BOOK RENTAL FEE
AND CONSUMMABLE MATERIAL COST, 1957

Book Rental Fee

1st grade	$3.00
2nd grade	3.50
3rd grade	3.75
4th grade	4.00
5th grade	4.00
6th grade	4.25
7th grade	4.50
8th grade	1.25 (per subject except for band, home economics, agriculture and commercial subjects)

Consumable materials and the Weekly Reader cost

1st grade	$1.50
2nd grade	2.00
3rd grade	1.50
4th grade	1.50
5th grade	1.50
6th grade	1.50
7th grade	1.50

Source: The Kenbridge-Victoria Dispatch, August 15, 1957.

APPENDIX C

TABLE 3:

VOTING BY PRECINCT IN LUNENBURG COUNTY, 1952

Precinct	Byrd	Miller
Brown's Store	374	101
Columbian Grove	65	16
Crymes Store	41	3
Dodson's Store	29	13
Knights & Olivers	32	8
Lewiston	113	39
Lochleven	113	39
Meherrin	43	30
Plantersville	63	10
Pleasant Grove	38	27
Plymouth	285	321
Rehoboth	61	17
Totals	**1177**	**600**

Source: The Kenbridge-Victoria Dispatch, July 18, 1952.

APPENDIX D

TABLE 4:

LUNENBURG VOTES BY PRECINCT, 1953

Precinct	Stanley	Dalton
Brown Store	350	86
Columbian Grove	57	7
Crymes Store	33	1
Dodson's Store	31	3
Knights & Oliver	23	2
Lewiston	40	7
Lochleven	115	7
Meherrin	48	18
Plantersville	45	8
Pleasant Grove	38	6
Plymouth	352	182
Rehoboth	43	9
Totals	**1175**	**336**

Source: The Kenbridge-Victoria Dispatch, November 6, 1953.

APPENDIX E

TABLE 5:

LUNENBURG COUNTY PUBLIC SCHOOLS ENROLLMENT, FALL 1969

| | STUDENT ENROLLMENT | | | | | TEACHERS | | |
| | | | | | | *figures do not include principals | | |
School (Grade levels)	White	%	Negro	%	Total	White	Negro	Total
Central Sr. High (10-12)	309	55%	257	45%	566	22	12	34
Lunenburg Jr. High (8-9)	184	39%	292	61%	476	14	14	28
Victoria Elementary (4-7)	263	56%	205	44%	468	12	8	20
Kenbridge Elementary (4-7)	154	34%	303	45%	457	11	8	19
Kenbridge Primary (1-3)	100	28%	262	72%	262	7	8	15
Lunenburg Primary (1-3)	131	45%	157	55%	288	6	8	14
West End Elementary (1-6)	61	46%	72	54%	133	5	2	7
Totals	**1202**	**43.7%**	**1548**	**56.3%**	**2750**	**77 (56%)**	**60 (44%)**	**137**

Source: School Board Minutes, November 7, 1969

APPENDIX F

APPLICATION FOR PLACEMENT OF PUPIL
IN THE
LUNENBURG COUNTY SCHOOLS

1. I, the undersigned parent/or legal guardian, request that the child named
Below be placed in the _____ School of the
Lunenburg County Public School System.

2. Full Name of Child: _____
         FIRST   MIDDLE   LAST

3. Address: _____

4. Will your child be a bus pupil? _____

5. Name of school attended in 1964-65 term: _____

6. Grade of session 1965-66: _____

7. Sex: _____

8. Birthdate: _____
         Month   Day   Year

9. Place of Birth: _____

10. My relationship to the above named pupil is _____.

11. Date _____ Signed: _____
                                   Parent or Guardian

                         Address: _____

IMPORTANT-If you wish to enroll your child in the first, second, eighth, or twelfth
      grade for the session 1965-66, you must fill out the above application.

Source: School Board Minutes, August 9, 1965.

APPENDIX G

SCHOOL ATTENDANCE AREAS
LUNENBURG COUNTY, VIRGINIA 1969-1970

ZONE A – All students in grades 1 through 6 would attend West End Elementary Schools; All 7th grade students would attend Victoria Elementary School.

ZONE B – All students in grades 1-3 would attend Lunenburg Primary School (formally Lunenburg Elementary School). All students in grades 4-7 would attend Victoria Elementary School.

ZONE C – All students in grades 1-3 would attend the Kenbridge Primary School (formally Kenbridge Graded School). All students in grades 4-7 would attend Kenbridge Elementary School.

ZONE A, B, C – All students in grades 8 and 9 would attend the Lunenburg Junior High (formally Lunenburg High School). All students in grades 10, 11, and 12 would attend Central High School.

Source: The Kenbridge-Victoria Dispatch, July 24, 1969.

LUNENBURG COUNTY SCHOOL SUPERINTENDENTS

1871 – 1906	Robert M. Williams
1906 – 1919	Isham T. Wilkinson
1919 – 1925	A. B. "Ben" Wilson
1925 – 1936	James T. Waddill, Jr.
1936 – 1943	Thomas F. Crittenden
1943 – 1967	Macon F. Fears
1967 – 1970	James T. Thweatt

LUNENBURG COUNTY JEANES SUPERVISORS

1909 – 1917	McNoah B. Cralle
1918 – 1952	Lucy M. Hinton Morrison
1952 – 1956	Clara A. Morse

AFTERWORD

The Trails and Trailblazers: Public Education and School Desegregation in Lunen-burg County Public Schools 1870-1970 documents the centennial history of public education in Lunenburg County, Virginia, and the local, state, and national events that influenced the system. This work also speaks of an era when people from different ethnic backgrounds were compelled by federal law to begin a new educational experience at the same school.

Members of this rural community in the Southside region of Virginia came together during a most difficult and uncertain time for the purpose of full school integration as ordered by the Courts. A life-changing, un-forgettable event was experienced, and success was achieved because of the support of family members, community leaders, school administra-tors, teachers, and students. These courageous young people have proven without doubt that when children are given equal accessibility to educa-tional opportunity—they can achieve, excel, and become productive con-tributing members of society. The equality of educational opportunity for *all* students in Lunenburg County became a reality on September 8, 1969, in spite of disparities in funding and resources; the personal beliefs of some people that African Americans are inferior; and the lack of legal protections in some cases. These factors—separate or in totality—did im-pede equal educational, economic, political, and social opportunities for African Americans.

The author presents the following conclusions: (1) Segregated public education in Lunenburg County developed slowly beginning in the late 1800s, and grew rapidly after the turn of the twentieth century into one of largest, most expensive functions of the county; (2) Historically, the black church and philanthropic organizations created opportunities for students to develop a sense of pride and personal value in the face of unrelenting Jim Crow restrictions; and (3) Unsung heroes, in spite of intolerable circumstances, left their comfort zone and opened the doors of educational opportunities that enriched the lives of others. Many students have experienced success because their lives were influenced by caring, supportive educators.

School desegregation is a non-issue since the Supreme Court decision in the *Brown* cases; and passage of the Civil Rights Act of 1964. Lunenburg citizens continue to expect and support "excellent" schools, and many patrons still view public education as a high priority for their children. It is believed that education is essential to an effective, productive life—and parents often seek out exceptional schools and programs. They desire their children to learn in an enriched and well-suited environment that represents the global world—including the experience of living and working within a diverse population. Each school in Lunenburg County offers equal access to educational opportunities for '*all*' children as they learn to work together.

The documentation of the Lunenburg County Public Schools' story would not have been possible without the legacies of its educational heroes. Truly, these trailblazers have paved the way for public education in Lunenburg County, Virginia.

Many, many thanks!

PHOTO AND IMAGE CREDITS

Photo of Isham Trotter Wilkinson courtesy of the Wilkinson Family.

Photo of Lucy M. Hinton Morrison courtesy of Daisy M. Garris.

1935 photo of West End School - Special Collections and University Archives, Archie G. Richardson Papers - Courtesy of Johnston Memorial Library, Virginia State University.

Photo of James T. Waddill, Jr. courtesy of the Victoria High School Preservation Foundation, Inc.

1938 Elementary Certificate for Leroy Davis courtesy of Shula F. Davis.

Photo of Macon F. Fears courtesy of Edna B. Jones.

2010 photo of the former Lunenburg County School Garage by Shirley R. Lee.

Two Dollar Bus Receipt courtesy of Norma Elloise Marable Callahan.

2012 photo of the Snead School by Shirley R. Lee.

Photo of Galvin Lewis Jenkins courtesy of Mildred H. Jenkins.

2012 photo of the former Lunenburg County Board of Education by Shirley R. Lee.

Photo of Ann W. Jackson courtesy of Ann W. Jackson.

BIBLIOGRAPHY

Archives

John Hope and Aurelia Elizabeth Franklin Library, Julius Rosenwald Fund Archives, Fisk University, Nashville, Tennessee.

Special Collections and University Archives - Archie G. Richardson Papers, Johnston Memorial Library, Virginia State University, Petersburg, Virginia.

Special Collection and University Archives Janet D. Greenwood Library, Longwood University, Farmville, Virginia.

Ripberger Public Library, Kenbridge, Virginia,

Books and Other Resources

Callahan, Elloise M. and Ruth C. Wood. *Historical Sketch of Lunenburg High School, 1917-1969*. Victoria, Virginia, 1985.

Central High School. *Sword and Shield*. Victoria, Virginia, 1967-1970.

Commonwealth of Virginia. *A History of Public Education in Virginia*. Richmond: Department of Education, 2003.

Courier-Record, July 7, 1966.

Deutsch, Stephanie. *You Need a Schoolhouse*. Evanston: Northwestern University Press, 2011.

Editors. *Pictorial History – Black America, Vol. I, II*. Chicago: The Johnson Publishing Company, and Nashville: Southwestern Company, 1971.

Gates, Robbins L. *The Making of Massive Resistance ~ Virginia's Politics of Public School Desegregation 1954 1956*. Chapel Hill: The University of North Carolina Press, 1962, 1964.

Gruver, J. S., *Virginia Teacher Directory*, Reliance, Virginia: Cutting & Wallihan, 1900.

Hamlett, Anne C. and Israel, Stephen S. *Victoria Then and Now: The Centennial Edition 1909 2009*. Raleigh: Lulu.com, 2009.

Irvine, Russell W. and Jacqueline J. Irving. *The Impact of the Desegregation Process on the Education of Black Students: Key Variables*, Journal of Negro Education, 52, no. 4, Autumn, 1983, pp. 410-422.

Israel, Stephen S. Kenbridge, *The First Hundred Years 1908 2008*. Raleigh: Lulu.com, 2008.

Kenbridge Chamber of Commerce. *Our Town 75th Anniversary*, Kenbridge, Virginia, October 1983.

Kenbridge Elementary School. *Classbook*. Kenbridge, Virginia, 1969.

Kenbridge Graded School. *Highlighter*. Kenbridge, Virginia, 1963.

Kenbridge High School. *The Comet*. Kenbridge, Virginia, 1966.

Kilpatrick, James J. *The Southern Case for School Segregation*. New York: The Crowell-Collier Publishing Company, 1962.

Lee, Shirley R. *West Hill Baptist Church History 1909-2010*, (unpublished). Kenbridge, Virginia, 2010.

Lochleven Hi Newsletter, Vol. 1, No. 5, June 1936.

Lunenburg County Public Schools, *Our Schools*. South Hill, Virginia: South Hill Enterprise, 1908.

Lunenburg County School Public Schools. *Board of Education Minutes*, Victoria, Virginia.

Lunenburg County School Public Schools. *Virginia Daily Register and Monthly Grade Record*, Victoria, Virginia.

Lunenburg County Teachers' Association Minutes, 1915.

Lunenburg High School. *Student Handbook 1960-1961*. Chase City, Virginia: The Middleton Press, 1960.

Lunenburg School Life Newsletter, Victoria, Virginia: October-November 1922, March 1923, February 1924.

Monnie, Bill. *Selma And Its Aftermath*. Merrimack, New Hampshire: A Snowy Day Distribution and Publishing, 2015.

Muse, Benjamin. *Virginia's Massive Resistance*. Bloomington: Indiana Press, 1969.

Neale, Gay W. *The Lunenburg Legacy*. Lawrenceville, Virginia: Brunswick Publishing Company, 2005.

Pulley, Mary C. *History of Lunenburg County In World War II*. Richmond, Virginia: The Dietz Press, Inc., 1949.

Rich, Sallie Berniece L. *An Overview of Early Black Education in Nottoway County, Virginia: From One, Two, Three Plus Rooms to Nottoway Training School Volume I – The end of the slavery era (1865 to 1950)*. Farmville, Virginia: Farmville Printing, 2006.

Richmond Times-Dispatch, July 21, 1953.

Scruggs, Eugene L. *A Man Called Nash ~ The Memoirs of Eugene L. Scruggs*.

Smith, Bob. *They Closed Their Schools, Prince Edward County, Virginia 1951-1964*. Farmville, Virginia: Robert Russa Moton Museum, 2008.

Smith, George E. *Kenbridge Elementary School History*, 1993.

Sullivan, Neal V., Maynard, Thomas L., and Yellin, Carol L. *Bound For Freedom: An Educator's Adventures in Prince Edward County, Virginia*. Farmville, Virginia: Robert Russa Moton Museum, 1965.

The Lunenburg Call. Victoria, Va., 1913-1924.

The Victoria Dispatch. Victoria, Virginia, 1925-1933.

The Kenbridge Victoria Dispatch. Victoria, Virginia, 1933-1970.

Victoria High School. *The Panther*, Victoria, Virginia, 1966.

Victoria High School. *The Victoria Newsletter*, Victoria, Virginia, 1940.

Virginia Department of Education. *A Report of the Superintendent of Public Instruction*. Richmond, Virginia: March 28, 1870.

Virginia Department of Education, *Pupil Transportation in Virginia School Systems*. Richmond, Virginia: April 1974.

Virginia Students' Civil Rights Committee Newsletter, February 1967.

Walker, Vanessa S. *Their Highest Potential: An African American Community in the Segregated South*. Chapel Hill: The University of North Carolina Press, 1996.

Wood, Oscar. *Development of Education for Negroes in Lunenburg County, Virginia 1870 1952*, Master's Thesis, Virginia State College, Petersburg, Virginia, 1953.

Web Resources

Disclaimer: All the Internet addresses (URLs) given in this book were valid at press time. Due to the dynamic nature of the Internet, readers should be aware that the web sites offered as citation and/or sources for further information may have changed or are no longer available. While the author and publisher regret any inconvenience this may cause readers, no responsibility for such changes can be accepted by either the author or publisher.

CTE Resource Center. "History of Public Education." CTEresoure.org. http://www.cteresource.org/TFTfinalWebFiles/OtherDocuments/history_public_ed.pdf

"The Presidents of the United States of America." Whitehouse.gov. http://www.whitehouse.gov/about/presidents/franklindroosevelt

House of Delegates. "Constitution of Virginia." Virginiageneralassembly.gov. http://legis.state.va.us/Laws/search/ConstitutionPrint.htm (Retrieved: 3 November 2010).

U. S. Department of Education. "A Selected History of the Department of Education and Key Legislation." Ed.gov.http://www2.ed.gov/pubs/strat-plan2001-05/title.doc (Retrieved: 18 January 2012)

Virginia Center for Digital History. "Rosenwald Schools of Virginia." Vcdh.virginiaedu.http://www.2vcdh.virginia.edu/schools/school.php?id=257

Virginia Foundation for the Humanities, "Massive Resistance." http://www.en-cyclopediavirginia.org/Massive_Resistance (Retrieved: 19 August 2010)

Botsch, Carol S. "The Jeanes Supervisors." Aiken, South Carolina: http://www.usca.edu/aasc/jeanes.htm (Retrieved: 28 July 2012)

INDEX

Chapters in bold

U

Underwood Constitution, 1
Underwood, Ralph, 90, 199
Uniform Examination for Teachers' Certification, 73, 219
Union Central School, 26, 104
Union Ridge School, 7
United Services Organization, 59
United States Fourth Circuit Court of Appeals, 152
United States Department of Education, 82, 86
United States District Court, 132, 150
United States Supreme Court, 95, 109, 110, 113-123, 126-127, 131, 134, 139, 152, 184, 206, 234
Unity School, 34, 90, 107, 167-168, 197

V

Valentine, Maude E., 34
Vance, John, 130
Varick School, 26, 77, 105, 106
Vaughan, Beulah, 160
Vaughan, Carl E., 90
Vaughan, Sherman C., 86, 101, 129, 163-164
Victoria Community House, 127, 128, 129, 134
Victoria Elementary School, 50, 62, 101, 107, 108, 126, 127, 150, 154, 155, 156, 159, 169-170, 171, 192, 202, 207, 208, 227, 232
Victoria High School, 20, 22, 23, 25, 26, 36, 40, 45, 47, 48, 57, 66, 71, 72, 73, 81, 84, 85, 88, 89, 90, 91, 97, 98, 107, 126, 127, 149, 159, 161, 163, 169, 183, 189-192, 194, 199, 200, 202
Victory Loan, 48
Virginia Commission on Accredited Schools, 94
Virginia Committee for Public Schools, 132,
Virginia Constitution of 1902, 6
Virginia Council on Human Rights, 117
Virginia Crusaders for Constitutional Government, 129
Virginia Education Commission, 67, 112
Virginia Normal and Collegiate Institute, 74
Virginia State Conference of the NAACP, 117
Virginia Students Civil Rights Committee, 62, 142, 143, 147

NOTES

Preface

[i]   Jim Crow laws were local and state laws enacted—between 1876 and 1965—in the United States. These laws mandated racial segregation, a separate but equal status, in all public facilities in Southern states starting in 1890 for African Americans. Jim Crow laws applied to the segregation of public schools, public transportation and public places—restrooms, restaurants, and drinking fountains. The U.S. military was also segregated.

[ii]   *Plessy v. Ferguson*, 163 U.S. 537 (1896).

[iii] *Brown v. Board of Education of Topeka*, 347 U.S. 483 (1954). Brown II, a 1955 United States Supreme Court decision under Chief Justice Earl Warren, includes the phrase "all deliberate speed."

[iv]   *Civil Rights Act*, Pub. L. 88-352, 78 Stat. 241 (1964).

Chapter 1: Awakening of Public Education

[v]   *Annual Report of the Superintendent of Public Instruction of the Commonwealth of Virginia* (Richmond: Virginia State Board of Education), 1871.

[vi]   Mary C. Pulley. *History of Lunenburg County in World War II* (Richmond: The Dietz Press, Inc., 1949), xviii.

[vii] Stephen S. Israel. Kenbridge, *The First Hundred Years 1908-2008* (Lulu.com, 2008), 5.

[viii] Pulley, xix.

[ix]   Gay W. Neale. *The Lunenburg Legacy*, (Lawrenceville: Brunswick Publishing Com-

pany, 2005), 115; *History of Public Education in Virginia* (Richmond: Virginia Department of Education, 2003), 5.

x   Ibid., 6; Heinemann, Ronald L., John G. Kolp, Anthony S. Parent Jr., and William G. Shade. *Old Dominion, New Commonwealth: A History of Virginia, 1607-2007.* Copyright 2007 by the Rector and Visitors of the University of Virginia, 254. Heinemann and others emphasized the major themes that play throughout Virginia history—change and continuity, a conservative political order, race and slavery, economic development, and social divisions—and have related that story to national events. Included in this story is the transition of Virginia from the dominant mainstream model of British North American settlement and development (up to 1820) to a defensive, tradition-bound, inward-looking, and different version of American development (1820-1960) and back again to a progressively conservative society in the late twentieth century.

xi   Ibid., 255.

xii   *Annual Report of the Superintendent of Public Instruction* (Richmond: Commonwealth of Virginia, Virginia State Board of Education), 1871.

xiii   Ibid., 1872.

xiv   Neale, *The Lunenburg Legacy*, (Lawrenceville: Brunswick Publishing Company, 2005), 116.

xv   Oscar Wood, *Development of Education for Negroes in Lunenburg County, Virginia 1870-1952* (Petersburg: Virginia State College, 1953), 25. Wood is a retired public school administrator. This is a thesis submitted to the faculty of the Division of Graduate Studies of Virginia State College in partial fulfillment of the requirements for the degree of Master of Science in Education in 1952. Wood's research documents eighty-two years of the development of education for Negroes in Lunenburg County, Virginia.

xvi   *Lunenburg School Life Newsletter*, 1922; Richard May was the superintendent of his magisterial district.

xvii   Wood, 29. Interview by Oscar Wood with Pattie Callahan, a former student of the Methodist School, Victoria, Virginia, July 15, 1952.

xviii   Ibid. Interview by Oscar Wood with Maude Callahan, a former student of the Baptist Church School, Victoria, Virginia, July 15, 1952.

xix   *Civil Rights Act*, Pub. L. 88-352, 78 Stat. 241 (1964).

xx   Wood, 23-25.

xxi   *Annual Report of the Superintendent of Public Instruction of the Commonwealth of Virginia*, (Richmond: Virginia School Report, Office of the Board of Education), 1881; Heinemann, 255.

xxii   School photo and information archived by the Victoria High School Preservation Foundation, Inc.; Neale, 183.

xxiii Neale, 172.

xxiv   Heinemann, 254.

xxv   *Plessy v. Ferguson*, 163, U.S. 537 (1896).

xxvi   Heinemann, 276.

xxvii *A History of Public Education in Virginia*, 8.

xxviii Ibid., 8.

xxix   Neale, 136.

xxx   Heinemann, 276.

xxxi   *A History of Public Education in Virginia*, 8.

xxxii Ibid., 9; Heinemann, 280-281; Wood, 40-41. Interview by Oscar Wood with Rosa Marable, August 15, 1952.

xxxiii Heinemann, 281.

xxxiv Ibid., 280; *A History of Public Education in Virginia*, 9.

xxxv   *The Victoria Dispatch*, 1925.

xxxvi *Our School*, (South Hill: South Hill Enterprise Print, Spring No. 1908), 29.

xxxvii Neale, 116.

xxxviii Stephen S. Israel. Kenbridge - *The First Hundred Years 1908-2008* (Lulu.com, 2008), 187.

xxxix Heinemann, 280; *A History of Public Education in Virginia*, 9.

xl   *Our School*, 28.

xli   Ibid., 29.

xlii   *Richmond Times-Dispatch*, 1953.

xliii Kenbridge Chamber of Commerce, Our Town October 1983, 28.

xliv   John 'Shug' W. Callahan, Sr., at his home in Kenbridge, Virginia, February 26, 2012; Callahan was a retired farmer, public worker, and student at West Hill School. Eugene L. Scruggs. *A Man Called Nash: The Memoirs of Eugene L. Scruggs* (Tennessee: 2001), 9.

xlv   Obituary of Professor W. E. Nash, Athens, Tennessee, April 30, 1996.

xlvi   Shirley R. Lee, *West Hill Baptist Church History, March 5, 1909 – March 26, 2010* (Kenbridge, Virginia [Unpublished], 12; John W. Callahan, Sr.; Neale, 120.

xlvii David Jones, Jr., interview at West Hill Baptist Church, Victoria, Virginia, July 11, 2010. Jones is a former student of the West Hill School.

xlviii *The Lunenburg Call*, 1971; *The Lunenburg Call* became *The Victoria Dispatch* in 1924.

xlix   *A History of Public Education in Virginia*, 12.

[l]   *Richmond Times-Dispatch*, 1953; Israel, 187-188; *Kenbridge-Victoria Dispatch*, December 3, 1937.

[li]   Wood, 43, 59.

[lii] Sallie B. Rich, *An Overview of Early Black Education in Nottoway County, Virginia: From One, Two, Three Plus Rooms to Nottoway Training School Volume I – The end of the slavery era (1865 to 1950)* (Farmville: Farmville Printing, Virginia, 2006), 17-21. Rich is a graduate of Luther H. Foster High School in Nottoway County, Virginia. She returned to Nottoway County following early retirement from the IBM Corporation in 1993. A love of history prompted her to publish a history of early black education from the end of slavery [1865] to the Nottoway Training School closing in 1950.

[liii] *A History of Public Education in Virginia*, 10-11; Records of the Jeanes Supervisors can be found in the archives of the Southern Education Foundation in the Atlanta University Center Library on the Clark-Atlanta University campus and in the Anna T. Jeanes Foundation Papers at the Rockefeller Archive Center in Pocantico Hills, N.Y.

[liv] Rich, 21.

[lv]   The name Cralle is pronounced "Crawley."

[lvi] Wood, 45.

[lvii] Ibid., 54

[lviii] *Lunenburg County Teachers' Association Minutes*, 1915.

[lix] *A History of Public Education in Virginia*, 13.

[lx]   Obituary of L. M. Morrison, February 25, 1973.

[lxi] Barbara Nelson Shell, interview at her home in Kenbridge, Virginia, January 2, 2013.

[lxii] *The Kenbridge-Victoria Dispatch*, February 19, 1960.

[lxiii] *The Victoria Dispatch*, August 18, 1952; *The Kenbridge-Victoria Dispatch*, August 24, 1956; The 1960-1961 *Lunenburg High School Student Handbook* (Chase City: The Middleton Press, 1960), 6.

[lxiv] *A History of Public Education in Virginia*, 11; Carol S. Botsch, Jeanes Supervisors, Aikens, South Carolina, August 9, 1998.

[lxv] Virginia Center for Digital History, "Rosenwald Schools of Virginia," Vcdh.virginia.edu, http://www2.vcdh.virginia.edu/schools/school.php? id=257. The Rosenwald Fund was established by Julius Rosenwald in 1917. Created as an extension of Rosenwald's personal philanthropies, which were initiated as early as 1913, the first period of the fund's work (1917-28) focused on building Negro rural schoolhouses in the South by providing a monetary incentive for Negro

communities that were willing to raise funds to support the building of schools. The fund was reorganized in 1931 to broaden its focus to "the well-being of mankind." In 1932, it concluded its rural school-building program. For a break-down of Rosenwald expenditures by state, see Work, *Negro Yearbook*, 84-85; Smith, 14; Heinemann, 243.

Chapter 2: Building A Public School System

[lxvi] *Lunenburg School Life*, October-November, 1922. Copies of this newsletter (1922, 1923, and 1924) are archived at the Ripberger Public Library in Kenbridge, Virginia; Wilson was called "Ben" according to Richard Kirby, retired insurance agent. Superintendent Wilson purchased the Kirby's family home in Victoria.

[lxvii] *A History of Public Education in Virginia*, 12.

[lxviii] *Lunenburg School Life*, October-November 1922.

[lxix] Ibid., March 1923; Virginia Center for Digital History.

[lxx] *Lunenburg School Life*, March 1923.

[lxxi] *Lunenburg School Life*, February 1924.

[lxxii] Michael A. Tisdale, interview on June 7, 2011. Tisdale is a graduate of Victoria High School, retired school administrator and the grandson of Sarah Virginia Love.

[lxxiii] *The Victoria Dispatch*, 1925-1933.

[lxxiv] Ibid., April 23, 1925.

[lxxv] Ibid., May 14, 1925.

[lxxvi] Ibid., May 2, 1941.

[lxxvii] *The Victorian*, 1940.

[lxxviii] Michael A. Tisdale.

[lxxix] Margaret Cushwa Cocks, interview in her home in Kenbridge, Virginia, June 11, 2011. Cocks was an English teacher at the Kenbridge High School and librarian at Central High School.

[lxxx] Alvester L. Edmonds, interview at his home in Kenbridge, Virginia on March 27, 2012. Edmonds is a former school board member; 1970 graduate of Central High School; and a member of the Lunenburg County Board of Supervisors representing the Brown's Store District.

[lxxxi] Barbara Nelson Shell.

[lxxxii] *The Victoria Dispatch*, May 2, 1941.

[lxxxiii] Barbara Thomas Reese, interview at her home in Victoria, Virginia, June 9, 2011

& April 2, 2012. Reese is a retired physical education teacher in Lunenburg County.

lxxxiv Hamlett and Israel, 43.

lxxxv *The Victoria Dispatch*, October 2, 1925.

lxxxvi Ibid., June, 1926.

lxxxvii Ibid., July, 1926; September 13, 1926.

lxxxviii *The Kenbridge-Victoria Dispatch*, November 1996; June 11, 1954.

lxxxix *The Victoria Dispatch*, June 4, 1926.

xc Wood, 57-58; School Board Office archives, *Virginia Daily Attendance Register and Monthly Grade Record*; The Central School mentioned is not the Central High School constructed in 1966.

xci *The Victoria Dispatch*, September 3, 1926.

xcii Ibid.

xciii *The Victoria Dispatch*, February 3, 1928.

xciiv *The Victoria Dispatch*, April 13, 1928.

xcv *The Victoria Dispatch*, February 8, 1929.

xcvi *The Victoria Dispatch*, April 19, 1929.

xcvii Pulley, xxi.

xcviii Heinemann, 179.

xcix Editors of Ebony, *Pictorial History – Black America, Vol. I* (Chicago: The Johnson Publishing Company and Nashville: The Southwestern Publishing Company, 1971), 145.

c Ibid., Vol. I, 173; Wood, 10; Israel, 21. A stone marker of the 1865 Trinity School has been placed on Hound's Creek Farm by the Jennings family for preservation.

ci Editors of Ebony, Vol. I, 173; Vol. II, 17.

cii Wood, 42-43.

ciii Heinemann, 313-314.

civ Roosevelt Crowder, interview by at his home in Kenbridge, Virginia, October 31, 2010. Crowder is a life-long resident of Lunenburg County, a retired farmer and public worker.

cv Bernice Stokes Charlton, interview at the Stokes' family farm in Rehoboth, Virginia, June 7, 2011. Charlton is a 1942 graduate of Lunenburg Training School.

cvi Margaret Cushwa Cocks.

cvii *A History of Public Education in Virginia*, 16.

cviii *The Victoria Dispatch*, November 20, 1931.

cix *The Victoria Dispatch*, November 27, 1931.

cx *The Victoria Dispatch*, January 22, 1932.

[cxi] *History of Public Education in Virginia*, 16.

[cxii] *The Victoria Dispatch*, February 12, 1932; March 11, 1932.

[cxiii] Ibid., August 19, 1932.

[cxiv] Ibid., August 11, 1933.

[cxv] Ibid., December 1, 1933.

[cxvi] *Kenbridge-Victoria Dispatch*, March 20, 1936; March 27, 1936.

[cxvii] Ibid., April 1, 1936.

[cxviii] *A History of Public Education in Virginia*, 16.

[cxix] *Kenbridge-Victoria Dispatch*, September 25, 1936.

[cxx] Ibid., October 2, 1936.

[cxxi] Ibid., March 12, 1937.

[cxxii] Ibid., April 16, 1937.

[cxxiii] *The Victoria Dispatch*, January 13, 1939.

[cxxiv] *A History of Public Education in Virginia*, 16.

[cxxv] *Kenbridge-Victoria Dispatch*, April 21, 1939.

[cxxvi] *A History of Public Education in Virginia*, 16, 17.

Chapter 4: Schools, World War II and Post-War Developments

[cxxvii] Pulley, 1-2, 16-33.

[cxxviii] Neale, 239.

[cxxix] Helen Wilkinson Buchanan, interview at her home in Kenbridge, Virginia, May 11, 2011. Buchanan is retired educator.

[cxxx] Pulley, 13-14.

[cxxxi] *The Victoria Dispatch*, October, 4, 1940.

[cxxxii] *School Board Minutes*, December 6, 1940.

[cxxxiii] *The Victoria Dispatch*, January 3, 1941.

[cxxxiv] Ibid., January 24, 1941.

[cxxxv] *School Board Minutes*, March 6, 1942.

[cxxxvi] Neale, 238.

[cxxxvii] Ibid., Neale, 240.

[cxxxviii] *The Victoria Dispatch*, October 9, 1942.

[cxxxix] *Kenbridge-Victoria Dispatch*, 1952.

[cxl] *The Victoria Dispatch*, December 10, 1943.

[cxli] *School Board Minutes*, May 5, 1944.

[cxlii] Florence Hayes Hatchett, interview at the West Hill Baptist Church, Victoria,

Virginia, July 10, 2010. Hatchett is a former student at the West Hill School.

[cxliii] Shirley R. Lee. *West Hill Baptist Church History* 1909-2010, July 10, 2010. A copy of the report card is included in the unpublished scrapbook located at the West Hill Baptist Church, Victoria, Virginia; and an abbreviated version is archived at the Ripberger Public Library, Kenbridge, Virginia, and The Bluestone-Harmony Baptist Association Headquarters, Keysville, Virginia.

[cxliv] *The Victoria Dispatch*, August 18, 1944.

[cxlv] *The Victoria Dispatch*, October 20, 1944.

[cxlvi] Pulley, xxii.

[cxlvii] Richard L. Kirby.

[cxlviii] *The Victoria Dispatch*, November 9, 1945.

[cxlix] Heinemann, 311.

[cl] Neale, 300.

[cli] Ibid., 303; *A History of Public Education in Virginia*, 18-19.

[clii] Ibid., 18.

[cliii] *School Board Minutes*, June 1, 1945.

[cliv] *The Victoria Dispatch*, June 8, 1945.

[clv] Ibid., June 8, 1945.

[clvi] *School Board Minutes*, May 6, 1949; September 8, 1966.

[clvii] *The Victoria Dispatch*, September 7, 1945.

[clviii] *The Victoria Dispatch*, June 21, 1946.

[clix] *The Victoria Dispatch*, September 5, 1947.

[clx] *School Board Minutes*, April 2, 1948.

[clxi] *A History of Public Education in Virginia*, 20.

Chapter 5: School Transportation

[clxii] *Highlighter*, Kenbridge Graded School, 1963. This is an excerpt of a comment by Macon F. Fears, Superintendent of Schools, included in this publication. The Highlighter was a Kenbridge Graded School yearbook in the 1960s. This publication contains photos of the faculty, staff, students, and other school-related information.

[clxiii] *Pupil Transportation in Virginia School Systems*, (Richmond: Virginia Department of Education, April 1974), 1.

[clxiv] *Kenbridge-Victoria Dispatch*, November 1996.

[clxv] Neale, 182.

clxvi *Pupil Transportation in Virginia School Systems*, April 1974.

clxvii *The Victoria Dispatch*, July 15, 1927.

clxviii Hilda Bagley Hawkins, interview at her home in Kenbridge, Virginia, October 31, 2010. Hawkins was a retired educator.

clxix *Pupil Transportation in Virginia School Systems*, April 1974.

clxx Wood, 50; Wood's interview with George Holloway, School Board Representative from the Rehoboth District; and Rosa Marable, retired teacher, Rehoboth, Virginia, 1952.

clxxi Elloise Marable Callahan, interview at her home, Victoria Virginia, May 12, 2011.Callahan is a retired educator.

clxxii *The Victoria Dispatch*, August 12, 1932.

clxxiii *School Board Minutes*, August 4, 1939.

clxxiv Wood, 50. Interview George Holloway and Rosa Marable, 1952.

clxxv Ibid., 49, 52; Superintendent of Public Instruction (Richmond: *Virginia School Report*, Virginia Board of Education, 1920, 1930, 1940).

clxxvi Russell Lacy Callahan, interview at his home in Kenbridge, Virginia, January 11, 2013.

clxxvii *School Board Minutes*, April 5, 1940.

clxxviii *The Victoria Dispatch*, January 31, 1941.

clxxix *School Board Minutes*, August 1, 1941.

clxxx *The Victoria Dispatch*, August 15, 1941.

clxxxi *The Kenbridge-Victoria Dispatch*, June 9, 1961.

clxxxii *The Victoria Dispatch*, September 20, 1940; School Board Minutes, August 2, 1940.

clxxxiii *The Victoria Dispatch*, March 20, 1942.

clxxxiv *Pupil Transportation in Virginia School Systems*, April 1974.

clxxxv *School Board Minutes*, May 1, 1942.

clxxxvi Ibid, August 2, 1940; Wood, 51.

clxxxvii Neale, 300; *The Victoria Dispatch*, August 7, 1942; October 2, 1942.

clxxxviii Ibid., November 6, 1942

clxxxix *School Board Minutes*, January 8, 1943.

cxc *The Victoria Dispatch*, January 22, 1943.

cxci *School Board Minutes*, February 5, 1943; Wood, 51, 52.

cxcii *The Victoria Dispatch*, September 3, 1943.

cxciii Survey of Lunenburg County Schools, "Transportation System, (Richmond: Virginia State Department of Education), October, 1943.

cxciv *School Board Minutes*, February 5, 1943.

cxcv Janis Taylor Whitehead, interview on May 16, 2011. Whitehead is a daughter of the late Reverend and Mrs. Joseph E. Taylor, Sr. She is a 1963 graduate of Lunenburg High School, retired school guidance counselor, and former Lunenburg County School Board member representing the Meherrin River District.

cxcvi Verna Hurt Spencer, interview on June 8, 2011.

cxcvii *School Board Minutes*, September 1, 1944.

cxcviii Wood, 52.

cxcix *Survey of Lunenburg County Schools*, Transportation Systems (Richmond: Virginia Department of Education, October 1943), 1-2; Wood, 51-53.

cc Early Mason Reese, interview at his home in Kenbridge, Virginia, June 8, 2011; Neale, 238.

cci *The Kenbridge-Victoria Dispatch*, September 1, 1966.

ccii Virginia Students' Civil Rights Committee Newsletter, February 1967.

cciii *School Board Minutes*, September 9, 1968.

cciv Ibid., August 7, 1969.

ccv *The Kenbridge-Victoria Dispatch*, September 4, 1969.

ccvi *School Board Minutes*, September 8, 1969.

Chapter 6: Educational Disparities and Other Issues

ccvii Neil V. Sullivan. *Bound For Freedom: An Educator's Adventures in Prince Edward County, Virginia* (Farmville: Robert Russa Moton Museum, 1965), xlv.

ccviii *The Kenbridge-Victoria Dispatch*, November 4, 1938.

ccix Wood, 60.

ccx *The Victoria Dispatch*, November 25, 1927.

ccxi *A History of Public Education in Virginia*, 16.

ccxii Virginia Education Commission, (Richmond: Virginia Department of Education, 1944), 180-187.

ccxiii Wood, 21.

ccxiv *Our School*, 28. School Board Office, *Virginia Daily Register and Monthly Grade Record*, 1922.

ccxv Wood, 24.

ccxvi *The Victoria Dispatch*, March 4, 1927.

ccxvii *The Victoria Dispatch*, September 9, 1927; July 20, 1928.

ccxviii *The Victoria Dispatch*, August 8, 1930.

ccxix *Tax Levy for Magisterial Districts in Lunenburg County, 1931*. The amount was listed on the back of each tax form.

ccxx *The Victoria Dispatch*, February 20, 1931.

ccxxi Ibid., August 21, 1931.

ccxxii Ibid., August 18, 1939.

ccxxiii Wood, 24; *Virginia School Report* (Richmond: Commonwealth of Virginia, Office of the Board of Education, 1871.

ccxxiv Ibid., 1910-1911; Heinemann, 255.

ccxxv *Virginia School Report* (Richmond: Commonwealth of Virginia, Office of Board of Education), 1910-1911.

ccxxvi Wood, 59.

ccxxvii Ibid.

ccxxviii *School Board Minutes*, April 5, 1940; Wood, 59.

ccxxix Wood, 59; Virginia State Board of Education (Richmond: *Annual Report of the Superintendent of Public Instruction of the Commonwealth of Virginia*),1940, 1950.

ccxxx *School Board Minutes*, April 2, 1942.

ccxxxi *School Board Minutes*, May 7, 1943.

ccxxxii Ibid., May 5, 1944.

ccxxxiii Margaret Lawing Collier, *Contract with Teachers*, 1945. Information was provided with permission by Phylis Jones Adams, Collier's niece. Collier retired as principal of the Kenbridge Graded School in June of 1969.

ccxxxiv *School Board Minutes*, May 4, 1945.

ccxxxv Ibid., June 1, 1945.

ccxxxvi Ibid., March 1, 1947.

ccxxxvii Ibid., April 1, 1949. A History of Public Education in Virginia, 18.

ccxxxviii *School Board Minutes*, April 2, 1948; May 7, 1948; April 1, 1949; April 6, 1951; February 5, 1952.

ccxxxix *Virginia School Report* (Richmond: Annual Report of the Superintendent of Public Instruction of the Commonwealth of Virginia, Office of the Board of Education, 1881); Wood, 55.

ccxl *A History of Public Education in Virginia*, 13; *Lunenburg School Life Newsletter*, March 1923; *Virginia School Report*, (Richmond: Annual Report of the Superintendent of Public Instruction of the Commonwealth of Virginia, Office of the Board of Education), Uniform Examination For Teachers' Certificate, 1900.

ccxli *The Victoria Dispatch*, Virginia, November 8, 1929.

ccxlii Heinemann, 254-255, 258; Editors of Ebony, Vol. II, 63-64; Smith, 14.

ccxliii Rich, 88-89.

ccxliv *The Victoria Dispatch*, November 8, 1929.

ccxlv *A History of Public Education in Virginia*, 13, 17.

ccxlvi *School Board Minutes*, May 4, 1945; April 6, 1951; February 5, 1952.

ccxlvii *A History of Public Education in Virginia*, 25.

ccxlviii *School Board Minutes*, November 7, 1969.

ccxlix *The Victoria Dispatch*, February 11, 1927.

ccl Ibid., September 30, 1927.

ccli Ibid., September 16, 1927.

cclii Ibid., February 17, 1928.

ccliii Neale, 177.

ccliv *Kenbridge-Victoria Dispatch*, February 3, 1939.

cclv *The Victoria Dispatch*, June 21, 1940.

cclvi Ibid., September 13, 1940.

cclvii Neale, 303.

cclviii *The Victoria Dispatch*, September 16, 1949.

cclix Wood, 49; *Annual Report of the Superintendent of Public Instruction of the Common-wealth of Virginia* (Richmond: Virginia State Board of Education), 1940, 1952.

cclx *School Board Minutes*, September, 1969.

Chapter 7: New School Programs

cclxi *The Victoria Dispatch*, June 4, 1926.

cclxii *School Board Minutes*, June 4, 1943; May 5, 1944.

cclxiii *School Board Minutes*, May 4, 1945.

cclxiv *The Victoria Dispatch*, June 2, 1950; *A History of Public Education in Virginia*, 25; *School Board Minutes*, June 30, 1969.

cclxv Wood, 45.

cclxvi *Our Town*, 28; *The Victoria Dispatch*, April 22, 1927.

cclxvii Ibid., April 29, 1927.

cclxviii Ibid., May 11, 1928.

cclxix Neale, 225.

cclxx Wood, 10-11.

cclxxi *Kenbridge-Victoria Dispatch*, September 8, 1939; Neale, 225.

cclxxii Bessie Chatmon Hopkins, retired teacher, interview at her home in Kenbridge, Virginia, November 9, 2010.

cclxxiii Pulley, 39.

cclxxiv *Title 1 of the Elementary and Secondary Education Act*, 20 U.S.C. 6301 et. seq.,

1965.

cclxxv *A History of Public Education in Virginia*, 25.

cclxxvi Ann W. Jackson, interview by at her home in Victoria, Virginia, October 25, 2010.

cclxxvii *School Board Minutes*, February 7, 1966.

cclxxviii U.S. Department of Education: A Selected History of the Department of Education and Key Legislation. http://www2.ed.gov/pubs/stratplan2001-05/title.doc (accessed January 18, 2012).

cclxxix Stephanie Deutsch, *You Need A Schoolhouse-Booker T. Washington, Julius Rosenwald and the Building of Schools for the Segregated South* (Illinois: Northwestern University Press, 2011), 21-22.

cclxxx *Lunenburg School Life Newsletter*, 1923.

cclxxxi Virginia Center for Digital History.

cclxxxii Wood, 62; *Historical Sketch of Lunenburg High School* (1917-1969).

cclxxxiii "The Presidents of the United States of America," Whitehouse.gov, http://www.white-house.gov/about/presidents/franklindroosevelt.

cclxxxiv The Civil Works Administration (CWA) was a school construction program initiated by President Roosevelt in 1933.

cclxxxv *The Victoria Dispatch*, April 12, 1935.

cclxxxvi *Kenbridge-Victoria Dispatch*, August 23, 1935; July 9, 1937; May 13, 1938.

cclxxxvii Ibid., August 18, 1939.

cclxxxviii *The Victoria Dispatch*, July 31, 1942.

cclxxxix *The Kenbridge-Victoria Dispatch*, August 18, 1939.

ccxc Ibid., September 8, 1939.

ccxci Ibid., September 22, 1939.

ccxcii Helen F. Snead, interview at her home in Kenbridge, Virginia, February 29, 2012.

ccxciii *The Victoria Dispatch*, July 21, 1944.

ccxciv Neale, 242-243.

ccxcv *The Victoria Dispatch*, June 25, 1948.

ccxcvi *The Victoria Dispatch*, August 26, 1949.

ccxcvii Ibid., August 11, 1950.

ccxcviii *The Kenbridge-Victoria Dispatch*, September 7, 1946; August 24, 1950.

ccxcix August 15, 1952; *The Cub*, Lunenburg High School Yearbook, 1953.

ccc Nathaniel Harvey Jeter, interview at his home in Victoria, Virginia, June 7, 2011. Jeter was a retired agricultural-vocational education teacher.

ccci *The Kenbridge-Victoria Dispatch*, January 21, 1955.

[cccii] *A History of Public Education in Virginia*, 23-24.

[ccciii] *The Kenbridge-Victoria Dispatch*, September 1, 1966.

[ccciv] Violet W. Johnson Harris, interview, August 25, 2011.

Chapter 8: Curriculum and Instruction

[cccv] *A History of Public Education in Virginia*, 7, 9.

[cccvi] Ibid., 9, 10; Heinemann, 280-281; Neale, 116.

[cccvii] *A History of Public Education in Virginia*, 9-11; Monthly School Report of Thelma Harding, November 30, 1910.

[cccviii] *A History of Public Education in Virginia*, 10-11; Wood, 60, 62.

[cccix] 347 U.S. 483, (1954); Brown II (1955); *A History of Public Education in Virginia*, 21.

[cccx] Ibid., 21-23.

[cccxi] Ibid., 26-27.

[cccxii] Edwin S. Sheppe, *Word Study Textbook* (Richmond: B. F. Johnson Publishing Company, 1908). Sheppe was a superintendent of Schools in Mount Airy, North Carolina. This book was used by Annie Thelma Harding, mother of N. Harvey Jeter, during her studies at the Kenilworth School in 1909.

[cccxiii] *A History of Public Education in Virginia*, 12.

[cccxiv] *The Victoria Dispatch*, October 2, 1925; September 2, 1927.

[cccxv] Willie Lucretia Maddux McAllister, interview at the Heritage Hall Healthcare and Rehabilitation Center, Blackstone, Virginia, May 12, 2011.

[cccxvi] *The Victoria Dispatch*, August 21, 1931.

[cccxvii] Ibid., September 4, 1931.

[cccxviii] Ibid., March 10, 1933.

[cccxix] Ibid., February 10, 1939.

[cccxx] Ibid., March 31, 1941; Bernice Stokes Charlton. Interview at the Stokes' Family Farm, Rehoboth, Virginia, June 7, 2011. Charlton is a retired business secretary & bookkeeper; and 1942 graduate of the Lunenburg Training School.

[cccxxi] *The Kenbridge-Victoria Dispatch*, December 15, 1939.

[cccxxii] Ibid., January 12, 1940.

[cccxxi] Ibid., June 14, 1940; *School Board Minutes*, August 2, 1940.

[cccxx] *The Victoria Dispatch*, November 25, 1932; *The Kenbridge-Victoria Dispatch*, September 1, 1944.

[cccxxv] Ibid., May 4, 1945.

cccxxvi Ibid., June 1, 1945.

cccxxvii Ibid.

cccxxviii *The Victoria Dispatch*, March 22, 1946.

cccxxix *The Kenbridge-Victoria Dispatch*, August 15, 1957.

cccxxx Sherman C. Vaughan, interview at his home in Blackstone, Virginia, May 12, 2011. Vaughan was an assistant principal and seventh grade teacher at Lunenburg Elementary School from 1959 to 1965.

cccxxxi *The Kenbridge-Victoria Dispatch*, September 1, 1966.

cccxxxii *School Board Minutes*, August 7, 1969; September 8, 1969.

cccxxxiii *The Kenbridge-Victoria Dispatch*, August 27, 1970.

Chapter 9: Trend of School Consolidation

cccxxxiv *Our School*, 28.

cccxxxv *The Victoria Dispatch*, August, 6, 1926.

cccxxxvi Neale, 181; *The Kenbridge-Victoria Dispatch*, October 23, 1996.

cccxxxvii Neale, 178-179; *The Victoria Dispatch*, August 39, 1940. The Nonintervention School last year of operation was 1940-1941.

cccxxxviii *A History of Public Education in Virginia*, 20; Lucy Arvin, History of Ledbetter School, January 1997.

cccxxxix *School Board Minutes*, August 1939; Wood, 46; Note: The Lunenburg School was a one-room log school not the Lunenburg Training School.

cccxl George E. Smith, *Kenbridge Elementary School History*, February 26, 1993. A copy is archived at the Ripberger Public Library in Kenbridge, Virginia.

cccxli Wood, 57-58; Note: The Central School mentioned here was a one-room log structure for Negro pupils erected in 1900. The second frame building was erected on the same site in 1925; *Survey of Lunenburg County Schools*, 1943.

cccxlii Neale, 300.

cccxliii *The Victoria Dispatch*, March 10, 1944.

cccxliv Ibid., November 9, 1945.

cccxlv *The Kenbridge-Victoria Dispatch*, September 20, 1946.

cccxlvi Ibid., September 5, 1947.

cccxlvii Gracie Knott-Barksdale Saunders, interview at her home, July 14, 2011.

cccxlviii *School Board Minutes*, April 2, 1948; *The Kenbridge-Victoria Dispatch*, June 11, 1954.

cccxlix Ibid., August 11, 1961; Alvester L. Edmonds.

[cccl] *The Kenbridge-Victoria Dispatch*, August 11, 1961.

[cccli] Ibid., December 22, 1961, November 9, 1962.

[ccclii] *School Board Minutes*, 1969; *A History of Public Education in Virginia*, 20.

Chapter 10: Public Education Issue of the Century

[cccliii] *347 United States Supreme Court 482* (1954).

[cccliv] Smith, 27-35, 45-47; http://www.encyclopediavirigina.org/Massive_Resistance, August 19, 2010; *Davis et al. v. County School Board of Prince Edward County*, 103 F. Supp. 337 (1952).

[ccclv] *The Kenbridge-Victoria Dispatch*, June 26, 1953.

[ccclvi] Ibid.

[ccclvii] Ibid., July 28, 1961; Richmond Times-Dispatch, October 21, 1966.

[ccclviii] Wilkinson III, 4.

[ccclix] Ibid.

[ccclx] Ibid., 6.

[ccclxi] Wood, 16; Heinemann, 333-334, 337; *The Victoria Dispatch*, August 5, 1949; *A History of Public Education in Virginia*, 20.

[ccclxii] *The Kenbridge-Victoria Dispatch*, May 16, 1951.

[ccclxiii] Ibid., February 15, 1952.

[ccclxiv] Ibid., July 18, 1952.

[ccclxv] Ibid., November 6, 1953; January 22, 1954.

[ccclxvi] *347 United States Supreme Court 482* (1954); Bob Smith. *The Closed Their School, Prince Edward Couth, Virginia 1951-1964*; (Farmville: Robert Russa Moton Museum, 2008), 83-86; *Southern School News*, September 3, 1954; *The Victoria Dispatch*, June 17, 1960.

[ccclxvii] Smith, 83-86.

[ccclxviii] Benjamin Muse. *Virginia's Massive Resistance* (Indiana, 1961), 7.

[ccclxix] *A History of Public Education in Virginia*, 20.

[ccclxx] U.S. Census Bureau (1950); J. H. Wilkinson III, *Harry Byrd and the Changing Face of Virginia Politics 1945-1966* (Charlottesville: The University Press of Virginia, 1968), 114; http://www.encyclopeidavirginia.org/Massive Resistance, August 19, 2010.

[ccclxxi] *A History of Public Education in Virginia*, 20.

[ccclxxii] Smith, 104; *Southern School News*, July 6, 1955.

[ccclxxiii] *Richmond Times-Dispatch*, May 21, 1954.

ccclxxiv Smith, 90.

ccclxxv *The Kenbridge-Victoria Dispatch*, November 5, 1954.

ccclxxvi Ibid., November 12, 1954.

ccclxxvii Ibid., October 28, 1955.

ccclxxviii Ibid., November 1955.

ccclxxix Smith, 98.

ccclxxx Muse, 8.

ccclxxxi *The Kenbridge-Victoria Dispatch*, December 2, 1955.

ccclxxxii Ibid., December 23, 1955.

ccclxxxiii Ibid.

ccclxxxiv Ibid.

ccclxxxv Ibid., January 6, 1956.

ccclxxxvi Smith, 151-171.

ccclxxxvii Sources for all quotations from the various resolutions and for roll-call votes thereon, *Journal of the Senate of Virginia*, Session 1956, 143-48; *Journal of the House of Delegates of the Commonwealth of Virginia*, Session 1956, 78-80, 143-48, 171-73.

ccclxxxviii *The Kenbridge-Victoria Dispatch*, February 10, 1956.

ccclxxxix Ibid., February 24, 1956.

cccxc Ibid., March 16, 1956; Smith, 143; Southern School News, April, 1956.

Chapter 11: The Massive Resistance Movement

cccxci *The Kenbridge-Victoria Dispatch*, March 16, 1956.

cccxcii Ibid., January 6, 1956.

cccxciii Robbins L. Gates, *The Making of Massive Resistance, Virginia's Politics of Public School Desegregation 1954-1956*, (North Carolina: The University of North Carolina Press, 1962), 124.

cccxciv Leonard "Stanley" Lambert, telephone interview with author, November 13, 2010. Lambert was one of two African American males to enroll in grade twelve at Kenbridge High School in fall of 1965. He was one of the three students (male) to ever graduate from a white high school (Kenbridge and Victoria) in the history of public education in Lunenburg County, Virginia.

cccxcv *The Kenbridge-Victoria Dispatch*, July 13, 1956.

cccxcvi Ibid., July, 1956. This is an excerpt from an editorial.

cccxcvii Ibid., August 31, 1956; http://www.encyclopediavirginia.org/Massive Resistance.

cccxcviii *The Kenbridge-Victoria Dispatch*, September 7, 1956.

cccxcix Ibid., September 14, 1956.

cd *Editors of the Farmville Herald*, (printed in the *Kenbridge-Victoria Dispatch*), February 17, 1957; Smith, 83-86.

cdi *The Kenbridge-Victoria Dispatch*, October 11, 1957.

cdii Ibid., November 13, 1957.

cdiii Ibid., January 24, 1958; Smith 141.

cdiv *School Board Minutes*, August 7, 1958.

cdv *The Kenbridge-Victoria Dispatch*, February 13, 1959.

cdvi *The Kenbridge-Victoria Dispatch*, March 20, 1959, March 27, 1959; April 3, 1959.

cdvii Ibid., November 20, 1959.

cdviii Ibid.

cdix *A History of Public Education in Virginia*, 21; Smith, 151; *The Kenbridge-Victoria Dispatch*, February 6, 1959; http://www. encyclopediavirginia.org/Masssive_Resistance. November 19, 2010.

cdx *The Kenbridge-Victoria Dispatch*, February 6, 1959; A History of Public Education in Virginia, 21-22.

cdxi Smith, 152.

cdxii Smith, 151, 152, 260; The Kenbridge-Victoria Dispatch, February 6, 1959.

cdxiii Smith, 198, 240, 258.

cdxiv Rebecca Lee Randolph, interview, November 14, 2010 and November 18, 2010. Randolph was one of several students who attended Lunenburg County Public Schools when public schools in Prince Edward County closed (1959-1964). She is a retired senior accounts payable bookkeeper, Prince Edward County Public Schools, Farmville, Virginia; 377 U.S. 218, (1964); Smith, 258.

cdxv Neale, 76, 118.

cdxvi *The Kenbridge-Victoria Dispatch*, February 27, 1959; March 6, 1959.

cdxvii Smith, 152-174; Southern School News, February, 1960.

cdxviii *The Kenbridge-Victoria Dispatch*, July 22, 1960.

cdxix Smith, 168.

cdxx *The Kenbridge-Victoria Dispatch*, March 31, 1966; April 28, 1966.

cdxxi Ibid., April 14, 1966.

cdxxii Ibid., May 5, 1966.

cdxxiii Marjorie B. Powers, interview at her home in Kenbridge, Virginia, October 8, 2012.

cdxxiv *The Kenbridge-Victoria Dispatch*, January 23, 1969; January 30, 1969.

Chapter 12: Civil Rights Movement At Home

cdxxv 163 U.S. 537 (1896); 328 U. S. 373 (1946); 391 U. S. 430 (1968); 388 U.S. 1 (1967).

cdxxvi Dorothy Bell, interview at her home in Kenbridge, Virginia, March 1, 2013.

cdxxvii Vanessa s. Walker. *Their Highest Potential*, (North Carolina: The University of North Carolina Press, 1996), 3; Civil Rights Act, *Public Law 99-352*, July 2, 1964.

cdxxviii Russell L. Callahan, interview at his home in Kenbridge, Virginia, on January 12, 2013.

cdxxix Author's point of view based on personal experience.

cdxxx *The Washington Post*, December 6, 1965.

cdxxxi Ibid.; Bill Monnie. *Selma And Its Aftermath*, New Hampshire: A Snowy Day Distribution and Publishing, 2015), 96-97.

cdxxxii *The Washington Post*, December 6, 1965; Margie W. Fitzgerald, interview at her home in Kenbridge, Virginia, September 17, 2010. Fitzgerald is the daughter of the late Reverend W. H. Winston.

cdxxxiii *The Washington Post*, December 6, 1965.

cdxxxiv Alfonza Webster Stokes, interview at his home in Victoria, Virginia, June 16, 2011.

cdxxxv *Virginia Students' Civil Rights Committee Newsletter*, February 1967, 4.

cdxxxvi Carolyn V. Callahan, email dated May 10, 2011. Callahan is a 1968 graduate of the Lunenburg High School.

cdxxxvii Annie Holloway Holmes, interview at her home in Meherrin, Virginia, July 20, 2011; Holmes is a retired school administrator and guidance counselor at Lunenburg High School. She was a key factor in the employment of African American students at the Peebles Supermarket, Victoria, Virginia in the spring of 1969.

cdxxxviii Stanley C. Lee is a member of the Central High School Class of 1970. Lee is a retired City of Richmond Police Officer from Chesterfield County, Virginia; Reflection sent via email on September 14, 2011.

cdxxxix *The Evening Star*, December 12, 1966.

cdxl *School Board Minutes*, June 7, 1965.

cdxli *School Board Minutes*, August 9, 1965.

cdxlii *Virginia Students' Civil Rights Committee Newsletter*, February 1967, 4.

cdxliii *The Comet*, Kenbridge High School, 1966; The Panther, Victoria High School, 1966; John Croslin, interview in Chesterfield, Virginia, May 29, 2012; Msonga-Mbele Andre Parvenu, interview, September 24, 2011.

cdxliv Easter Smith Crowder, interview at her home in Kenbridge, Virginia, October

31, 2010. Crowder is a retired school cafeteria employee.

[cdxlv] Margaret Cushwa Cocks.

[cdxlvi] *School Board Minutes*, August 9, 1965; January 21, 1969.

Chapter 13: A "Done" Deal

[cdxlvii] Announcement made by Chief Justice Earl Warren of the United State Supreme Court, May 1954.

[cdxlviii] *The Kenbridge-Victoria Dispatch*, February 9, 1967.

[cdxlix] *Kenbridge-Victoria Dispatch*, September 1, 1966; School Board Minutes, September 9, 1968. Darlena Marshall (Biggers) was the first African American assigned to the library at Kenbridge and Victoria Elementary Schools during freedom of choice for the 1966-67 school term; The Elementary and Secondary Education Act, (1966) funded Marshall's assignment as librarian at the Lunenburg Elementary School; *The Evening Star*, December 12, 1966.

[cdl] *The Kenbridge-Victoria Dispatch*, September 5, 1968.

[cdli] *Phemie D. Hawthorne, etc., et al., Appellees v. County School Board of Lunenburg County, Virginia, Civil Rights Action No 5949-R*, December 30, 1968; Ellen Hawthorne (Wright) and Nathaniel L. Hawthorne, Jr., interview at the home of E. H. Wright in Richmond, Virginia, July 27, 2011; The Kenbridge-Victoria Dispatch, January 23, 1969, January 30, 1969.

[cdlii] Claude Littleton "C.L." Barnes, Jr., interview at his home in Kenbridge, Virginia, May 31, 2011; School Board Minutes, January 3, 1969.

[cdliii] Ibid.

[cdliv] *School Board Minutes*, January 21, 1969; The Kenbridge-Victoria Dispatch, January 23, 1969.

[cdlv] *The Kenbridge-Victoria Dispatch*, February 13, 1969.

[cdlvi] Ibid., January 30, 1969; March 6, 1969; July 17, 1969.

[cdlvii] Claude Littleton "C.L." Barnes, Jr.

[cdlviii] Bessie Chatmon Hopkins interview at her home, Kenbridge, Virginia, November 9, 2010.

[cdlix] *The Daily Progress*, December 19, 2010.

[cdlx] Dr. Howard "Hank" W. Allen, interview at his home in Charlottesville, Virginia, April 13, 2012.

[cdlxi] *The Kenbridge-Victoria Dispatch*, February 13, 1969.

[cdlxii] *School Board Minutes*, 1965-1969. Note: The number teachers listed are estima-

tions based on names identified in the local paper (fall of the 1967-68 and 1969-1970 school terms) and does not include instructional staff who may have been employed later.

[cdlxiii] H. R. Watkins, Sr. was the first African American assigned the position as ESEA Coordinator at the School Board Office in 1969. Reverend Watkins, a Baptist minister, had been employed as an assistant principal and teacher at the Kenbridge Graded School.

[cdlxiv] Chester L. Conyers was the first African American assistant principal at the Central High School in the fall of 1969. Conyers had been the coach and teacher of boys' physical education at the Lunenburg High School.

[cdlxv] Carl Hardy Jones, a Baptist minister, was the first African American guidance counselor at Central High School in 1969. Prior to this assignment, Reverend Jones was an assistant principal, history and social studies teacher at the Lunenburg High School.

[cdlxvi] Allen S. Bridgforth was the first African American school administrator at the Kenbridge Elementary School in the fall of 1969.

[cdlxvii] Isaiah G. Hopkins was the first African American school administrator assigned to the Victoria Elementary School in the fall of 1969. Hopkins had taught at the Camp School in the 1950s, and was a seventh grade teacher at the Lunenburg Elementary School prior to his assignment at Victoria Elementary.

[cdlxviii] Jacqueline Sanford Haskins replaced Darlena Marshall (Biggers) as the librarian at the Victoria Elementary and Kenbridge Elementary Schools during the freedom of choice in the fall of 1968.

[cdlxix] Bessie Reese Callahan worked in the library at the West End Elementary School during the freedom of school. She was the first African American secretary at a white school in the Lunenburg County Public School system.

[cdlxx] Special* refers to a reading program specifically designed to assist students with developing their reading skills. These programs were made possible through the Title I funds provided to the Lunenburg County Public School in 1966.

[cdlxxi] *The Kenbridge-Victoria Dispatch*, September, 18, 1969.

[cdlxxii] Ibid., August 27, 1970.

Chapter 14: Hallowed Grounds

[cdlxxiii] Neale, 174.

[cdlxxiv] *The Victoria Dispatch*, 1930.

[cdlxxv] Ibid., June 13, 1941; *School Board Minutes*, July 2, 1941.

[cdlxxvi] Claude Swanson Thompson, interview at the Heritage Hall Healthcare and Rehabilitation Center, Blackstone, Virginia, August 3, 2012.

[cdlxxvii] June Banks Evans, Lunenburg County Historical Society Historian, via email, August 14, 2015.

[cdlxxviii] Neale, 153; George E. Smith, *Kenbridge Elementary School History*, Ripberger Library, Kenbridge, Virginia, 1993.

[cdlxxix] Ibid.; *Kenbridge-Victoria Dispatch*, September 1, 1966.

[cdlxxx] *The Kenbridge-Victoria Dispatch*, January 2, 1969; August 21, 1969.

[cdlxxxi] Nathaniel Harvey Jeter.

[cdlxxxii] *Historical Sketch of Lunenburg High School*, 1917-1969; Wood, 61.

[cdlxxxiii] Sherman C. Vaughan.

[cdlxxxiv] *The Kenbridge-Victoria Dispatch*, September 1, 1966.

[cdlxxxv] Ibid., January 23, 1969. Franklin D. Warren became the first white principal of Lunenburg Primary School as part of the desegregation plan.

[cdlxxxvi] Thomas Ross Irby, interview, Kenbridge, Virginia, September 17, 2011; Real Estate Deed, Office of County Clerk, Lunenburg, Virginia, April 25, 1921.

[cdlxxxvii] Wood, 29-30; *Virginia Daily Attendance Register and Record of Class Grades for Oak Grove School*, 1925-1926; Kenbridge-Victoria Dispatch, July 9, 1937; July 21, 1944; September 7, 1945.

[cdlxxxviii] *Plantersville School Minutes*, March 1, 1934; Elloise M. Callahan is a former student of the Plantersville School.

[cdlxxxix] Gracie Barksdale Knott-Saunders, interview at her home in Drakes Branch, Virginia, July 14, 2011.

[cdxc] Charles Eugene Welborn, interview at his home in Kenbridge, Virginia on July 20, 2011. C. E. Welborn and J. M. Welborn are property owners of Robertson School; Neale, 175.

[cdxci] *The Victoria Dispatch*, September 25, 1925; Wood, 41. Wood's interviews with [cdxcii] Lucy M. Morrison, July 19, 1952; and LaNelle Shields, August 26, 1952.

[cdxciii] *The Kenbridge-Victoria Dispatch*, July 9, 1937; September 7, 1945; August 15, 1952.

[cdxciii] Neale, 280-281.

[cdxciv] Interview by Oscar Wood with Bettie Hinton, July 15, 1952. Hinton was an eld-

erly citizen and member of Unity Baptist Church in Kenbridge, Virginia. Hinton reported Hannie Almond as a white lady from New York.

cdxcv Lewis Carl Reese, interview at his home in Kenbridge, Virginia, November 7, 2010.

cdxcvi *The Kenbridge-Victoria Dispatch*, July 9, 1937.

cdxcvii Ibid., August 15, 1952; August 27, 1954; September 2, 1955; August 26, 1960.

cdxcviii Early Mason Reese, interview at his home in Kenbridge, Virginia on June 8, 2011.

cdxcix Hamlett and Israel, 44.

d *The Kenbridge-Victoria Dispatch*, September 1, 1966.

di Ibid., August 21, 1969.

dii Hamlett and Israel, 45; *The Victoria Dispatch*, February 3, 1950.

diii Ibid., August 15, 1952.

div Ibid., August 28, 1953.

dv Ibid., September 2, 1954.

dvi Ibid., August 20, 1964.

dvii Glada Jarvis Dunnavant, interview at her home in Victoria, Virginia, March 13, 2012.

dviii *The Kenbridge-Victoria Dispatch*, September 1, 1966.

dix Bessie Reese Callahan, interview at the Lunenburg Senior Citizens, Inc., Victoria, Virginia, June 22, 2011; Gracie B. Knott-Saunders.

dx *The Kenbridge-Victoria Dispatch*, August 21, 1969.

dxi Frances Price Wilson, via email on September 27, 2011.

dxii *Kenbridge-Victoria Dispatch*, November 4, 1938; November 25, 1938; *School Board Minutes*, June 1, 1945; *The Victoria Dispatch*, June 8, 1945; November 2, 1945.

dxiii *School Board Minutes*, March 1, 1947.

dxiv *The Kenbridge-Victoria Dispatch*, March 12, 1964; March 19, 1964.

dxv *School Board Minutes*, August 9, 1965.

dxvi *The Kenbridge-Victoria Dispatch*, September 1, 1966.

dxvii Ibid., February 9, 1967.

dxviii Ibid.

dxix *Sword and Shield*, Central High School, 1969-1970.

dxx *The Kenbridge-Victoria Dispatch*, August 24, 1969.

dxxi *School Board Minutes*, November 7, 1969.

dxxii *Sword and Shield*, 1969-1970.

dxxiii *The Kenbridge-Victoria Dispatch*, October 30, 1969.

dxxiv *Our Town 75th Anniversary*, October 29, 1983; Lucy Arvin, Historical Sketch of the Ledbetter School, January, 1997.

[dxxv] *Kenbridge High School, Graduation Announcement*, May 15, 1915. This document is archived at the Ripberger Public Library in Kenbridge, Virginia.

[dxxvi] Smith, 1993.

[dxxvii] Neale, 225.

[dxxviii] Bessie C. Hopkins.

[dxxix] *The Comet*, 1966.

[dxxx] Helen Wilkinson Buchanan, interview at her home in Kenbridge, Virginia, May 11, 2011.

[dxxxi] *The Kenbridge-Victoria Dispatch*, August 26, 1965; The Comet, 1966.

[dxxx] *The Victoria Dispatch*, September 22, 1933; May 17, 1935; September 5, 1947;

[dxxix] Neale, 182-183.

[dxxiii] Claude Littleton "C.L." Barnes, Jr.; *The Victoria Dispatch*, August 19, 1932.

[dxxxiv] *Courier-Record*, July 7, 1966.

[dxxxv] Smith, 1993; *School Board Minutes*, June 25, 1943.

[dxxxvi] Ibid., June 2, 1944.

[dxxxvii] Elsie Parrish Moore Almand, interview at her home in Dundas, Virginia, August 19, 2011.

[dxxxviii] *The Kenbridge-Victoria Dispatch*, August 15, 1952; August 28, 1953.

[dxxxix] Ibid., August 24, 1956.

[dxl] C.L. Barnes, Jr.; Neale, 67.

[dxli] Bob Smith, 14.

[dxlii] *The Lunenburg High School Student Handbook*, 1960, 3-4.

[dxliii] *Lunenburg School Life*, March 1923; Note: Second grade certification mentioned here referred to the teachers' certification level set by the state not grade level.

[dxliv] Virginia Center for Digital History, "Rosenwald Schools of Virginia," Vcdh.virginia.edu; Wood, 61-62.

[dxlv] *The Lunenburg High School Student Handbook*, 1960, 3.

[dxlvi] Wood, 61-62.

[dxlvii] *Souvenir Journal*, Lunenburg High School Alumni First Reunion, Victoria, Virginia, 1985, 17. The second grade certificate mentioned refers to level of secondary education completed, not second grade at the elementary level; Neale, 182.

[dxlviii] Wood, 62.

[dxlix] *School Board Minutes*, April 2, 1943.

[dl] Joanna Jackson Bell, interview at her home in Meherrin, Virginia, June 29, 2011. Bell is a retired public school librarian.

[dli] Wood, 62; *Historical Sketch of Lunenburg High School* (1917-1969); *Souvenir Jour-*

nal, Lunenburg High School Alumni First Reunion, 16.

dlii *The Victoria Dispatch*, Victoria, Virginia, June 14, 1940; September 7, 1945.

dliii *The Kenbridge-Victoria Dispatch*, June 14, 1940; School Board Minutes, June 1, 1945.

dliv Wood, 62.

dlv *School Board Minutes*, August 3, 1945.

dlvi Wood, 62-64.

dlvii *The Kenbridge-Victoria Dispatch*, February 22, 1952.

dlviii Ibid., August 28, 1953.

dlix *The Lunenburg High School Student Handbook*, 1960, 6.

dlx Ibid.

dlxi Ibid., 27.

dlxii Ibid., 4.

dlxiii Neale, 182; Annie Holloway Holmes, interview at her home in Meherrin, Virginia, July 20, 2010; *The Lunenburg High School Student Handbook*, 1960.

dlxiv *The Kenbridge-Victoria Dispatch*, November 16, 1962.

dlxv Ibid., August, 29, 1963; October 3, 1963.

dlxvi Ibid., October 24, 1963

dlxvii Ibid., December 5, 1963.

dlxviii Ibid., February 20, 1964, March 12, 1964, March 19, 1964.

dlxix *The Torch*, Lunenburg High School Yearbook, 1966.

dlxx D. B. Carnes, interview at his home, Victoria, Virginia, August 18, 2011. Currently, Carnes serves as chairman of the Lunenburg County School Board representing the Plymouth District.

dlxxi Mildred H. Jenkins, interview in her home in Victoria, Virginia, October, 12, 2010; May 24, 2012. Jenkins is a retired elementary school teacher and wife of the late G. L. Jenkins.

dlxxii Pulley, xxiv; Hamlett and Israel, 44.

dlxxiii *The Lunenburg Call*, September 11, 1924.

dlxxiv *The Victorian*, 1941. *The Victorian* was a newsletter printed at the Victoria High School in the 1940s. This newsletter is archived at the former Victoria High School building.

dlxxv Hamlett and Israel, 44.

dlxxvi Richard L. Kirby.

dlxxvii *The Kenbridge-Victoria Dispatch*, January 22, 1943.

dlxxviii *School Board Minutes*, April 2, 1943.

dlxxix Richard L. Kirby.

[dlxxx] Bessie M. Callahan, Bobbie A. Crane, John R. Croslin and Marcia A. Slacum have been added to the Victoria High School history based on interviews and their photo in *The Panther*, 1966.

[dlxxxi] Easter Smith Crowder.

[dlxxxii] Joanna Jackson Bell is an aunt of Marcia A. Slacum (Greene).

[dlxxxiii] Nathaniel Harvey Jeter.

[dlxxxiv] *The Panther*, 1966.

[dlxxxv] Hamlett and Israel, 48-49.

[dlxxxvi] *Kenbridge-Victoria Dispatch*, April 12, 1935.

[dlxxxvii] Hamlett and Israel, 48; *The Kenbridge-Victoria Dispatch*, August 1967.

[dlxxxviii] Neale, 243.

[dlxxxix] *School Board Minutes*, December 3, 1943.

[dxc] Ibid., June 5, 1959.

[dxci] *The Victoria Dispatch*, July 21, 1944, September 7, 1945, August 15, 1952.

[dxcii] Edith Craig Hurt, interview at her home in Victoria, Virginia, August 12, 2011.

[dxciii] *School Board Minutes*, February 4, 1944.

[dxciv] Mary Locust Baker, interview at her home in Victoria, Virginia, May 12, 2011.

[dxcv] Daisy C. Jones, interview at her home in Victoria, Virginia, June 9, 2011.

Chapter 15: IN THEIR OWN WORDS

[dxcvi] Bessie Reese Callahan.

[dxcvii] Leonard Stanley Lambert, interview on November 13, 2010. Lambert was one of ten African American students to enroll at the white school in Kenbridge. He was the first and only of two black students to graduate from the Kenbridge High School in 1966. Now retired, he was employed as a Technical Information Specialist with Defense Logistics Agency Aviation in Richmond, Virginia.

[dxcviii] Edward A. Almand, interview at his home in Dundas, Virginia, February 29, 2011. Almand is a former student of the Dundas Graded School.

[dxcix] Mildred H. Jenkins, interview at her home in Victoria, Virginia, May 3, 2011.

[dc] Shirley Underwood Haag, interview at her home in Victoria, Virginia, May 25, 2011.

[dci] Margaret Cushwa Cocks.

[dcii] William "Bill" M. Monnie, June 12, 2011. Monnie is a former civil rights worker and retired social worker from New Hampshire. Grogan mentioned here is Senator Nan Grogan Orrock who serves in the Georgia State Legislature in Atlanta, Georgia.

[dciii] Roberta C. Rickers, interview at the Ripberger Public Library in Kenbridge, Vir-

ginia, June 17, 2011. Rickers is a former public and private school educator, and former branch manager of the Ripberger Public Library, Kenbridge, Virginia.

[dciv] Ellen H. Wright and Nathaniel L. Hawthorne, Jr., interview at Wright's home in Richmond, Virginia, July 27, 2011; and via email on August 23, 2011; Classbook, Kenbridge Elementary School, 1969. The Classbook was the Kenbridge Elementary School's yearbook.

[dcv] Zella Reese Gray, via email on July 28, 2011.

[dcvi] Anne Cordle Hamlett, via email on August 9, 2011. Hamlett is a retired educator and member of the Lunenburg County Historical Society.

[dcvii] Msonga-Mbele Andre Parvenu, interview in Kenbridge, Virginia, May 24, 2012. Parvenue is identified as Ronald Andre Allen on the Virginia Teacher's Register, Victoria School, 1965-1966.

[dcviii] Violet W. Johnson (Harris), interview on August 12, 2012; and via email, August 25, 2011.

[dcix] Stanley C. Lee, via email on September 14, 2011.

[dcx] Frances Price Wilson, via email on October 18, 2011.

[dcxi] Howard W. Allen, interview at his home, Charlottesville, Virginia, April 13, 2012.

[dcxii] Phillip Gee, via email on June 7, 2012.

[dcxiii] Claude Swanson Thompson, interview Heritage Hall Healthcare and Rehabilitation Center, Blackstone, Virginia, August 3, 2012.

[dcxiv] Marjorie B. Powers, interview at her home in Kenbridge, Virginia, October 8, 2012.